W9-BRK-196

THE REFERENCE SHELF   VOLUME 42 NUMBER 3

TURMOIL
ON THE CAMPUS

EDITED BY
EDWARD J. BANDER

THE H. W. WILSON COMPANY
NEW YORK   1970

THE REFERENCE SHELF

The books in this series contain reprints of articles, excerpts from books, and addresses on current issues and social trends in the United States and other countries. There are six separately bound numbers in each volume, all of which are generally published in the same calendar year. One number is a collection of recent speeches; each of the others is devoted to a single subject and gives background information and discussion from various points of view, concluding with a comprehensive bibliography.

Subscribers to the current volume receive the books as issued. The subscription rate is $17 in the United States and Canada ($20 foreign) for a volume of six numbers. Single numbers are $4 each in the United States and Canada ($4.50 foreign).

PREFACE

There are two striking revelations for the editor of a book on student unrest. One is the sheer bulk of material on the topic, revealing the widespread interest it has aroused. The second is the attraction this topic has had for outstanding writers in all fields. The attraction is both dramatic and fundamental. It pits the young against the old, the liberal against the conservative (who may still think of himself as liberal), the individual against the institution. Also it raises the question: Can our society function on a crowded, impersonal, ravaged, poverty-stricken planet?

In reading the selections that follow in this book, one should bear in mind the fact that many of the writers generalize from different bases. One man sympathizes with students' discontent with the state of society, the war in Vietnam, the inertia of university administrators; another is outraged by the arrogance, innocence, and cynicism of some student activists. However, as in good fiction, the sides are never clearly drawn. Truth and wisdom and common grounds are scattered among all the combatants, and the inevitable conclusion is that the answer lies not on either side, or somewhere in between, but among the adversaries.

As this book went to press, a final section was added dealing with the tragic violence at Kent State University and Jackson State College, the Cambodian crisis, and the momentous effects these events have had on colleges and universities in all parts of the country.

The editor would like to thank the authors, publishers, and agents whose permission to reprint material has made this book possible. Acknowledgments are noted with each contribution.

EDWARD J. BANDER

May 1970

CONTENTS

III.   Universities in Turmoil

IV.   Black Studies

V.   The Over Thirty View

VI. LAW AND ORDER

VII. EPILOGUE

I. CAUSES OF STUDENT UNREST

EDITOR'S INTRODUCTION

This section provides a background for the confrontations and contradictions that appear in the later sections of the book.

The first article, taken from *Newsweek,* succinctly reviews the development of campus strife, and in the following selection Representative Brock (Republican, Tennessee) shows that there is substantial sympathy in Congress for the student and his grievances. President Kingman Brewster of Yale persuasively discusses some sobering problems faced by the university administration, not because of students or in spite of them, but by the nature of the task. The solution he proposes is "administrative accountability," a concept which he spells out in careful detail. The excerpt from "Who's in Charge?" which follows concerns itself with the student; the full report includes a discussion of the administration, the faculty, the alumni, and the public, as well as the student. In the concluding selection Russell Baker effectively ridicules both young and old. (No mention of humor can pass without a reference to Art Buchwald, whose syndicated columns in the New York *Post* and other newspapers on this problem are listed in the Bibliography.)

CLASS OF '69: THE VIOLENT YEARS [1]

As if arranged by an author quickly tying up the loose ends of his plot in the last act, the entire American academic year came together in Harvard Yard last week during commencement exercises.

[1] From article by Edwin Diamond, senior editor. *Newsweek.* 73:68-73. Je. 23, '69. Copyright Newsweek, Inc., 1969. Reprinted by permission.

The ceremony was tradition-laden and generally peaceful, just as the majority of the 2,400 colleges and universities in the United States have been this year. True, a dean praised President Nathan Pusey for defending Harvard against "anarchy and demagoguery, while not a few teachers and students went astray." But fortunately his salutation was in Latin. The major disruption, as in most of the campus disturbances this year, came from the Students for a Democratic Society, specifically from a suspended student named Bruce C. Allen of Cincinnati.

Allen had been given five minutes to speak by Pusey at the urging of student marshals who feared an SDS rush on the microphones. Allen exceeded his time limit, delivered some standard diatribes against the Puseys and the Rockefellers—and was eventually hooted and led off the podium.

Then, the regular student speaker arose, a law graduate named Meldon Levine. The voice of the moderate majority was heard. It was, as so often this year, angry, slightly arrogant and wholly effective. Said Levine:

> For attempting to achieve the values which you have taught us to cherish, your response has been astounding. It has escalated from the presence of police on the campuses to their use of clubs and gas. I have asked many of my classmates what they wanted me to say today. "Talk with them about hypocrisy," most of them said. "Tell them they have broken the best heads in the country. . . . Tell them they have destroyed our confidence and lost our respect."

Levine received an ovation from his peers and from some —but by no means all—of the faculty, parents and alumni present. And that, too, fitted in with the pattern of the year.

And so commencement for the 750,000 members of the Class of 1969 found both students and adults divided and angered. The Class of '69 had entered college just after the first wave of student dissent broke loose at Berkeley and swept across the United States. In the four years since, there have been more disorders on campus than in the comparable years of labor unrest in the 1930s. The article that follows

. . . examines the implications of student unrest for American society.

The students have forced universities to reexamine their purposes, faculties to reexamine their careers and adults to reexamine their consciences. It is clear that the movement that has done this represents something more than youthful exuberance, more than a transitory stage of growing up ("they'll settle down when they get married"), more than symbolic Freudian parricide, more than Dionysian energies released by sex and drugs—indeed, something more than can be encompassed by any of the other unitary approaches that "explain" the young. It is now recognized that a culturally distinct and apparently permanent youth class is emerging. This grouping is worldwide, but its distinguishing modes of behavior are most evident on U.S. campuses, where the conditions that have created it exist in their most powerful forms.

The emergence of a new class is most easily observed among the nonwhite U.S. students. Before 1965, they were Negroes; today they are blacks—a profound psychological transformation. Though the break is just as sharp between white youth over and under twenty-five, no one as yet has hit upon a precisely descriptive set of labels. Margaret Mead, for one, calls the young "natives" of a totally new technological world and over-twenty-five adults "foreigners" in this land. Perhaps the most accurate description is contained in Yale psychologist Kenneth Keniston's phrase "postmodern youth"—the first generation to be brought up by modern parents influenced by the emancipating social doctrines of the 1930s.

Postmodern youth, as Yale's Robert Brustein notes, has already been sufficiently praised, even overpraised, for its qualities of commitment, spontaneity, humanitarian values and personal authenticity. America has always valued youth. But now there is a kind of cult of divine youth that suggests that the young are intrinsically superior to the old. The most objective neutral statement that can be made about the new youth class is that modern parents have got the children they professed they wanted. As Levine reminded faculty and parents: "You have convinced us that equality and justice were inviolable concepts and we have taken you seriously."

These new students live in a period of extended youth. Adolescence now begins earlier and lasts longer. The affluence brought on by economic growth and increasing productivity has made it both economically possible and desirable for thousands of individuals to postpone work and a career to the mid- or late twenties. Whereas only one third of U.S. high school graduates went on to college in 1940, almost half were entering college by the mid-1960s. In theory, the technological society needed these highly trained people to take their places in the work force along with the machine; California made college, heretofore a privilege of the well-to-do, a right for every resident. But fewer people—and bigger computers—were already producing more goods. College is often a holding pattern for students. But few fidget about a career: the Depression memories of their parents rarely touch them.

Within this period of extended and often disengaged youthhood, a cluster of distinct characteristics has developed. The new class often appears to be intelligent but not intellectual. Penalties for any mental risk-taking frequently are built into their education. "The kids who reach the elite colleges," says Dr. Benson Snyder, a psychiatrist and newly appointed dean of university relations at MIT, "have gone through twelve years of schooling where they are systematically punished with poor grades when any attempt is made to go outside the system or question the teacher. So they learn how to use the system and make it work for them. The tendency is to say, 'Okay, they say that this is right, but I'm going to play it cool and make up my own mind.'"

Finally, the young have developed a firm sense of identity as a group. This is due to awareness of their sheer numbers (nearly 7 million in college this year), to shared tastes in dress, music and speech—and to the media, which accord them the attention given "newsmakers" like Jackie Onassis. Like many newsmakers, they have learned the arts of self-promotion.

The Knowledge Biz

This emergence of a new youth class coincides with the emergence of a new kind of university. When the academic envisions the university he sees a disinterested community of scholars devoted to reasoned discourse, the pursuit of truth and the education of the young. The classic statement of this idea of the university was delivered in 1852 by John Henry Cardinal Newman. The university was to be an "alma mater, knowing her children one by one, not a foundry or a mint or a treadmill." The aim was a "liberal education"—and not mere vocational or technical instruction—for the elite leaders of tomorrow. This is the vision that still inspires commencement speakers and mists over the present turmoil on campus. But it is more chimerical than real.

Actually, the American university has followed a different model. The accepted date for the beginning of the modern American university is the appointment of President Charles Eliot of Harvard in 1869. Eliot's Harvard imitated the German university with its emphasis on graduate research and study. Yale, Columbia and the newly created universities like Johns Hopkins, Chicago and Stanford also followed the German model. This marked the triumph of "professionalism" in U.S. education, the development hailed by David Riesman and Christopher Jencks as "the academic revolution."

There were efforts to restore the primacy of undergraduate education at the professional, research-oriented universities, most notably at Chicago under Robert Hutchins in the 1930s. These efforts were vaporized, ironically enough, by the atomic bomb which was developed at Hutchins's own school and which ushered in the most recent phase of university development. In July 1939, Enrico Fermi and the other physicists working on the idea of a nuclear chain reaction needed $6,000 worth of graphite. No university physics department in the nation could even consider granting such an astronomical sum—and it took no less than the famous Einstein letter to FDR himself to get the project going.

That was the end of the university's political innocence: the academics went to war; radar developments, proximity fuses, navigation devices—as well as The Bomb—came out of the academy during World War II. Scientific and technical knowledge became, in Clark Kerr's words, "the focal point for national growth." And at the center of the knowledge process, Kerr proudly pointed out, was the new university, or multiversity—a term meant to convey that the academy was now serving a variety of worldly needs. By the mid-1960s, in fact, Kerr's own University of California was itself operating two national nuclear laboratories for the Government on a budget of more than $200 million a year.

Masters and Servants

By this time, too, alma mater had become precisely that foundry and treadmill Newman had abhorred. With 40,000 students on campus, the multiversity had to put the names of its students on IBM cards, send grades out by code number and install TV monitors in the back of vast lecture halls so students could see the tiny creature at the distant podium. Often, this might be the student's only glimpse of the professor. The knowledge business has catapulted the star faculty member and the rising researcher from a local to a national constituency; his time and his loyalty no longer belonged to his university, but to his discipline—and to those in government and industry who wanted to pay for his specialized consultation. With the new academic entrepreneur spending so much time on the shuttle run to Washington, the actual teaching became the responsibility of section heads, often graduate students. "When a man's reputation is national," observes Berkeley Professor Neil Smelser, "he does the things that enhance his reputation—and teaching isn't one of them."

Cardinal Newman might not have recognized the place, but both the faculty and the administration had good reasons to be satisfied. For the professor, there was the good pay, short hours, sabbaticals, and a ready supply of cheap help in the form of graduate students. He was now part of corporate America—or at least an "in-and-outer"—yet he still had the traditional privileges, a sustaining atmosphere for critical thought and control over the curriculum.

For the administrator, there was new power. In the past, university administration had seemed to be vaguely custodial and somewhat beneath the dignity of faculty men (administrators sometimes were men who didn't make it as scholars or researchers). In the multiversity, however, university governance proved to be much more substantive than providing football tickets for alumni, and making sure there were lights and heat in the classrooms. Some universities developed specialists adept in prowling the corridors of government and industry for new contracts. New research offices proliferated under the benevolent green thumb of the Government. By 1968 the Federal Government was spending $17 billion for research and development. More than half the funds for such universities as MIT came from the Government.

The Naked Emperor

The first student complaints about the multiversity were particular rather than general, self-centered rather than cosmic. After the souped-up curriculum of a good high school, the college classroom, grail of all those hard-working years, seemed anticlimactic. Many students had experience with sex and drugs before they reached college, and they objected to rules that required them to live in campus dorms or restricted their hours or visitors. Parietal rules are still among the major causes of white student protest in the South and Midwest. As one student said: "Students don't have the power to get a girl in their room when they want to, and we're talking about ending the Vietnam war!"

The first major mobilization of student dissent came at Berkeley with the Free Speech Movement in 1964. This episode has set the style for subsequent student demonstrations and university responses around the country. FSM centered on a specific grievance—the right for students to have a microphone and political recruiting tables in Sproul Plaza. It involved the tactics of sit-ins and confrontations with authority—techniques that Martin Luther King, Jr., used so effectively. At Berkeley, as in Montgomery, authority responded with police, mass arrests, court injunctions, suspensions—and, eventually, negotiations that culminated in the granting of the protesters' demands. Today Sproul at noon is as good a show as *Hair*—and administrators pridefully show it off.

This belated acknowledgment of the reasonableness of the original student demand is part of a pattern too: students protest an injustice; after turmoil and dissension, the university admits that the wrong existed. Moreover, there is evidence that the wrong would have continued to exist uncorrected if the activists, like the boy in *The Emperor's New Clothes,* had not insisted: "But the emperor *is* naked."

Thus the dismissal of Marlene Dixon at Chicago pointed up the fact that there weren't many women on the faculty and that academic departments value research ability over classroom flair. The seizure of the Applied Electronic Laboratory by the April 3 Coalition at Stanford jogged the university's memory about how deeply it was involved in secret military research. The crisis between black and white students at Cornell led to the recognition that the university had a "communications failure"—and that its chief faculty committee of seventeen men did not fairly represent the 1,400-member faculty. The demands of black and Puerto Rican students at CCNY for a separate orientation program that would be more "meaningful" caused a faculty team to look into the program and find that it wasn't any good for white students either.

Crisis Managers

If many student demands are not unreasonable (in hindsight), then why the failure of so many university officials to grasp this fact? The radical's answer would be that the officials are too corrupt; the cynical might say that they aren't too bright. A more accurate answer might be that administrations, by and large, simply forgot about the students and the professed ideals of the university during the heady, aggrandizing days of the multiversity's growth. At the same time, they failed to appreciate fully the quantum change in student attitudes. The present turmoil is in part the due bill for the years of outward growth and internal indifference.

As a result the administrations on the more volatile campuses have become "crisis managers"—no more than glorified firemen running here and there to put out the conflagrations. Like firemen, these administrators concentrate on each specific emergency as it comes up; they have little time to work out a theory of arson or the design of fireproof communities. Each man is judged by his tactics: Columbia's Grayson Kirk and Harvard's Nathan Pusey "failed" because they called in the police; Cornell's James Perkins erred because he didn't grasp the impact of the news pictures showing black students brandishing guns on campus. Chicago's Edward Levi and Brandeis's Morris Abram, on the other hand, were good tacticians. When student radicals took over Levi's office, Levi simply let them have the building. He mobilized moderate opinion and let the faculty (a body too diffuse to become a target) deal with the nettlesome task of discipline. Abram kept the "lines of communication" open when blacks occupied a Brandeis building—using his powers of persuasion, as lawyers do, rather than bringing on police action. Yale's Kingman Brewster is credited with "staying one step ahead of trouble" by seeking out students and anticipating their needs. Minnesota's Malcolm Moos, too, is a sympathetic and imaginative administrator. When some funds were needed this year for black-studies activities at state-supported Minnesota, Moos agreed to find private money to pay some of the cost.

This tactical approach, by definition, cannot resolve the campus crisis for several reasons.

First of all, it cannot head off the effectiveness of the Students for a Democratic Society. SDS aims are thought to be generally Marxist, and most discussions center on the tactics of opposition and disruption. Actually Marx wouldn't have approved of SDS any more than contemporary Marxists do: to them, SDS is a band of Bakunin revolutionaries—all action and no organization.

The crisis managers have not yet realized that the revolutionaries' demands can be endless. Columbia's SDS served a list of six demands on the university last year. An SDS leader was asked what the group would do if all six demands were accepted. He replied: make six more demands. The tactic of constant pressure is an old revolutionary strategy; the object is not reform but to bring down the "corrupt" university as a step toward bringing down the "corrupt" society.

This may sound like bravado, since SDS is small as campus groups go—there are perhaps 70,000 SDS members spread over some 350 campus chapters—and often these chapters are split into warring factions. The impulsiveness of the romantic revolutionaries is usually opposed by the "moderation"—in this context—of the more orthodox Progressive Labor wing, or "short hairs"—so-called because they are presenting a neat appearance in order to win over blue-collar opinion in factories this summer [1969]. Moreover, according to Berkeley Chancellor Roger Heyns, who has more experience in these matters than most, on some campuses there is a hard-core group of ten or twelve radical leaders interested not as much in revolution as in the personal exercise of power *qua* power.

But whether SDS is united or divided does not matter ultimately: the university's ideals and geography make it vulnerable—and it can be tied up by a few determined activists.

Many administrators appreciate how vulnerable the university is. Before the crisis occurs, they are attentive (like Brewster and Moos) to the moderate students' wishes. After trouble begins, they seek (like Levi and Abram) to avoid "radicalizing" the moderates, refusing to call in the police or the guard. But these good tacticians miss the wider meaning of what has been happening to students over the last few years—and this is the second reason they will fail to cool off the campuses. The reputed moderates are really like the SDS: they, too, cannot be bought off with tactical concessions—though for a different reason. The members of the new student class seek a truly radical—as opposed to political —goal. The most unadorned way to phrase this goal is, "They want control of their lives." It is a demand, in its several variations, that is as familiar to parents as to university administrators.

Whose University?

In sum, the present generation of students wants a hand in controlling most phases of university affairs. This goal means demands for an end to the university's role of *in loco parentis* and to other efforts to limit personal freedom, no matter how reasonable to adults. It means demands for "more relevant" courses and a student voice in choosing and promoting faculty. If anything, the moderates' desire for control is more of a "threat" to the university than all the nonnegotiable demands of the political revolutionaries. Unlike the SDS, the moderates are serious about wanting to run the university.

This difference between rhetorical goals and real goals was reflected at Harvard . . . [in] April [1969] in the contrasting behavior of the SDS group and the moderate students. The SDS wanted to "shut the place down" while the moderates wanted to "make it a better place." The latter carried the day at the remarkable meeting of some 10,000 students in Soldiers' Field on April 14. "The yearning of

this appealing group of young people for a better community was very nearly palpable," remembers economist
Robert Lekachman. He also recalls the meeting's emotional
high point, the moment when a graduate student called for
a vote to condemn the "threat" made by the Harvard Corporation—"these seven old men"—to close "our" university.
The motion passed by acclamation.

The campus crisis managers cannot be blamed for the
third reason for their failure. As more than one commencement speaker noted last week, this is an era of pervasive and
passionate questioning of the legitimacy of all who hold
power in society. Harvard's Franklin Ford has referred to
this as "the particular malaise of the sixties." But it goes
beyond recent events. Everyone knows by now that the Vietnam war and the draft are central concerns of the new student class; what is less appreciated is the fact that even if
the war and the draft were to end tomorrow, this would not
fatally dampen the present assault on authority. Canada has
no draft and no war and yet Canadian students are considered perhaps the most militant in the world. What has
happened in the United States is that the war, the race issue,
the befouled environment and all the other perceived gaps
between professed ideals and reality have precipitated a crisis
for all authority.

This crisis has been building for decades all over the
world. It is easier to describe than explain. At the time of
the Sorbonne riots last year one French politician thought
society had reached a point when, like Rome, civilizations
collapse because belief is dead. For Archibald MacLeish the
exact opposite is true. Passionate belief in the value of man,
he said recently at the University of California, "had come
alive for the first time in the century and with it rage and
violence."

University administrators may protest that they are not
responsible for all of society's ills, that they are—like the
students—just passengers aboard the sinking ship of authority. They blame the political leaders at the controls for the

troubles. The continuing unrest on the campus, Amherst President Calvin Plimpton concluded in an extraordinary "all campus" statement addressed to President Nixon, "results from a shared sense that the nation has no adequate plans to meet the crisis of our society." Equally to the point, many on campus now share a sense of horrifying helplessness. They fear the holders of political power have lost the will to do anything about this crisis—except to call out the full forces of law and order to suppress those who protest.

Many in authority are myopic to the conditions Plimpton referred to. In a remark of towering complacency, Attorney General John Mitchell said, "We have today in this nation more equality in the law, more honesty in politics, more ethics in science, more people employed and less people hungry, and more religious dedication to the problems of society than at any other period in our history."

The burden for unrest is thus shifted back to the campus. Mr. Nixon himself blamed "permissive faculties," university administrators who need more "backbone"—and the small tyrannical minority of the students who are storm troopers, nihilists and/or paid agents of the enemy.

In truth many students today are subversive. But theirs seems to be a moral and not a political subversion. If the problem of student dissent were only political, then it would be relatively easy to deal with: the state could uproot the provocateurs; the university could continue to shorten its lines of vulnerability, correct its past ills and make concessions to various student groups in return for tranquillity. The universities have already done a great deal of political trading. Parietal rules have been reduced in many dorms to the vanishing point. Students have been added to disciplinary committees, administrators have reexamined their investment portfolios and military contracts in the light of student criticism and just last week Princeton University named two students—one a black activist—to its board of trustees.

These concessions, however, cannot satisfy the essentially *moral* principles being put forth under the student slogans of "community," "cocontrol," "relevance" and "legitimacy." There is only so much that the university administration can yield, for example, to satisfy the cry to get "war research" off campus. The point is eventually reached when to meet these claims means diminishing other principles which may not only be moral too, but also rooted in the tradition and the law. Two such principles are now under the most intense pressure.

"Justifiable" Violence

The first principle is the academic right of free inquiry. The university won the right for its members to pursue the work they chose after bitter battles in the 1930s and the 1940s with heresy hunters, right-wing legislatures, Red baiters and bluestockings (the late Dr. Alfred Kinsey was hounded mercilessly for his sex research). Now the threat comes from within the campus. In the past year student groups have disrupted the classes of teachers who support U.S. policy in Vietnam, prevented other students from attending interviews with military and industrial recruiters and occupied laboratories doing Pentagon research in order to stop faculty and staff members from going to work.

These coercive acts are clearly extralegal, a minority imposition on majority rights. They can be "justified" only by appeals to moral aims or to conscience. Thus, violence has come to be regarded by some students—and faculty—as acceptable in the short run (but not as an end in itself) because it dramatizes just grievances and brings them to public attention. Thus, too, free speech and free assembly have become in this view relative rather than absolute: no one, a recent campus broadside declares, "has a 'right' to utilize the university for racist, militarist or imperialist activities."

These are vague catchall terms. They suggest an intimidating self-righteousness and certitude. As Princeton President Robert Goheen remarked last week: "It must be the awareness of human fallibility which we all carry within us that makes the man without error so obnoxious to us." But this mode of objection is an ancient one; Antigone was among the first militants to put morality over laws of state, and history is filled with the violent episodes brought on when the frustrated evoke higher, natural law against authority.

Still, it is one thing for faculty men to discuss the conflicts of Sophocles's drama in the abstract and quite another thing for them to face intimidation on the campus. Professor Herbert Marcuse, the philosopher who provides the most closely argued justification for "repressive intolerance" and "acceptable violence" on the left, himself has recently exempted the universities from destruction on the ground that quite a few of them are "still oases of relatively critical thought. . . ."

This still leaves unsettled the faculty's response once coercion begins. To "call the cops" entails demonstrable risks. Phil C. Neal, dean of the University of Chicago Law School, recently observed that a university cannot ask the protection of civil authority without sacrificing its distinct qualities—just as a household that must fall back on the law to regulate the conduct of its members thereby ceases to be what it was.

Neal's alternative solution is to appeal beyond the law to the intangibles of "university spirit and motive"—and at the same time limit access to the university. The Harvard Committee of Fifteen, appointed by the faculty of arts and sciences after the April upheavals, arrived at the same solution when it suspended sixteen students last week for their part in the seizure of University Hall. Students have responsibilities as citizens of the state, the committee said, and by accepting membership in the university they also acquire additional responsibilities to the whole university community. In Neal's words, the university must be reserved "for those who are prepared not only to renounce force and the threat of force but the idea of coercion itself as a means of making their views prevail." The university, he concludes, belongs to no one, but it does not follow that it belongs to everyone.

The second fundamental principle affected by the student claims is the matter of university ownership. The new students have come to regard the university as belonging to them as much as to any other of its constituencies. It is an identification that faculties themselves have presumed to make from time to time. But the legalities are quite incontrovertible. Private schools like Harvard are owned by chartered corporations; public schools like Berkeley, Illinois or CCNY, are operated by regents or boards either appointed by public officials or elected by the voters. The faculty may express its position, as CCNY's did recently on minority admissions, but the decision in the admissions case rests with the Board of Higher Education appointed by the mayor of New York.

This ownership is not likely to change hands bloodlessly; there were none of the niceties of spirit Professor Neal talked about in Berkeley . . . [in May 1969] when the university's rights were challenged in the name "of the people."

The episode involved People's Park, the property of the regents of the University of California. A year ago the land was "urban renewed" for future university use. Around mid-April, the "street people" of Berkeley took over the lot in the name of the "community." The university responded by putting up a chain-link fence. In a series of clashes, police and the National Guard killed one bystander, wounded some thirty others, arrested eight hundred people and tear-gassed the campus from a helicopter.

The first accounts of the People's Park battle emphasized the degree of terror all out of proportion to the matter at hand—a few hundred square feet of sod laid down by barefoot children and aging anarchs. Authority, it seems, might have met this bizarre challenge to property in kind with humor and, as one middle-echelon university official suggested, by rolling up the sod and blithely handing it back to "the people." But the proprietors were in no joking mood: they had to assert their legal right to ownership or face more people's parks—and people's libraries, people's classrooms and people's chancellors' offices. So authority reverted to crushing repression. The students, Berkeley political science professors John Schaar and Sheldon Wolin note, "identify spontaneity and unpredictability with all that is human and alive, and rule and control with all that is inhuman and dead."

Faculty Power

"Which side are you on?" go the words of an old labor-union song. Many faculty members are wondering if they stand on the side of change (even if that change affects the basis of U.S. corporate society) or on the side of authority. Their role will be critical. If it is not true that the faculty is the university, it is nevertheless accurate to say that without the faculty the administration would be hard put to keep the campus buildings open. Moreover, the knowledge industry would stagger without its clerks. The faculty also still enjoys a high status in the eyes of the students—at least until they come to college. According to a study by a young Columbia University graduate named Stanley Raffel, about half of Columbia College students, when asked about their plans before entering the university, said they wanted to become professors. By the senior year, however, those choosing an academic career had dropped to one sixth.

In recent months, faculty power has been belatedly asserted. At Chicago, ninety-one faculty members recently ran for the seventeen positions on the faculty-senate council, the group which disciplined eighty-one students for their roles in the Chicago sit-in. Normally half that number run. One year after the sit-ins that brought Columbia to a halt, the faculty has helped remake the university's system of governance—the first major change in two hundred years. When the Columbia SDS undertook a new offensive this spring there was little campus support and the offensive fizzled. (The reawakened faculty interest in their school has produced all sorts of dividends: one professor elected to the new council attended a reception and came away shaking his head in appreciation of "some of the really fascinating men we have here—when you get to know them.")

Faculty members have also lately taken a major role in the effort to bring black students and black studies onto the campus. This sometimes turns out to be a traumatic experience for many. First, they had to admit that the universities were in fact guilty of racial tokenism no less vicious because it was largely unconscious. As late as 1965, Northwestern, just a few miles north of one of the biggest black ghettos in the world, had fewer than thirty Negro undergraduates and twenty of these were "hired hands" on athletic scholarships.

Second, the faculty has had to examine more closely a set of attitudes which professed to see little academic substance in black studies—or else dismissed such studies as "ego development." Upon reexamination the faculty recalled that departmental concerns for "pure intellectual process" hadn't prevented the universities from taking on a whole range of applied studies, including Mickey Mouse courses in military science for the ROTC. They also discovered that, in any case, the principle of education for all—including the so-called "unqualified"—dates not from Stokely Carmichael but from the 1862 Morrill land-grant acts which have sustained such universities as Cornell, Michigan and California.

Finally, black-study programs have forced the faculty to reexamine some of its most cherished guild rules. It may well be that militant blacks like Professor Nathan Hare are taking the most extreme position when they demand that Afro studies be taught by blacks only from a radical, black perspective. The imposition of such tests sounds like thought control. Yet few scholars would contend any more that a Ph.D. degree is the chief test of fitness to teach.

Alternative Futures

What happens now? Few commencement speakers found in their hearts much cause for optimism, though not many were as pessimistic as Gunnar Myrdal. "Riots lead to repression, violence to counterviolence," he said. "At the end there is nothing left but the police state."

There are alternative futures, some not much better. The state and Federal governments can push through legislation increasing the penalties for campus disruption and cutting off funds to the universities involved. University administrators may decide to control admissions to eliminate "troublemakers." Officially, admissions officers say there is no reliable political test that can be applied to high-school seniors; but, privately, they acknowledge that they have studied the picture of campus dissent long enough now to detect some demographic patterns: East Coast and Bay Area, middle- and upper-middle class, third-generation Jewish or old-line Wasp.

The faculty may go into exile, abandoning the campuses in turmoil for research institutes like Brookings, for government service or for industrial laboratories where there are no courses to teach or students to worry about. Eventually, too, research-minded companies like IBM and Bell Laboratories might go into the degree-granting business. Such firms now give postgraduate training to engineers on the job and it would not be difficult to extend such programs. Then industry would no longer have to rely on angry young products of the university at all.

The students may emulate the faculty and flee the campus too. Student-run "counteruniversities" now exist in a score of U.S. cities alongside the straight campuses. The Free University of Berkeley catalogue provides a clue to what students attempt when they do their own thing. The description of Liberation Now reads: "A leaderless encounter group to which we all must contribute our love and concern."

The differences between IBM and FUB would seem too great for any university to bridge. Some scholars now hold that there is no chance of squaring the aims of the traditional university and the desires of the new student class. "If one asks one's students what the university is there for," reports

Professor Roger Poole of Nottingham in England, "they will answer that the university is there to experiment in. . . . The student doesn't want any more of the past. He wants the future."

But it is extraordinarily difficult for the university to be futural, to remake the age according to a vision of spontaneity, love and an immediate end to all injustices. The university's ideals of scholarship link it to the past, and its finances have tied it to government, industry and the established order. Students—black and white—are trying to break these ties. President Pusey reminded the graduates that "evils and shortcomings" cannot simply be willed away. "Your generation," he added, "has not brought into the world any such new commanding virtue capable of effecting a miracle of this sort."

Few would quarrel with Pusey, but the new student class can call upon other sources of power to achieve its ends. Some time during their school years, the Class of 1969 became members of a special-interest bloc that surpasses the farmers in numbers. This new power bloc has not yet made its numbers felt politically as the farm bloc still does. But it exerts a strong moral pull. As Berkeley's Frederick Crews says, "The unique strength of the black student movement is its claim on the conscience of the white majority. This is why a tiny group of black students in a college far removed from the ghetto can get results undreamt of by SDS."

Far beyond the campus, white students, too, have claims on conscience. Massachusetts Governor Francis Sargent said he would introduce legislation proposing that one voting member of the board of trustees of Massachusetts public colleges be elected by the student body of each institution. A Brahmin, moderate Republican, Sargent has undergone a dramatic change of mind about the student revolt. Friends attribute this in part to his son, a junior at Harvard. Like the faculty, parents are asking each other: "Which side are you on?"

CONGRESS LOOKS AT THE CAMPUS [2]

A deep concern about today's problem of unrest among our youth, and the realization that we possessed little reliable information about events on the American campus prompted us to go out to a variety of colleges and universities to talk with students, faculty, administrators, and other officials on their own ground. We had nothing to sell, no speeches to make, and offered only a desire to know and understand the factors which appear to threaten the destruction of many of our most respected institutions and the alienation of many of this nation's finest students.

The problems confronting higher education are so complex that no study or analytic effort yet mounted can really claim to be comprehensive. We recognize the need for continued in-depth research. Nonetheless, we believe we achieved substantial success with respect to our main concern—the acquisition of some degree of personal understanding of the nature of the problem.

We came away from our campus tour both alarmed and encouraged. We were alarmed to discover that this problem is far deeper and far more urgent than most realize, and that it goes far beyond the efforts of organized revolutionaries. By the same token, we were encouraged by the candor, sincerity and basic decency of the vast majority of students we met. Too often, however, we saw their idealism and concern vented in aimless or destructive ways.

If one point is to be emphasized in this report it is that violence in any form, in any measure, under any circumstances, is not a legitimate means of protest or mode of expression—and that it can no more be tolerated in the university community than in the community at large. If there is to be orderly progress and a redress of legitimate student grievances, student violence must be averted.

[2] From the preface to *Report of Campus Unrest Submitted June 17, 1969, to the President Following a Tour of Campuses by 22 Congressmen,* by Representative Bill Brock (Republican, Tennessee) and others. W. E. Brock. 115 Cannon House Office Bldg. Washington, D.C. 20515. mimeo.

As Erwin N. Griswold, solicitor general of the United States, has said:

> The right to disagree—and to manifest disagreement—which the Constitution allows to the individual . . . does not authorize them to carry on their campaign of education and persuasion at the expense of somebody else's liberty. . . .

It is clear that if violence on our campuses does not end, and if the reaction to it is on the one extreme too lax, or on the other extreme too harsh and indiscriminate, the vast moderate student majority may be forced into the arms of the revolutionaries, and those few who seek to destroy the fabric of higher education will have succeeded.

We agree with the editorial in the June 8 [1969] New York *Times*:

> If lasting damage to the independence of the universities is to be avoided, if the society's attention is to be redirected to its larger, more serious problems, violence has to cease and tranquillity has to be returned to the campuses.

There is on the campus today a new awareness of potential student power and the emergence of a large group, probably the vast majority of student leaders and a substantial number of intelligent, concerned and perplexed young people, which has genuine concern over what it feels is the difference between the promise and performance of America. While these students have no monolithic leadership or single set of goals, they are fairly united in questioning many of the values of our system. The revolutionaries on campus who desire to destroy our system are few in number. The vast majority of students are not poised on the edge of revolution and have not lost faith in our system. However, many students can be radicalized when violence or confrontation on campus occurs. Also disillusionment in our system by students can grow, even without violence, if we place one label on all students and fail to understand that they raise many areas of legitimate concern.

Perhaps our most important and pressing conclusion is that rash legislative action cutting off funds to entire institutions because of the actions of a minority of students would play directly into the hands of these hard-core revolutionaries. Legislation which treats innocent and guilty alike inadvertently confirms extremist charges that the establishment is repressive and indifferent to citizen needs and concerns. We must not put ourselves in the position of aiding the handful of anarchists.

In a period of conflict and turmoil, deep divisions on campus as well as between campus and community are understandable, but the danger exists that these divisions are polarizing America into two distinct camps. On neither side has there been enough willingness to listen and discuss problems before the fireworks have begun and emotions have been inflamed. Obviously it is time for our traditional American sense of fair play and tolerance to be evidenced by the responsible majority of this nation, young and old. The alternative of students, intolerant and unwilling to reason, and their elders, intolerant and unwilling to reason, constitutes the ingredients of chaos.

To the extent that our universities can foster an environment of trust, participation, involvement and interaction, we believe that the danger of violent confrontation (and the emotional climate which is its prelude) can be reduced. To the extent that this nation can foster an environment of quality, excitement and challenge throughout its total educational system, creative leadership can be developed. In this report we offer proposals aimed at implementing these goals. We can envision no greater tragedy for this nation and the free world than for us to allow our educational system to slowly settle into obsolescence, losing touch with reality and becoming incapable of responding to the needs of students and society.

We also suggest more positive contact between the campus community and the greater community—increased social action programs, volunteer projects and similar activities which provide students with an opportunity to work on pressing human problems side by side with other concerned citizens.

We are convinced that such experiences can be an important supplement to the classroom, acting to restore student faith in the basic soundness of the American system. Additionally, they can demonstrate in positive fashion the sincere good intentions of a significant portion of the adult community—which many students and faculty with whom we met so readily charged with hypocrisy.

Finally, this nation has an enormous stake in preserving our system of higher education. "The task of the university," as Alfred North Whitehead has written, "is the creation of the future as far as rational thought and civilized modes of appreciation can affect the issue." The creation of a better future will indeed be impossible if the free and orderly pursuit of knowledge is jeopardized by the destruction of our colleges and universities either through anarchy, or through a refusal to consider pleas for necessary improvements.

ADMINISTRATIVE ACCOUNTABILITY [3]

The answer to the legitimate student demand to have protection against incompetent and unresponsive administration is not formal *representation* in all matters. It is administrative *accountability*.

I would urge radical reform to make real the promise of administrative accountability precisely because I am skeptical in the reality of either participatory or representative democracy as a way of making final university decisions.

The first requirement of accountability is disclosure. Those affected by policies and decisions cannot hold those who make them to account unless there is full and adequate public access to the record of the process by which the decision was made. Reasons of good manners or simple humanity may make it from time to time desirable to impose

[3] From *The Politics of Academia*, remarks of Kingman Brewster, Jr., president of Yale University at the Yale Political Union, September 24, 1969. The Author. Yale University. New Haven, Conn. 06520. '69. mimeo. Reprinted by permission.

a seal of confidence on one man's opinion about another, in the admissions or appointment processes in particular. Unless opinion can be received in confidence in such cases it may well either not be given or be watered down into banalities in order to avoid offense or injury.

Also there may be situations where the intentions of the institution in its dealing with adversary outside interests make it very unwise to tip one's hand by public disclosure. In an impending real estate deal there is no reason why the university should be deprived of its bargaining power by having to reveal the inner thoughts about what the outside price would be. In a legal proceeding there is no reason why the university should forfeit its right to devise its strategy in confidential talks with counsel and others involved. But these are exceptions which can be reserved for executive sessions and confidential minutes. Hiatus could be noted in the record, specifying the nature of the problem and the reasons for exceptional confidentiality. Otherwise, it seems to me, that the record should be public. At the very least there should be a public communiqué. It might be even better if there were literal transcripts. Even if such transcripts were rarely resorted to, their availability would be the best assurance that the university could not be governed by conspiracy and that the reasons given by way of explanation were in fact the reasons for decision. Obviously the self-consciousness which this would impose might be an inhibition, it certainly will be opposed by traditionalists who value the men's club atmosphere of confidential deliberation. Some form of convincing access to the record of proceedings and the reason for decision seems to me far, far preferable to an ever widening and diluting of the responsibility for decisions. If accountability as an alternative to representation is to be convincing, disclosure must be as nearly complete as possible.

The second requirement of accountability is the right of petition by those affected by decisions. There has to be a legitimate, easy and reliable way in which critical opinion can be generated and communicated. Informal access through a variety of channels is the best way to do this in a relatively healthy situation. But if lack of confidence in authority spreads to a numerically significant minority of any of the constituent parts of the university—students or faculty (or alumni for that matter) then there should be an understood channel of petition to whatever level is responsible for the appointment to the post or office whose conduct is the subject of complaint.

If a large majority most of the time, or a significant minority all of the time, is willing to delegate the job of policy making and direction to faculty and administrative leadership, it is especially important to be sure that when this confidence is lost something can be done about it through legitimate channels. Accountability as a substitute for representation presupposes that those who are entrusted with responsibility will feel the hot breath of accountability day in and day out. This will be so only if petition can reach and gain response from those in a position to act, at a level above those complained of.

The third essential element if accountability is to be real is some regular, understood process whereby reappraisal of the competence of administration and the community's confidence in it can be undertaken without waiting for a *putsch* or rebellion.

At Yale this takes place pretty regularly in the case of college masters, department chairmen, and deans. Unlike many universities, every administrative appointment is for a term of years; three for chairmen, five for masters and deans. Naturally there is a presumption in favor of renewal if the man is willing. But after a second term there is generally an expectation that the man will revert to his purely academic status as a teacher and scholar.

This expectation of impermanent administrative appointment has many obvious virtues. It passes the burdens of academic administration around so that over the cycle of a generation more points of view are brought to bear, more people are involved and have seen the institution from the vantage point of important responsibility. Hardening of the academic arteries is less likely to set in. Most important of all, the relatively short term assures both the institution and the man that there is an honorable and humane discharge which does not imply dissatisfaction on either side. Given this opportunity for periodic reappraisal, the president is in a position to solicit and react constructively to criticisms and malaise without waiting for the mobilization of malcontentment in the form of petition. Recent experience with the appointment of new masters and new deans has shown that a little time and trouble can bring to bear on such appointments the authentic views of the students and faculty affected. This should be no less true when the issue is renewal of an existing appointment, and any self-respecting, self-confident dean would welcome it.

But what about the president himself?

For a couple of years now I have been toying with ways in which the president might be made more accountable to those whose lives and professional circumstance he crucially affects. While I do not think that his power can be fully shared by any legislative process, I do think that his own tenure should be at risk if he is to enjoy the latitude of executive decision which the job requires.

In thinking through the question of the president's responsibility in the case of a disruptive confrontation, I concluded that the power to act on the spot should not be stultified; but that in spite of all the risks of Monday-morning quarterbacks on the faculty, the president should submit his actions to review and should, if necessary, make the issue one of confidence. If he were to receive a vote of no confidence he should offer to resign. This conclusion is implicit in the "Dear John" letter of April 1969, in which I tried to spell out our thinking about the protection of dissent and the prevention of disruption.

The principle of executive accountability as the price which must be paid for the exercise of executive discretion has, up to now, been formally limited to the power of the trustees to fire the man they hired as president. This is a terribly limited and inhibited power, since it cannot be exercised without running contrary to the expectation of a lifetime tenure. There is no objective occasion or event which invites the appraisal. Even the most decorous and covert effort to remove an unsatisfactory president is at best a matter of intense personal anguish to everyone concerned.

Since it is likely to be resorted to only after deep rumblings of widespread dissatisfaction have been voiced in several quarters, the chances of concealing the reasons for premature retirement are very slight. If the malaise has erupted into rude, crude, and unattractive challenge, then of course the trustees are likely to get their defensive backs up, just to prove that they cannot be pushed around and that the institution will not be governed by mob rule. So, the worse the disease, the harder the cure.

The essence of the problem is that, while there is legal accountability to the trustees, there is no orderly way in which those most significantly affected by maladministration can invoke trustee action within a measurable time, without open challenge to the stability of the institution and the integrity of its processes.

It seems to me that the only way this problem can be solved is to require the periodic, explicit renewal of a president's tenure. I happen to think that ten or twelve years or so is about enough anyway, although there is no generalization valid for all times and places and people. More important than the length of average term, however, is the need for some shorter interval which permits periodic reassessment as a matter of course, without waiting for or requiring invidious or disruptive public complaint. Unless there is some such arrangement the hope for genuine accountability at all levels of authority is illusory.

I think Yale would be better off if it were understood that the trustees would make a systematic reappraisal and explicit consideration of the president's reappointment at some specified interval. This might be seven years after the initial appointment, perhaps at a somewhat shorter interval thereafter. I would urge the trustees right now to consider adoption of such a policy. This would mean a termination of my present appointment a year from June and an explicit judgment about the wisdom of my reappointment by that time. Under present circumstances the effect would be to make the office more attractive not only for initial appointment but also for continuation in it.

Of course the trustees could not, and should not, abdicate their ultimate responsibility for the exercise of their best judgment about the best interests of the institution. Occasions have arisen, and may well arise again, where defiance of popular student and faculty opinion is in fact justified by an issue of principle, just as may be the defiance of alumni or public opinion. Reservation of this duty and right, however, does not justify insulation of either the president or the trustees from a periodic, systematic assessment of what student and faculty opinion is.

Such accountability from top to bottom of the institution would require startlingly new measures for full disclosure of the meetings at which decisions were taken; and unorthodox revision of the terms of presidential appointment. Disturbing as they may seem from the perspective of inherited tradition, I would urge with great conviction that they would be far more consistent with the nature of a free academic community, and the administrative leadership it requires, than would the sharing of faculty and administrative responsibility for academic and institutional policies.

If such real accountability were achieved then I have no doubt whatsoever that consultation would become regular, widespread, and serious. This should include formal as well as informal participation, including elected groups where appropriate. No one with any sense, let alone pride and ambition, could fail to take seriously the importance of adequate consultation with those to whom he would in fact be held accountable at periodic intervals. Sometimes the

processes of consultation will be best served by an elective
process; sometimes it will best be done by trying deliberately
to impanel a group with a greater variety of interests and
viewpoints than would probably emerge from majority vote.
Also there are mixed solutions, relying in part on ballot, in
part on administrative selection. Most important there
should be no exclusive channel of communication or opinion,
nor any requirement that all consultation should be formal.

If it were limited for the most part to consultative arrangements, "legitimacy" might lose some of its rigidity.
Even if ultimate responsibility should lie with the full-time
faculty and administration, subject only to review by the
trustees, consultative participation is . . . good education for
the participants but also essential if the institution is to be
alert to its own needs in a fast-changing society.

I make these somewhat radical proposals because while
I do respect and share the dissatisfaction with a governance
which seems free to ignore the will of the governed, I think
that the sharing of faculty and administrative power with
students on a widely dispersed democratic basis would be a
disaster for our kind of academic institution. So I urge much
more strenuous examination of techniques of accountability.
They would be more fitting for university governance than
would techniques for the sharing of ultimate responsibility
with the transient student constituency. In order to further
serious consideration of these possibilities I submit the concrete proposals concerning disclosure and the terms of presidential appointment as worthy of consideration. Much more
thought and inquiry is in order before such notions could
harden into concrete proposals. They seem to me, however,
to point in a direction far more promising than expecting
actual direction of university affairs to come from a participatory democracy in which only a minority would participate, a representative democracy which would be unlikely
to be truly representative, and the substitution of a legislative power for what are inherently executive responsibilities.

WHO'S IN CHARGE? [4]

Who's in charge? Today a new group has burst into the picture: the college and university students themselves.

The issues arousing students have been numerous. Last academic year, a nationwide survey by Educational Testing Service found, the Number 1 cause of student unrest was the war in Vietnam; it caused protests at 34 per cent of the 859 four-year colleges and universities studied. The second most frequent cause of unrest was dormitory regulations. This year, many of the most violent campus demonstrations have centered on civil rights.

In many instances the stated issues were the real causes of student protest. In others they provided excuses to radical students whose aims were less the correction of specific ills or the reform of their colleges and universities than the destruction of the political and social system as a whole. It is important to differentiate the two, and a look at the *dramatis personae* can be instructive in doing so.

At the left—the "New Left," not to be confused with old-style liberalism—is Students for a Democratic Society, whose leaders often use the issue of university reform to mobilize support from their fellow students and to "radicalize" them. The major concern of SDS is not with the colleges and universities *per se,* but with American society as a whole.

"It is basically impossible to have an honest university in a dishonest society," said the chairman of SDS at Columbia, Mark Rudd, in what was a fairly representative statement of the SDS attitude. Last year's turmoil at Columbia, in his view, was immensely valuable as a way of educating students and the public to the "corrupt and exploitative" nature of U.S. society.

"It's as if you had reformed Heidelberg in 1938," an SDS member is likely to say, in explanation of his philosophy.

[4] From a report on the national picture of college governance. Editorial Projects for Education. 3301 N. Charles St. Baltimore, Md. 21218. Copyright © 1969 by Editorial Projects for Education, Inc. Reprinted by permission. Text from *Simmons Review*. Spring-Summer '69.

"You would still have had Hitler's Germany outside the university walls."

The SDS was founded in 1962. Today it is a loosely organized group with some 35,000 members, on about 350 campuses. [See "Class of '69: The Violent Years," above, for another estimate of SDS membership.—Ed.] Nearly everyone who has studied the SDS phenomenon agrees its members are highly idealistic and very bright. Their idealism has led them to a disappointment with the society around them, and they have concluded it is corrupt.

Most SDS members disapprove of the Russian experience with socialism, but they seem to admire the Cuban brand. Recently, however, members returning from visits to Cuba have appeared disillusioned by repressive measures they have seen the government applying there.

The meetings of SDS—and, to a large extent, the activities of the national organization, generally—have an improvisational quality about them. This often carries over into the SDS view of the future. "We can't explain what form the society will take after the revolution," a member will say. "We'll just have to wait and see how it develops."

In recent months the SDS outlook has become increasingly bitter. Some observers, noting the escalation in militant rhetoric coming from SDS headquarters in Chicago, fear the radical movement soon may adopt a more openly aggressive strategy.

Still, it is doubtful that SDS, in its present state of organization, would be capable of any sustained, concerted assault on the institutions of society. The organization is diffuse, and its members have a strong antipathy toward authority. They dislike carrying out orders, whatever the source.

Far more influential in the long run, most observers believe, will be the U.S. National Student Association. In the current spectrum of student activism on the campuses, leaders of the NSA consider their members "moderates," not radicals. A former NSA president, Edward A. Schwartz, explains the difference:

"The moderate student says, 'We'll go on strike, rather than burn the buildings down.' "

The NSA is the national organization of elected student governments on nearly four hundred campuses. Its Washington office shows an increasing efficiency and militancy—a reflection, perhaps, of the fact that many college students take student government much more seriously, today, than in the past.

The NSA talks of "student power" and works at it: more student participation in the decision-making at the country's colleges and universities. And it wants changes in the teaching process and the traditional curriculum.

In pursuit of these goals, the NSA sends advisers around the country to help student governments with their battles. The advisers often urge the students to take their challenges to authority to the courts, and the NSA's central office maintains an up-to-date file of precedent cases and judicial decisions.

A major aim of NSA this year is reform of the academic process. With a $315,000 grant from the Ford Foundation, the association has established a center for educational reform, which encourages students to set up their own classes as alternative models, demonstrating to the colleges and universities the kinds of learning that students consider worthwhile.

The Ford grant, say NSA officials, will be used to "generate quiet revolutions instead of ugly ones" on college campuses. The NSA today is an organization that wants to reform society from within, rather than destroy it and then try to rebuild.

Also in the picture are organizations of militant Negro students, such as the Congress for the Unity of Black Students, whose founding sessions at Shaw University last spring drew 78 delegates from 37 colleges and universities. The congress is intended as a campus successor to the Student

Nonviolent Coordinating Committee. It will push for courses on the history, culture, art, literature, and music of Negroes. Its founders urged students to pursue their goals without interfering with the orderly operation of their colleges or jeopardizing their own academic activities. (Some other organizations of black students are considerably more militant.)

And, as a "constructive alternative to the disruptive approach," an organization called Associated Student Governments of the U.S.A. claims a membership of 150 student governments and proclaims that it has "no political intent or purpose," only "the sharing of ideas about student government."

These are some of the principal national groups. In addition, many others exist as purely local organizations, concerned with only one campus or specific issues.

Except for those whose aim is outright disruption for disruption's sake, many such student reformers are gaining a respectful hearing from college and university administrators, faculty members, and trustees—even as the more radical militants are meeting greater resistance. And increasing numbers of institutions have devised, or are seeking, ways of making the students a part of the campus decision-making process.

It isn't easy.

The problem of constructive student participation—participation that gets down to the "nitty-gritty"—is of course difficult [Dean C. Peter Magrath of the University of Nebraska's College of Arts and Sciences has written]. Students are birds of passage who usually lack the expertise and sophistication to function effectively on complex university affairs until their junior and senior years. Within a year or two they graduate, but the administration and faculty are left with the policies they helped devise. A student generation lasts for four years; colleges and universities are more permanent.

Yale University's President Kingman Brewster, testifying before the National Commission on the Causes and Prevention of Violence, gave these four "prescriptions" for peaceful student involvement:

Free expression must be "absolutely guaranteed, no matter how critical or demonstrative it may be."

Students must have an opportunity to take part in "the shaping and direction of the programs, activities, and regulations which affect them."

Channels of communication must be kept open. "The freedom of student expression must be matched by a willingness to listen seriously."

The student must be treated as an individual, with "considerable latitude to design his own program and way of life."

With such guidelines, accompanied by positive action to give students a voice in the college and university affairs that concern them, many observers think a genuine solution to student unrest may be attainable. And many think the students' contribution to college and university governance will be substantial, and that the nation's institutions of higher learning will be the better for it.

"Personally," says Otis A. Singletary, vice-chancellor for academic affairs at the University of Texas, "my suspicion is that . . . the students are going to make a real impact on the improvement of undergraduate teaching."

Says Morris B. Abram, president of Brandeis University [1968-1970]:

Today's students are physically, emotionally, and educationally more mature than my generation at the same age. Moreover, they have become perceptive social critics of society. The reformers among them far outnumber the disrupters. There is little reason to suppose that . . . if given the opportunity, [they] will not infuse good judgment into decisions about the rules governing their lives in this community.

. . . The power of the public to influence the campuses will continue. The Carnegie Commission on Higher Education, in its important assessment issued in December, said that by 1976 Federal support for the nation's colleges and universities must grow to $13 billion a year.

"What the American nation now needs from higher education," said the Carnegie Commission, "can be summed up in two words: quality and equality."

How far the colleges and universities will go in meeting these needs will depend not basically on those who govern the colleges internally, but on the public that, through the Government, influences them from without.

"The fundamental question is this," said the State University of New York's Chancellor Gould: "Do we believe deeply enough in the principle of an intellectually free and self-regulating university that we are willing to exercise the necessary caution which will permit the institution—with its faults—to survive and even flourish?"

In answering that question, the alumni and alumnae have a crucial part to play. As former students, they know the importance of the higher educational process as few others do. They understand why it is, and must be, controversial; why it does, and must, generate frictions; why it is, and must, be free. And as members of the public, they can be higher education's most informed and persuasive spokesmen.

Who's in charge here? The answer is at once simple and infinitely complex.

The trustees are. The faculty is. The students are. The president is. You are.

IMPRISONED IN KIDHOOD [5]

Campus unrest can be easily solved once we recognize that its basic cause is America's refusal to wean its young.

For reasons that are largely economic, though not without sentimentalism, the average American today is compelled to spend a third of his natural life expectancy being thought of and treated as a "kid." It is a common occurrence nowadays to hear some broken father, wan before his years and

[5] By Russell Baker, New York *Times* columnist. New York *Times*. p E 3. D. 6, '68. © 1969 by The New York Times Company. Reprinted by permission.

teetering on the edge of premature senility, lament that he is killing himself to put "the kids" through college.

His kids, upon meeting, usually turn out to be women far advanced in the age of nubility or 210-pound brutes bearded like scouring pads and wiser in the ways of life than Casanova. The situation is as absurd for the kids as for the parent, but, oddly, it is the kids instead of the parents who conduct such little resistance as there is against it.

Materially, the kids would seem to be the beneficiaries. It is, after all, the parents who are "killing themselves" to sustain the system, and it is the kids who get all the material profit from the parental suicide.

Kids Catch On

The kids, however, have seen the catch; to wit, that one of these days they are themselves going to become parents and be compelled to keep a brood of fully-grown men and women suckled at the parental bosom through what might otherwise be the best years of their lives.

The weaning of *Homo sapiens* has always been a slow business compared to the weaning of cats, horses and antelopes, but until recently it was possible to have it well over with by mid-adolescence when the offspring finished high school. After World War II, the weaning age began to rise as employers became adamant about the college diploma as a condition for admittance to the privileges of expense-account living.

Once American industry chose to make the college diploma the visa to affluent living, it was inevitable that there would be a trend toward universal college education. This trend is now well advanced.

Since it is very hard to be truly independent and go to school at the same time, the weaning age rose and is still rising. Thus, both parents and colleges became victims; the parents by being saddled in perpetuity with kids, the colleges by being diverted from their natural academic function.

The colleges have suffered even more than the parents. It is no lark being overseer to a sentient adult sentenced to kidhood. By shipping the prisoner off to college the parents at least escape the daily agony of playing the prison screw for eight or nine months of the year.

The parent's relief is the college's affliction. Its limited resources are swamped by enormous influxes of persons with little or no interest in scholarship, research or learning who have come or been sent merely because it is universally understood that college is the place one goes to obtain the credentials necessary to partake of the national affluence. The colleges find themselves debased into credential-issuing centers, rather like the United States Passport Office.

Four years is an intolerable wait for a passport. Naturally, the applicants become restless. Frustrated in their natural urge to get on with life, they vent their restlessness by tearing up the goal posts, stealing underwear, burning down the physics lab.

Many of them want only to scream with boredom. These kids, whose natural aptitudes might have started them already down the road to happy lives in auto repair, barbering, cabinetwork and similar crafts vital to a civilized society, are forced, instead, to come to grips with Dryden, quantum theory, Keynes and Schopenhauer.

Those with a genuine interest in the academic life find themselves lost cyphers in vast campus populations that turn the lecture hall into Calcutta at high noon and make the scattering of good professors inaccessible to all but the most aggressive. Their frustration expresses itself in resentment against peripheral grievances—curriculum structure, the college president's social habits.

From all this the solution to campus unrest becomes obvious. It is to grant every student, upon graduation from high school, a college diploma. This would instantly reduce the college population to a level that our present educational resources could cope with, eliminate the agony of the four-year wait for a visa and allow grown men and women to enter the world in work at which they are competent without the stigma of lacking a degree.

Anyone who still desires to attend college, of course, should be permitted to do so, and no doubt a few would. They would be put on firm notice, however, that whatever they did in college no additional degrees would be forthcoming. Colleges would refuse to continue as credential offices.

Industry Would Scream

Industry would probably scream at having a huge new pool of young labor dumped upon it, but it is time that college ceased being a mere reservoir of manpower for American industry. As for the unemployment problem, the worst of it might be offset if parents were willing to continue killing themselves long enough to subsidize their offspring until they had learned to shave neatly, dress in the fashion approved by corporate managers and acquire fluency in the glibness that impresses personnel offices.

This should certainly not take four years, as college does now; hence, it would be not only cheaper for parents, but also healthier for the nation's educational system and more humane for its youth by releasing them at a decent age from the unnatural prison of kidhood.

II. UNIVERSITIES IN TRANSITION

EDITOR'S INTRODUCTION

This section synthesizes a good deal of the theorizing that must be faced before the concrete issues in student unrest can be discussed.

In the first article, David Riesman discusses the dollars-and-cents costs (in a period of desperate financial retrenchment for most academic institutions) of achieving the various goals and often contradictory ends that students, faculty, and administrators seek. Next, the head of Yale University's School of Drama, Robert Brustein, discusses the threat to a scholarly community posed by those who would substitute relevancy for competency. The education editor of *The Christian Science Monitor* provides a journalistic summary of successful "student power" excursions into administrative and academic affairs. In connection with the student disturbances at Harvard last year, Nathan Glazer suggests that it is incumbent upon administrators and faculty to determine the political motives behind ostensibly desirable changes in the university structure demanded by student activists. Alexander Bickel has some cautionary words to say to those who would obstruct the path to the "ideal university." And Russell Kirk, in the concluding article of the section, turns the relevancy question full circle by discussing what is not relevant.

UNIVERSITIES ON COLLISION COURSE [1]

When one considers the plight of our mental hospitals, of our prisons, of our inadequate welfare and our other starved public services, it is clear that higher education has been in many states the secular cathedral of our time. One wonders,

[1] Article by David Riesman, professor of social relations at Harvard University. *Trans-action*. 6:3-4. S. '69. Reprinted by permission.

though, whether colleges would have enjoyed all the public support they received in the past if people were as ashamed of having their children in college as they are of having relatives in mental hospitals or in jail, or if state legislators, trustees and others concerned with higher education got as little enjoyment and prestige from their involvements with colleges as they do from other public facilities.

The question is not entirely fanciful. For, as everyone knows, at the same time that higher education is under tremendous pressures to increase its services to its diverse constituencies, the taxpaying public, as represented in legislatures and boards of regents and the like, is growing somewhat disenchanted with at least some aspects of the whole enterprise. The result, as yet, is not an absolute diminution of support, but rather a relative falling off when measured against the expectations of rapidly rising support that most people in higher education have become accustomed to since the Second World War.

The faculties perhaps most of all. They assume the payroll will somehow be met and, in a remarkable example of self-fulfilling prophecy, that their courses will not be cut out and that the plateau on which they have been living will continue to rise. Indeed, as academic salaries have risen, teaching loads have dropped (which does not mean, necessarily, that less work is being done), and, because of the boom market for Ph.D.'s, colleges have had to offer faculty increasing amenities in order to recruit and retain them. In the thirteenth grade (that is, the freshman year of college), the faculty's teaching load tends to be half, or less, of what it was in the twelfth grade (or senior year of high school), and the salary generally somewhat higher. Also, as one goes on to the postgraduate level, the faculty/student ratio grows closer and closer to one-to-one. The result, when combined with the fact that it is rapidly becoming easier for almost every young person to go to college than not to, is a really enormous rise in the cost of higher education. Even the conservative projections of the Carnegie Commission on Higher

Education put the increase in these costs at about twice the national rise of wages, and maybe three times the level of inflation.

This general pattern of escalating costs persists at a time when students and communities are demanding more and more from academic institutions. Many of the affluent students who often lead the protest movements at colleges seem persuaded that the society is fully abundant and that nothing really costs anything. And many other people have also been persuaded, overpersuaded in my opinion, of the contributions that institutions of higher learning can make to the problems of contemporary society. Much of the overpersuasion has been done by the universities themselves, especially by the people in the social sciences. Having responded to so many demands in the past, especially from defense-related agencies, and having often overstated their claims to "relevance" to justify themselves to Philistine critics, the universities may now, however, be driven to bankruptcy by the demand for urban studies, black studies, courses that will help prepare students for the Peace Corps—all the new relevancies—while neither outside constituencies nor the faculty are prepared to cut down on the older ones.

At Chapel Hill, at Duke and many other places, I have noticed that black and white radical students are organizing the cafeteria workers and the buildings and grounds people to demand higher salaries. Medical students, once very conservative and now often radicalized, are making similar demands of the medical schools for more service in the ghettos. The trouble is that none of these and other like demands are self-sealing; all are self-escalating.

The most dramatic example is, perhaps, the effort of the colleges to expand greatly their recruitment of black students and, in many cases, to set up black-studies programs as well. But recruitment is expensive, and so is the increasingly elaborate system of orientation and counseling that colleges find necessary to help students, black and white alike, to cope with the often new situation they encounter in college. And black-studies programs are expensive, too. The problem of resources is made almost desperate by the fact that it is not easy to cut down on Far Eastern studies, for example, just because one is developing a program in ethnic studies; and after a point, one cannot visibly do less for, let us say, Italians, just because one wants to do more for blacks, for Spanish Americans and for other deprived groups.

A subtler but no less costly demand for reform is for more imaginative teaching. Because of what I have come to think of as a contemporary cult of intimacy, pressures in the general society, as well as within the university, tend to drive both students and faculty to demand small groups. I suspect that research would show that there has been a general decline in the span of control (i.e., the number of individuals to whom a person feels he can relate) that individuals feel they can manage and in which they believe they can learn and grow. There is a decline of belief in the vicarious, such as the big lecture provides; and our current ideology, in my judgment, often confuses the authoritative with the authoritarian and dispenses with both. At the University of New Hampshire and elsewhere it has been proposed that the senior faculty give freshmen seminars with 15 or fewer students, but rarely do these proposals cope with the logistical problems of where the money will come from or recognize that there is no educational reform that does not cost money and take its toll of faculty time (which also of course costs money).

All this is happening as an extraordinary tacit alliance between the Right and the Left puts pressure on the universities from both sides. Paranoia is a convenient state of mind because one is never disappointed. If one is on the Left and can prove to oneself that the "power structure" is invariably racist and fascist, then he will never be surprised, even by the most desperate efforts of the university to accede to his demands. And if right-wing paranoids can prove to themselves that the lapse in authoritarian controls leads to "anarchy," they need not distinguish between Clark Kerr

and Mark Rudd in deciding which better represents the
university their taxes or contributions are supporting.

For all of us, the world is perplexing and disorienting.
How are we to interpret the war in Vietnam, or the intervention in the Dominican Republic, or the hegemony over
the budget that the military and their civilian allies, including the labor unions, possess? Do these things represent the
true reactionary nature of our society, which can only be
corrected by revolution? Or are we to see them as evils that
perhaps can be moderated through existing democratic and
institutional channels? Many young radicals are not sure of
the answer to this, nor of their own courage and beliefs. By
acting dramatically and decisively, they seek to persuade
themselves of their solidarity with each other; by getting a
reaction from adults, they sometimes feel confirmed in what
they are only tentatively seeking to become. The adults
whom they confront in the universities are even more evi-
dently unsure of themselves: We often lack a feeling of
legitimacy. In our defensiveness, we sometimes become *like*
the young, and sometimes we overreact to their defiance of us.

I do not myself believe that the Left can gain in the
United States by forcing the Right to act repressively. If one
raises the issue of long-range consequences with the students
who are helping to bring about this repression, they are apt
to say that their violent tactics work. They do sometimes
work, locally; the problem is in their cumulative and national impact. In 1964, I talked to some FSM activists in Berkeley,
who also said that their tactics—mild enough in hindsight—
worked. I commented that maybe they did work at Berkeley
but that they might make Ronald Reagan governor, or perhaps President. Some students only replied: "That's fine.
That will uncover the Fascist face of our society." But under-
neath that euphoria about confrontation, it seems to me, is
a terrible despair that would find release in an apocalyptic
showdown.

A consequence of these combined developments, in which
higher education becomes more and more omnivorous of

resources while it becomes less and less able to elicit community support, is a collision course. The most obvious casu-
alties now appear to be the great state universities where
overcommitment and underfinancing go hand in hand as
bond issues are defeated and as state legislators respond in
often punitive ways to white and black student protests and
to the alleged softness of faculty and administration in seeking to control them. But the private colleges, too, are already
facing at least equally severe financial pressures. Those that
depend on tuition and have miniscule endowments may find
themselves in the position of Sarah Lawrence College, where
students sat in to enforce their demands for lower tuition,
the recruitment of more impoverished black and white girls,
and the maintenance of small class size. Andrew Greeley of
NORC [National Opinion Research Center] has done a recent study of private college alumni seven years out, work
that indicates a certain amount of resentment against institutions of higher learning on the part of their recent beneficiaries. Certainly in the endowed private prestige colleges,
some alumni are disenchanted when they find that their
sons and daughters cannot get in, while places are being
found for what they feel are ungrateful blacks and cantan-
kerous whites.

The balancing act, in all these situations, has to be per-
formed by the administration; yet it seems to me that one
of the consequences of what is happening in universities
today is a loss of administrative flexibility. Top administrators would like to experiment with cost-cutting devices, but
experience has taught them that what they may gain in
dollar savings they more than lose in faculty and student
morale. Departmental power, and now student power, tend
to rob administrators of whatever residual room for ma-
neuver they have to resist outside pressures and cope with
budgetary stringencies. Students and faculty are in the American grain in finding the enemy in administrative "bureaucracy"; but actually the undernourished and understaffed
academic administrations often behave inflexibly because

lack of personnel means that decisions cannot be individuated but must be handled by rules. In a recent book, *Mirror of Brass,* Mark Ingraham observes that administrators lack the fringe benefits that faculty have, receive few vacations, get no sabbaticals, and have no way of retiring gracefully.

In his much abused but penetrating book, *The Uses of the University,* Clark Kerr described a new breed of academic administrators who were in effect brokers among the various commitments and constituencies of higher education. He saw these men much as I see them, as having minimal power and limited leverage over their departments, their students, their alumni, and their sources of financial and other public support. But if we are to get through the years ahead and preserve some of the autonomous functions of the university, where the commitment to action is oblique rather than direct, I think we will need to find a still newer breed of administrators, men who will be capable of resisting some constituencies in order to satisfy others. They will have to inspire students and faculty and others in the university to accept their leadership in making these choices, and their leadership will have to be persuasive rather than arbitrary. They will have to help institutions to make a better division of academic labor, to decide for example that a particular university will continue its mission to foreign students even if it is at the cost of blocking more forceful pressures for more black students. Another administrator may decide that he will go ahead with a concentration on the needs of black students and resist pressures to do something for the Chicanos; and so on around the ethnic map and the wider map of possible commitments to action.

The academic leaders who can help institutions make these hard decisions are going to be even more unpopular and unfashionable than the men who now wish they could step gracefully out of office. If we do not find these other leaders, however, we will see higher education spread increasingly thin over the landscape, seldom committed to reflection, often committed to impulse, often ending in the bankruptcy both of treasuries and of hopes.

THE CASE FOR PROFESSIONALISM [2]

In such a state of society [*a state of democratic anarchy*], *the master fears and flatters his scholars, and the scholars despise their masters and tutors; young and old are alike; and the young man is on a level with the old, and is ready to compete with him in word and deed; and old men condescend to the young and are full of pleasantry and gaiety; they are loth to be thought morose and authoritative, and therefore they adopt the manners of the young....*

Plato, *The Republic,* Book VIII

Among the many valuable things on the verge of disintegration in contemporary America is the concept of professionalism—by which I mean to suggest a condition determined by training, experience, skill, and achievement (by remuneration, too, but this is secondary). In our intensely romantic age, where so many activities are being politicalized and objective judgments are continually colliding with subjective demands, the amateur is exalted as a kind of democratic culture hero, subject to no standards or restrictions. This development has been of concern to me because of its impact upon my immediate areas of interest—the theatre and theatre training—but its consequences can be seen everywhere, most conspicuously in the field of liberal education. If the amateur is coequal—and some would say, superior—to the professional, then the student is coequal or superior to the professor, and "the young man," as Plato puts it in his discourse on the conditions that lead to tyranny, "is on a level with the old, and is ready to compete with him in word and deed."

As recently as five years ago, this proposition would have seemed remote; today, it has virtually become established

[2] From article "Whose University? The Case for Professionalism," by Robert Brustein, dean of the Yale School of Drama. *New Republic.* 160:16-18. Ap. 26, '69. Reprinted by permission of *The New Republic,* © 1969, Harrison-Blaine of New Jersey, Inc.

dogma, and its implementation is absorbing much of the
energy of the young. Although student unrest was originally
stimulated, and rightly so, by such external issues as the war
in Vietnam and the social grievances of the blacks and the
poor, it is now more often aroused over internal issues of
power and influence in the university itself. Making an analogy between democratic political systems and the university
structure, students begin by demanding a representative
voice in the "decisions that affect our lives," including questions of faculty tenure, curriculum changes, grading, and
academic discipline. As universities begin to grant some of
these demands, thus tacitly accepting the analogy, the demands escalate to the point where students are now insisting
on a voice in electing the university president, a role in
choosing the faculty, and even a place on the board of
trustees. . . .

Clearly, it is absurd to identify electoral with educational
institutions. To compare the state with the academy is to
assume that the primary function of the university is to
govern and to rule. While the relationship between the administration and the faculty does have certain political over-
tones, the faculty and administration can no more be considered the elected representatives of the student body than
the students—who were admitted after voluntary application
on a selective and competitive basis—can be considered free-
born citizens of a democratic state: the relationship between
teacher and student is strictly tutorial. Thus, the faculty
member functions not to represent the student's interests in
relation to the administration, but rather to communicate
knowledge from one who knows to one who doesn't. That
the reasoning behind this analogy has not been more frequently questioned indicates the extent to which some
teachers are refusing to exercise their roles as professionals.
During a time when all authority is being radically questioned, faculty members are becoming more reluctant to accept the responsibility of their wisdom and experience and

are, therefore, often willing to abandon their authoritative position in order to placate the young.

The issue of authority is a crucial one here, and once again we can see how the concept of professionalism is being vitiated by false analogies. Because *some* authority is cruel, callow, or indifferent (notably the government in its treatment of certain urgent issues of the day), the Platonic *idea* of authority comes under attack. Because some faculty members are remote and pedantic, the credentials of distinguished scholars, artists, and intellectuals are ignored or rejected, and anyone taking charge of a classroom or a seminar is open to charges of "authoritarianism." This explains the hostility of many students towards the lecture course—where an "authority" communicates the fruits of his research, elaborating on unclear points when prodded by student questioning (still a valuable pedagogical technique, especially for beginning students, along with seminars and tutorials). Preferred to this, and therefore replacing it in some departments, is the discussion group or "bull session," where the student's opinion about the material receives more attention than the material itself, if indeed the material is still being treated. The idea—so central to scholarship—that there is an inherited body of knowledge to be transmitted from one generation to another—loses favor because it puts the student in an unacceptably subordinate position, with the result that the learning process gives way to a general free-for-all in which one man's opinion is as good as another's.

The problem is exacerbated in the humanities and social sciences with their more subjective criteria of judgment; one hardly senses the same difficulties in the clinical sciences. It is unlikely (though anything is possible these days) that medical students will insist on making a diagnosis through majority vote, or that students entering surgery will refuse anesthesia because they want to participate in decisions that affect their lives and, therefore, demand to choose the sur-

geon's instruments or tell him where to cut. Obviously, some
forms of authority are still respected, and some professionals
remain untouched by the incursions of the amateur. In liberal education, however, where the development of the individual assumes such weight and importance, the subordi-
nation of mind to material is often looked on as some kind
of repression. One begins to understand the current loss of
interest in the past, which offers a literature and history veri-
fied to some extent by time, and the passionate concern with
the immediate present, whose works still remain to be ob-
jectively evaluated. When one's educational concerns are
contemporary, the material can be subordinated to one's
own interests, whether political or esthetic, as the contemporary literary journalist is often more occupied with his
own ideas than with the book he reviews.

Allied to this problem, and compounding it, is the problem of the black students, who are sometimes inclined to
reject the customary university curriculum as irrelevant to
their interests, largely because of its orientation towards
white culture and history. In its place, they demand courses
dealing with the history and achievements of the black man,
both in Africa and America. Wherever history or anthro-
pology departments have failed to provide appropriate
courses, this is a serious omission and should be rectified:
such an omission is an insult not only to black culture but
to scholarship itself. But when black students begin clamor-
ing for courses in black law, black business, black medicine,
or black theater, then the university is in danger of becoming
the instrument of community hopes and aspirations rather
than the repository of an already achieved culture. It is only
one more step before the university is asked to serve propaganda purposes, usually of an activist nature: a recent course,
demanded by black law students at Yale, was to be called
something like "white capitalist exploitation of the black
ghetto poor."

On the one hand, the demand for relevance is an effort
to make the university undertake the reparations that society

should be paying. On the other, it is a form of solipsism, among both black students and white. And such solipsism is a serious threat to that disinterestedness that Matthew Arnold claimed to be the legitimate function of the scholar and the critic. The proper study of mankind becomes contemporary or future man; and the student focuses not on the outside world, past or present, so much as on a parochial corner of his own immediate needs. But this is childish, in addition to being Romantic, reflecting as it does the student's unwillingness to examine or conceive a world beyond the self. And here, the university seems to be paying a debt not of its own making—a debt incurred in the permissive home and the progressive school, where knowledge was usually of considerably less importance than self-expression.

In the schools, particularly, techniques of education always seemed to take precedence over the material to be communicated; lessons in democracy were frequently substituted for training in subjects; and everyone learned to be concerned citizens, often at the sacrifice of a solid education. I remember applying for a position many years ago in such a school. I was prepared to teach English literature, but was told no such subject was being offered. Instead, the students had a course called Core, which was meant to provide the essence of literature, history, civics, and the like. The students sat together at a round table to dramatize their essential equality with their instructor; the instructor—or rather, the coordinator, as he was called—remained completely unobtrusive; and instead of determining answers by investigation or the teacher's authority, they were decided upon by majority vote. I took my leave in haste, convinced that I was witnessing democracy totally misunderstood. That misunderstanding has invaded our institutions of higher learning.

For the scholastic habits of childhood and adolescence are now being extended into adulthood. The graduates of the Core course, and courses like it, are concentrating on the development of their life styles, chafing against restrictions of all kinds (words like *coercion* and *cooption* are the current jargon), and demanding that all courses be geared to their personal requirements and individual interests. But this is not at all the function of the university. As Paul Goodman has observed, in *The Community of Scholars,* when you teach the child, you teach the person; when you teach the adolescent, you teach the subject through the person; *but when you teach the adult, you teach the subject.* Behind Goodman's observation lies the assumption that the university student is, or should already be, a developed personality, that he comes to the academy not to investigate his life style but to absorb what knowledge he can, and that he is, therefore, preparing himself, through study, research, and contemplation, to enter the community of professional scholars. In resisting this notion, some students reveal their desire to maintain the conditions of childhood, to preserve the liberty they enjoyed in their homes and secondary schools, to extend the privileges of a child- and youth-oriented culture into their mature years. They wish to remain amateurs.

One can see why Goodman has concluded that many of the university young do not deserve the name of students: they are creating conditions in which it is becoming virtually impossible to do intellectual work. In turning their political wrath from the social world, which is in serious need of reform (partly because of a breakdown in professionalism), to the academic world, which still has considerable value as a learning institution, they have determined, on the one hand, that society will remain as venal, as corrupt, as retrogressive as ever, and, on the other hand, that the university will no longer be able to proceed with the work of free inquiry for which it was founded. As an added irony, students, despite their professed distaste for the bureaucratic administration of the university, are now helping to construct—through the insane proliferation of student-faculty committees—a far vaster network of bureaucracy than ever before existed. This, added to their continual meetings, confrontations, and demonstrations—not to mention occupations and sit-ins—is leaving precious little time or energy either for their intellectual development, or for that of the faculty. As a result, attendance at classes has dropped drastically; exams are frequently skipped; and papers and reports are either late, underresearched, or permanently postponed. That the university needs improvement goes without saying. And students have been very helpful in breaking down its excesses of impersonality and attempting to sever its ties with the military-industrial complex. But students need improvement too, which they are hardly receiving through all this self-righteous bustle over power. That students should pay so much attention to this activity creates an even more serious problem: the specter of an ignorant, uninformed group of graduates or dropouts who (when they finally leave the academic sanctuary) are incompetent to deal with society's real evils or to function properly in professions they have chosen to enter.

It is often observed that the word *amateur* comes from the Latin verb, to love—presumably because the amateur is motivated by passion rather than money. Today's amateur, however, seems to love not his subject but himself. And his assault on authority—on the application of professional standards in judgment of his intellectual development—is a strategy to keep this self-love unalloyed. The permanent dream of this nation, a dream still to be realized, has been a dream of equal opportunity—the right of each man to discover wherein he might excel. But this is quite different from that sentimental egalitarianism which assumes that each man excels in everything. There is no blinking the fact that some people are brighter than others, some more beautiful, some more gifted. Any other conclusion is a degradation of the democratic dogma and promises a bleak future if universally insisted on—a future of monochromatic amateurism in which everybody has opinions, few have facts, nobody has an idea.

CAN STUDENT POWER REFORM THE SYSTEM? [3]

Student power is moving in new directions on the American university campus.

"What's happening is that students are asking for a new partnership role in education," declares Roland Hinz, dean of students at Northwestern University. "They are asking for a piece of the action, not to run the university but to input their views into the power structure."

Not all administrators and faculty members agree with Dean Hinz. But interviews with university officials reveal a swelling tide of opinion that—Vietnam, the draft, the Reserve Officers Training Corps, and similar protests aside—students have a point when they demand a change in the educational system. Wayne Booth, dean (of undergraduates) at the University of Chicago, speaks for a great many of his academic colleagues across the United States when he says: "We must revise the university in fundamental ways."

Not only must change come, these officials insist, but students must play a meaningful role in bringing it about. Students "have much to tell us about the learning experience they are having," Dean Hinz emphasizes.

Broad Base of Support

University spokesmen who share this view base it on the firm conviction that the vast majority of students want to see reform in the university structure and curriculum and are willing to work within the democratic framework to that end. . . .

Many Americans believe that handfuls of radicals are responsible for all campus commotion and that controlling them will restore preprotest tranquillity to the groves of academe.

Perspective is found in a Gallup Poll which reports that students subscribe overwhelmingly to the proposition that

[3] From article "Student Power: Can It Help Reform the System?" by Kenneth G. Gehret, education editor, *Christian Science Monitor.* p 9. Jl. 21, '69. Reprinted by permission from *The Christian Science Monitor.* © 1969 The Christian Science Publishing Society. All rights reserved.

members of the student body should sit on university policy-making groups. According to Gallup, not only campus activists but 81 per cent of nondemonstrating students agree on this point.

The Gallup finding shifts the spotlight from the minority that makes the headlines to the great bulk of students. The effect is to downgrade the significance of the 35,000 youths who reportedly belong to Students for a Democratic Society (SDS) and even the 600,000 who, according to a recent Roper Poll, can be termed radicals. Of correspondingly greater importance then are the 6 million students (out of some 7 million enrolled in higher education), who insist that decision-making power must be shared.

A *College Management* magazine survey shows 75 per cent of university deans of students agreeing that students should share such power. Hence it is not surprising to find large numbers of young people on many campuses already involved in the policy-making process or in advisory roles to the policy makers on various levels.

Details vary considerably, of course. In some places dormitory rules and other aspects of student life are still at issue. But nearly everywhere demands include, and usually center on, academic matters and university governance—getting "a piece of the action."

Two months ago news headlines hailed the first meeting of the Columbia University Senate. Against a background of months of campus turbulence had emerged a plan that symbolized and, hopefully, gave substance to structural reform at Columbia. Of the 101 senate members, 21 were students elected from the various graduate and undergraduate schools of the university.

Less heralded but equally significant are similar developments on other campuses. Shortly before the Columbia move, New York University expanded its university senate by adding student representation, and Rutgers University last month enlarged its senate to include 18 students, who now sit with 75 faculty and administrators in deciding academic policy.

Graduate Elected

Students are joining faculty and administrators on standing committees within university senates at New York University, Syracuse University, Florida Atlantic University, and the Irvine and Santa Barbara campuses of the University of California. Such developments suggest a trend.

Too, more students are serving on formerly all-faculty committees that deal with curriculum changes and other departmental matters, as well as with many university-wide issues. Extensive publicity has been given to student participation in planning black-studies courses and programs. Actually, student involvement is probably fully as great in other areas of curriculum change.

Universities are drawing on students in other ways, too.

Princeton, Vanderbilt, and the University of Maine have announced plans to elect each year a member of the graduating class to the board of trustees, and the Governor of Massachusetts has introduced legislation to achieve a similar result among state universities and colleges in the commonwealth.

Syracuse University named 11 students to a 33-member committee to select a new chancellor; three students of the University of California at Irvine joined faculty members in a search for a vice chancellor; a special student-alumni-faculty committee has been appointed to advise the board of trustees of Northwestern University on the appointment of a new president of the institution.

Seven students of the University of the Pacific worked with 12 faculty members in a six-week, foundation-financed study aimed at redefining the role of that institution, one of many such reevaluations of universities or their departments and programs now under way.

Freshmen-to-be helped to determine, before the doors opened, the direction and programs of Old Westbury College, part of the State University of New York, and of Livingston College, to open next fall as a unit of Rutgers University.

How significant are these developments?

The issue spurs lively debate wherever students or faculty and administrators gather. Viewpoints vary. The question itself takes on distinctive nuances among different groups.

Question of "Sincerity"

To students the question means: Is the administration sincere; is it really willing to share power, or is it merely going through the motions? One test commonly applied to "sincerity" is the kind and degree of power that is offered. Students are demanding sizable chunks of influence, and they want it now. Delay suggests insincerity.

To Michael Rabinowitz, a graduate student and teaching assistant at the University of Chicago, student participation on his campus is "a rubber stamp. There is an impression of power without real power. They haven't given up a thing, and won't unless pushed hard."

Earlier administration-student relations sometimes cast a pall over a university. This is true at Columbia, where student reaction to the new university senate often reflects a residue of bitterness.

Said one Columbia student: "It's just more window dressing. The trustees hold the power and refuse to share it. We've been through all this before."

Despite skepticism on the part of some students, others are hopeful and even expectant of progress. A West Coast senior appeared to reflect the position of many moderates when he commented: "Our administration is moving ahead steadily with student participation. All of the necessary changes won't come overnight. But the university is committed, and improvements are being made."

For their part, many university officials attach major significance to plans for increased student involvement. By and large they appear committed to the principle of student participation in university affairs formerly closed to them. Some have been forced by events to this viewpoint, but most seem to find positive value in power-sharing. Not all are responding defensively to campus pressure.

The emerging issue in academic circles is not whether the university should move toward providing for enlarged participation. The questions are: How best to do it? To what extent can power be effectively shared?

In discussing the limits of student power, Lawrence Silverman, dean of students at Roosevelt University, favors student involvement "in all areas where they can make a contribution—not on the board of trustees or on the budget committee."

Others would extend the "out-of-bounds area" to include particularly the hiring and firing of faculty and matters related to promotion and tenure.

Yet students sometimes demand—and on some campuses are getting—a voice in decisions concerning the faculty. This may take the form of membership on committees responsible for passing on instructors' or professors' qualifications. Or in the case of tenure, students through course ratings in effect "grade" the instructor. These ratings become part of the aspiring professor's file, to be examined when he is up for tenure, a faculty position for life.

Student Role Minimized

Most of the power gained to date by students has come from the authority formerly reserved to the administration. The faculty has given up little of its tremendous power. In fact, the faculty has often won concessions simultaneously with students, as when the Columbia University Senate was formed, affording both groups representation in the governing body.

In areas where authority is vested in the faculty, students find their enlarged role restricted principally to that of advisers.

"Students and faculty are not equal to each other," says Dr. Howard Babb flatly. Dr. Babb, chairman of the English department at the University of California at Irvine, adds: "A teacher is intellectually superior to a student. Students should suggest but not make decisions."

Students also face several other kinds of resistance to their quest for power. One of these springs from their very transiency on campus; they spend there on the average less than four years, in contrast to perhaps decades for the tenured faculty.

Then too, students' lack of experience in knotty university affairs and limited free time for the "nitty-gritty" of committee work militates against their achieving greater influence. Administrators also point out that students often become disenchanted with participation when they learn how much time and effort it requires. On one campus students are asking for dollar compensation for committee work; on another they seek academic credit for this effort.

Yet despite all the objections that can be raised, all the obstacles that will have to be overcome, the emerging fact is that students are concerned about the quality of their university education—concerned enough to want to improve it for themselves and for those who follow. They aren't likely to abandon the effort.

"New Legitimacy"

Continuing confrontations will probably be resolved through a kind of campus-by-campus negotiated settlement involving trustees, administration, faculty, and students. Progress will depend on patience, improved communication, and a backing off from fixed positions.

For their part, students will have to temper their rigidity (call it idealism or self-righteousness). Said one professor: "Students think if they fight hard, they should win. They will have to learn that even if you're right, you don't always get what you want."

The process of negotiation may be long and difficult, but a new structure of university governance seems sure to evolve. This is the outcome envisioned by McGeorge Bundy when he spoke ... of

a new legitimacy given to a kind of authority in the institution ... an authority which rests upon the consent and participation of the academic community itself. That kind of legitimate body can and will be established, can and will keep peace, can and will command the overwhelming support of students and faculty. . . .

The evolving of new forms goes on. The end of confrontations is not yet in sight. But there is a glimmer of light visible through the tunnel, raising expectations that student power can be effectively employed in the restructuring of higher education.

STUDENT POLITICS AND THE UNIVERSITY [4]

The script [of student revolt] was played out before Columbia, at Berkeley in 1964 and 1966, and it is now being played out at Harvard. In 1966 at Berkeley, radical students blocked military recruiters. Police were called onto the campus to eject and arrest them. What was the faculty's response? To set up a commission on governance.

Making New Radicals

The logic of these events is truly wonderful. The blocking of recruiters on campus has nothing to do with the governance of an educational institution. Whether it was run by the state, the trustees, the faculty, the students, or the janitors, any university might consider it reasonable to give space for recruiters to talk to students, and if these were blocked, any administration might well decide at some point to call police. But then the liberal students and faculty move into action. First, shocked at the calling of police, they de-

[4] From article "The Campus Crucible: Student Politics and the University," by Nathan Glazer, professor of education and social structure at Harvard University. *Atlantic.* 224:43-53. Jl. '69. Copyright © 1969, by the Atlantic Monthly Company, Boston, Mass. Reprinted with permission. This excerpt deals with the student unrest at Harvard in 1968.

mand that new governance arrangements be created. Then, because they dislike the tactics chosen to remove the disrupters, they demand amnesty for them. Finally, because they have been forced into a tactical alliance with the disrupters—after all, the liberals are defending them against the administration—they begin to find the original positions of the disrupters, with which the liberals had very possibly originally disagreed, more attractive.

We are all aware that calling in the police radicalizes the students and faculty (so aware that many students and faculty protesting President Pusey's action at Harvard said, "Why did he do it, he knows it radicalizes us"—they spoke as if they knew that, according to the scenario, they were *supposed* to be outraged, and they were). We are less aware that the radicalization extends not only to the police issue and the governance issue but to the content of the original demands. A demand to which one can remain indifferent or opposed suddenly gains enormously greater moral authority after one has been hit on the head by the police for it. Thus, the first mass meeting of the moderate student element [at Harvard] after the police bust, in Memorial Church, refused to take a position on ROTC and asked only for a student referendum, and referenda, as we know, generally turn out in favor of retaining ROTC in some form on campus. It is for this as well as for other reasons that SDS denounces votes and majority rule as "counterrevolutionary." But the second meeting of the moderate students, in the Soldiers Field Stadium a few days later, adopted a far more stringent position, hardly different from SDS's. And a few days after that, the distinguished faculty, which had devoted such lengthy attention to ROTC only a short time before, returned to discuss it again, and also took a more severe position.

The recourse to violence by the radical students at Harvard was therefore successful. The issue of ROTC, which was apparently closed, was reopened. The issue of university expansion, which excited few people, became a major one.

The issue of black studies, which everyone had thought had been settled for a time, and decently, with the acceptance of the Rosovsky report, was reopened by the black students. It might have been anyway, but certainly the SDS action encouraged the reopening.

The SDS takes the position that these are no victories—by the nature of their analysis of the structure of society, government, and university in this country, there can be no victories, short of the final, indefinable "basic social change." Thus, the fact that the university faculty and corporation have now adopted a resolution which will remove the ROTC from campus entirely (even the rental of facilities, according to the mover of the new faculty resolution, would be improper) demonstrates, according to SDS, that the university has not given an inch. Why? Because the resolution says the university will facilitate student efforts to take ROTC as an outside activity, off campus, presumably in the way it facilitates student efforts to find jobs or nearby churches. "Abolish ROTC," the SDS ROTC slogan, it now appears, means that not only must students not be allowed to take ROTC on campus; the university must not give them the address where they might take it off campus. One can be sure that if this "facilitating" clause were not in the resolution, the SDS would find other means of claiming that the university is intransigent—by definition, the power structure must be—and that there has been no victory.

On university expansion, the corporation and the various schools of the university have come up with the most detailed account to demonstrate that the direct impact of the university on housing has been minor and moderated. The indirect impact is hardly controllable—psychoanalysts want to live in Cambridge, millionaires' children want to live in Cambridge (and some of those after all contribute to radicals' causes), students want to live there, and faculty members want to live there. Any reasonable attempt to moderate the situation—as, for example, Harvard's effort to build low-cost or moderate-cost housing—is denounced by the radicals.

Could there be any more convincing demonstration that the demands are tactical, not designed to improve the housing situation (if it were, it might prevent the anger that hopefully leads to the revolution), but to serve as a rallying slogan whereby liberals can be turned into radicals?

The issue of the black demands is a different matter; these are raised by the black students and are not tactical. They are deeply felt, if often misguided. Thus, the key demand of formal student equality in recruiting faculty goes against one of the basic and most deeply held principles of the university—that the faculty consists of a body of scholars who recruit themselves without outside interference, whether from government, trustees, or students. For the purpose of maintaining a body of scholars, students *are* an "outside" force—they are *not* part of the body of scholars. But if the black demands are not raised tactically by the black students, they are adopted tactically by the white radicals—as they were at Harvard, with the indescribably simple phrase, "accept all Afro demands."

Once again, this is the kind of slogan that is guaranteed to create the broadest measure of disruption, disorder, and radicalization. Just as in the case of "abolish ROTC" or "no expansion," "accept all Afro demands" has a wonderful accordionlike character, so that no matter what the university does in response, the SDS can insist that nothing really has been accomplished, the ruling class and the corporation still stand supreme, and the work of building toward the revolution must continue.

There is only one result of a radical action that means success for the radicals—making new radicals. In this sense, the Harvard action has been an enormous success. Those who know something of the history of Marxism and Leninism will be surprised to see this rather esoteric definition of success for true radical movements now emerging full-blown in the midst of the SDS, which began so proudly only a few years ago by breaking with all previous ideology and dogma. "Build the cadres" was the old slogan: "build the cadres," because any *reform* will only make the peasants and workers happier or more content with their lot, and will thus delay the final and inevitable revolution.

The aim of action, therefore, is never its ostensible end —the slogan is only a tactic—but further radicalization, "building the cadres," now "the movement." The terrible effect of such an approach is to introduce corruption into the heart of the movement, and into the hearts of those who work for it, because the "insiders" know that the *ostensible* slogans are only tactical, that one can demand anything no matter how nonsensical, self-contradictory, and destructive, because the aim is not the fulfillment of demands, but the creation of new radicals who result from the process that follows the putting forward of such demands: violence by the revolutionaries, counterviolence by the authorities, radicalization therefore of the bystanders, and the further "building of the movement."

What justifies this process, of course, is the irredeemable corruption of the society and all its institutions, and therefore the legitimacy of any means to bring it all down.

The Failure of the Liberals

Liberals like to make the distinction between themselves and radicals by saying to radicals, "We approve of your aims but disapprove of your means." This in effect is what the liberal student body and faculty of Harvard did. It disagreed with the occupation of University Hall, the physical ejection of the deans, the breaking into the files. But it said, in effect, by its actions, we think the issues you raised are legitimate ones. Thus, we will revise our carefully thought-out position on ROTC, and we will change our position on black studies.

On university expansion, the faculty acted just as a faculty should; it accepted the proposals of a committee that had been set up some time before, a committee on the university and the city, chaired by Professor James Q. Wilson. It followed its agenda and its procedures rather than the agenda set for it by the radicals. It received neither more nor less abuse for this action than for its efforts to accommodate radical demands on ROTC. I think the proper liberal response was: "We disagree totally with your means, which we find abhorrent, we disagree totally with your ends, which are the destruction of any free and civil society; some of the slogans you have raised to advance your ends nevertheless point to real faults which should be corrected by this institution, which has shown by its past actions on various issues that it is capable of rational change without the assistance of violence from those who wish to destroy it, and we will consider them."

Oddly enough, the discussion of the ostensible aims, even though the liberal position was that the aims *were* valid, was terribly muted. The liberals were hampered in their discussion first by lack of knowledge of the issues (how many had gone into the intricacies of relocation and the provision of housing for the poor?), and second by the feeling that some of these issues were not really the business of the faculty. In the case of ROTC, the key issue, the faculty tried to find an "educational" component to justify the action that might assuage the passions of student radicals. Thus, the argument on ROTC was carefully separated from any position on the Vietnam War, and a resolution was passed ostensibly for educational purposes, simply because it had been determined that ROTC did not have any place in a university.

This was nonsense. The educational reasons for action against ROTC were settled when it was determined the courses should not get academic credit and the ROTC instructors should not get faculty standing. Why was it necessary to go on and specify that no facilities should be provided? Space is given or rented for all sorts of noneducational purposes on the campus—religious, athletic, social, and so on. What had happened was that under the guise of responding as an educational body to political demands, the faculty had accepted a good part of the political demands, and implicitly a good part of the political analysis, that led to them. It would have been more honest to denounce the Vietnam war than to remove ROTC. After all, what role has ROTC played in getting us into that quagmire? It was civilians, such as Presidents Kennedy and Johnson, who did that.

By denying to students the right previously established to take military training on the campus, the faculty was in effect taking the position that all the works of the United States Government, and in particular its military branches, are abhorrent, which is exactly the position that SDS wishes to establish. It wishes to alienate students from their society and Government to the point that they do not consider how it can be reformed, how it can be changed, how it can be prevented from making mistakes and doing evil, but only how people can be made to hate it.

This may appear an extravagant view of the action of the Harvard College faculty, and yet the fact is that there was little faculty debate on the demands. The liberals implicitly took the stand, "We agree with your aims, we disagree only with your tactics," and in taking this stand were themselves then required to figure out how by their procedures they could reach those aims without violence.

But the aims themselves were really never discussed. The "Abolish ROTC" slogan was never analyzed by the faculty. It was only acted upon. All the interesting things wrapped up in that slogan were left unexplored: the rejection of majority rule (explicit in SDS's rejection of the legitimacy of a referendum on ROTC) ; the implication that American foreign policy is made by the military; the assumption that the American military is engaged in only vile actions; the hope that by denying the Government access to the campus it can be turned into a pariah—and once we manage to turn someone by our actions into a pariah, we can be sure the proper emotions will follow.

The expansion demand was never really discussed, or at any rate insufficiently discussed. It never became clear how different elements contributed to the housing shortage and to the rise of rents in Cambridge. It was never pointed out that the popular demand for rent control would inevitably mean under-the-table operations in which the wealthier Harvard students and faculty could continue to outbid the aged and the workers. The issues of the inevitable conflicts over alternative land uses, and the means whereby they could be justly and rationally resolved, were never taken up.

The faculty did most to argue against the new demand for equal student participation in the committee developing the program of Afro-American studies and recruiting faculty. Even there, one can hardly be impressed with the scale and detail of the faculty discussion. . . . The key questions of the nature of a university, the role of students within it, the inevitable limits that must be set on democracy and participation if an institution designed to achieve the best, in scholarship and in teaching, is to carry out its functions—all these played hardly any role in the discussion. The students were not educated. To their eyes, reasonable and sensible demands were imposed by force on a reluctant faculty. They were right about the force. This was hardly a manly posture for the faculty—at least they should have argued.

There was thus to my mind a serious educational failure at Harvard. All the education, after the occupation and the police bust, was carried on by the radicals. They spoke to the issues they had raised; others did not, or countered them poorly. They established that these issues were important, and thus in the minds of many students their tactics were justified. By student, faculty, and corporation response, their view that the university reacts only to violent tactics was given credence. If this was a failure, of course the chief blame must rest on the faculty. It is their function to educate the students, and the corporation follows their lead and their analysis, when they give one.

There were of course administration failures, too, in not consulting sufficiently widely with students and faculty, and perhaps in calling the police. But these did not justify the faculty in its failure to analyze and argue with the radical demands, and in giving up positions it had just adopted.

I agree with the SDS that the issues should have been discussed—ROTC, campus expansion, black demands. But more than that should have been discussed. The reasons SDS had raised the issues should have been discussed. The basic analysis they present of society and government should have been discussed. The consequences of their analysis and the actions they take to achieve their demands should have been discussed. They should have been engaged in debate. They were not. Instead, they were given an open field and all possible facilities for spreading their view of the world, a view that to my mind is deficient in logic, based on ignorance and passion, contradictory, committed to unattainable aims, and one in which a free university could not possibly operate.

The university now suffers from the consequences of an untempered and irrational attack on American society, government and university, one to which we as academics have contributed, and on which we have failed to give much light. The students who sat in, threw out the deans, and fought with the police have, after all, been taught by American academics such as C. Wright Mills, Herbert Marcuse, Noam Chomsky, and many, many others. All these explained how the world operated, and we failed to answer effectively. Or we had forgotten the answers. We have to start remembering and start answering.

STUDENT DEMANDS AND ACADEMIC FREEDOM [5]

As students return to university campuses, so no doubt will turbulence. Some of the turbulence will again reflect despair over the war and have little to do with the university itself, except as it happens to be a place where the young are.

[5] Article by Alexander M. Bickel, a professor of law at Yale and a frequent commentator on civil rights themes. *New Republic.* 161:15-16. S. 20, '69. Reprinted by permission of *The New Republic,* © 1969, Harrison-Blaine of New Jersey, Inc.

The force of many other storms will turn specifically to the campus. At the center will be various momentary issues. We have, however, now reached the stage where one campus issue underlies most of the stated ones. It is academic freedom.

The fight is not really—at any rate, it is not yet—over "the governance of the university" as the current cliché goes, for we cannot very well decide how and through whom to govern the university until we know to what ends, and subject to what norms, it should be governed. The essential ends of the university and the norms that should govern its governors have in the past been summarized in the phrase, academic freedom. Today's students deserve to have their teachers restate and reexamine the conditions of academic freedom. Then today's students, as yesterday's, are entitled to have their teachers defend those conditions to the last.

With good cause, but not without difficulty, our society has, by and large, been persuaded to the belief that new knowledge and insight, like art, are the products of independent minds following each its own bent, and will not often be attained otherwise. That is why we value the freedom of qualified men and women to pursue self-directed work. The universities are places where professionals of many disciplines can follow lines of inquiry that are determined by themselves, individually and collegially, and not dictated by anyone else, on either ideological or practical grounds.

Not all universities, and certainly not all colleges, pretend to be such places, and different sorts of foundations—research institutes and "think-tanks" of one and another variety—can be. But only in a university can inquiry and teaching constitute one creative whole, so that the knowledge and insight of the scholar, and the methods by which he gained them, may be shared with the student; so that students may be the scholar's company, nourishing him, giving as well as taking, in a word, collaborating. To this end, teachers must be free to teach their work, as free in their teaching as in their scholarship, and the enterprise must be judged by professional criteria and none other. The twin freedoms of inquiry and of teaching are best secured by faculty self-rule in matters of appointments, curriculum, and academic standards.

No one will claim that the ideal university exists, or that all members of all faculties are intent on their independent intellectual labors. But we will make no closer approach to the ideal by compromising it. We will collect no more of the kind of people the ideal calls for, and allow no more of them to function as they should, if we let avowedly non-professional and nonintellectual criteria play a role in their recruitment, or in prescribing their activities.

To be sure, the young as well as society at large have their own perceptions, which may not coincide with a faculty's intellectual interests, of the skills the young should be trained in and of the information that should be transmitted to them. Academic freedom is limited as the universities pay their way by meeting the felt needs of their clients, which change over time. Society has an instrument at its disposal for bringing its needs home to the university. It is the market, inside the university and out, and it is quite effective in the aggregate, over time. Students vote with their feet, choosing the university they prefer and then, within it, accepting or rejecting parts of the elective curriculum, and their parents vote with their pocketbooks. The curriculum of every university is witness to that.

Nevertheless, like many other institutions, universities are seen to be sluggish in times of rapid change. One way to counteract sluggishness is to engage students in the professional decision-making process by putting them on committees, and giving them access to other, though not to all, faculty deliberations. Students are that part of the larger society which is most easily accessible to the university, and they are, in a sense and for a brief time, most immediately concerned, even if they are by no means alone in their concern.

But the university as the practical servant of the society can all too readily swallow up the university as the haven of independent inquiry; and it would do so, to the ultimate detriment, of course, of the society itself, if students were given a decisive voice in setting the curriculum, or otherwise directing the intellectual life of the university, just as if alumni, or government, or churches, or labor unions, or business, or professional associations were given such a voice.

The disruptive tactics of some students have at times amounted to the assumption of control in faculty decision making, and they are not to be tolerated for this fundamental reason, as well as for other more obvious ones. But whatever the tactics of students, even if they are entirely civil, and however embarrassingly unfashionable it may be to insist on power and privilege, administrators and faculties should realize that inroads on the autonomy of the latter are inroads on academic freedom; the abandonment of faculty control or any part of it, over appointments, curriculum and academic standards is the abandonment of the ends of the university.

WHAT'S RELEVANT? [6]

With reason, today's student on every campus often objects that his course of study "isn't relevant." This mood is not unhealthy, provided that one has more patience than did jesting Pilate, and stays for an answer. Indeed, the question of relevance is so moot nowadays that I took it for my theme in my commencement address at Mercy College, Detroit.

What do students mean when they raise the question of relevance? Relevant to what? I suppose that they mean, or ought to mean, relevant to wisdom—though some of them think only of relevance to current affairs. The higher learning is supposed to open the way to the acquisition of wisdom.

[6] Article by Russell Kirk, a frequent contributor to the *National Review* on educational topics, and a well-known conservative spokesman. *National Review*. 20:699. Jl. 16, '68. Reprinted by permission of *National Review*, 150 East 35th Street, New York 10016.

There exist students, of course, to whom nothing seems relevant—because these students have no interest in any of the primary purposes of a true university or college.

Permit me, then, to say something about what is *not* relevant—which head includes much of the activity of the typical campus, especially of the multiversity which endeavors, in a non-Pauline sense, to be all things to all men.

First of all, the exploded notion of adjustment to modern society is not relevant to the true higher learning. Those who have read Evelyn Waugh's little novel, *Scott-King's Modern Europe,* will recall how its luckless hero learns by a summer's experience of modern society that it would be infinitely wicked to teach young men to adjust to life in the modern world. To adjust to the age of the mass state, of the concentration camp, the secret police, and injustice triumphant, would be sin and shame. The higher learning is not meant to inculcate conformity to passing fad and foible, nor necessarily to present dominations and powers. It is intended, rather, to reveal to us the norms, the enduring standards, for the person and the republic. Adjustment to abnormality is ruinous policy.

Second, college and university do not exist to promulgate the latest quasi-intellectual novelties; for those are not relevant to enduring truth. Some subjects which are puffed up as related directly to the moment's reality are hopelessly unrealistic, actually. Some colleges and high schools offer courses in Swahili, for instance, as a token of interest in African peoples. Now while Swahili would be most useful to persons like your servant, who travel in Africa, it never will be employed by even one tenth of 1 per cent of a college's graduates; and no literature exists in that language. What a notion of relevance!

Similarly, the typical popular "non-Western studies" program in the typical college is irrelevant: an omnium-gatherum of isolated facts and opinions about every point east of Suez tells us nothing about normality; and if a student does not know his own culture first—especially when it is the world's triumphant culture—he cannot apprehend a culture he never has beheld.

Also the representative "current awareness" course, meant to inform the student of journalism or of international affairs, is a boondoggle, and irrelevant. For one can understand the events of the hours only in the perspective of history and great literature and philosophy—true subjects for college study. The present is merely a thin film upon the surface of the deep well of the past, and the future is unknowable; so the genuine college wisely confines itself to study of the permanently significant, rather than of ephemeral events with doubtful meaning.

Third, a misplaced vocationalism in the college is irrelevant to the pursuit of truth. This is especially so with attempts to prepare young people for taking a place in modern industry. Modern technology alters so rapidly that the college cannot possibly keep abreast of industrial methods. What the college should do is to discipline the intellect so that it may be applied in future to productive processes, as to many other matters. The university at which the student is "prepared for a job" is the university which condemns its graduates to the lot of base mechanicals.

To be succinct, the truly relevant things in a college are the permanent things, in T. S. Eliot's phrase. They are the body of knowledge not undone by modern conflagration of will and appetite. The truths of the fifth century before Christ, or of the first century of the Christian era, possess as much meaning today as they did many centuries ago. Studying the permanent things, we are fortified in our contest against the multitudinous distresses of private life and of the commonwealth in this twentieth century. Among the genuinely relevant disciplines—supposing them to be taught by lovers of wisdom, and not by lovers of mere opinion—are theology, philosophy, humane letters, political theory, and of the sciences as means to the philosophical habit.

A hastily-got-up course in "urban problems," for instance, is irrelevant if the students—and perhaps the professor—are ignorant of the history of urban growth, of economics, of political thought, and of the other disciplines connected with the life of the city. Yet a course in urban affairs may be highly relevant to truth, and productive of good, if it integrates genuine intellectual studies and relates them to our present urban discontents.

If a formal education does not bear at all upon our personal and social difficulties today, of course it is a sham, and worthless: in that, the students of the New Left are quite right. But no modern authors are more genuinely relevant than are Plato and Augustine, say. Preoccupation with the passing pageant is merely the sort of "relevance" which the big commercial book-clubs sell; and college and university were not endowed for that purpose.

III. UNIVERSITIES IN TURMOIL

EDITOR'S INTRODUCTION

If there is one section of this book that captures the volatile nature of the campus crisis, it is this. A *Saturday Review* editor reviews the Cox Commission Report on the Columbia troubles and this serves as a starting point for analysis and self-analysis of an academic institution. Three thousand miles away, a professor of history brings the Berkeley crisis up to date. Next, a student participant in the Columbia upheaval presents a convincing summary from young eyes. Following this, in a sharp debate, two professors view the violence at San Francisco State University. Most commentators have agreed that former President Morris B. Abram was a most capable administrator at Brandeis University. His comments, the final selection in this section, show an objectivity about the failures of the university and its role as educator as well as the lessons to be learned from the student revolt at Brandeis, where the police were conspicuous by their absence.

What have the violence, the subsequent changes, the comparative quiet of the early part of 1970 taught students, faculty, administrators, and trustees? Like many of the titles in this compilation, a question mark ends this sentence. It is difficult to judge at this early date whether any substantive results have yet appeared. The United States power structure, the universities, the war, and environmental pollution (is this the new battleground or just a cynical ploy?) still appear to have similar profiles. Possibly the answer lies in how much effect the young have had on the nonacademically situated adults. This will be discussed in Section V.

WHEN THE YOUNG LIONS ROARED [1]

In the turmoil that followed "the bust" last spring at
Columbia University, when police dragged more than five
hundred students from five campus buildings they had occupied for a week, the Executive Committee of the Faculties
appointed a fact-finding commission to investigate the student uprising and its causes. The commission, headed by
Archibald Cox of Harvard University Law School, has submitted its report to Columbia and to the public. It is a
measured and serious indictment of a major university.

While a small group of radicals served as the catalyst that
sparked the eruption, the commission found discontent and
mistrust of the administration widespread throughout the
student body and parts of the faculty. Although it was the
"more radical factions in the Students for a Democratic Society (SDS) who alone sought the confrontation and whose
deliberately contemptuous manners had tended to freeze the
administration's response," the factors that fed a full-scale
revolt "were faults resulting from Columbia's own organizational structure, from the attitudes of the faculty, and from
the administration's and trustees' prior handling of matters
of intense student concern, including problems involving
increasingly self-conscious black students."

In retrospect, a clash seemed almost inevitable between
a "sophisticated and liberal" student body and an authoritarian administration. Tensions were heightened on the
campus by the draft and the war in Vietnam, by the growing
militance of the peace and civil rights movements, and by
the frustration about these issues felt by the socially conscious
young. "Yet it would be a mistake to conclude," states the
report, "that Columbia experienced last spring's disturbances
because she was caught in a broader movement beyond her
control." The structure and style of the university had for

[1] A review, by Bonnie Barrett Stretch, of *Crisis at Columbia: The Cox
Commission Report* (Vintage. '68.). Miss Stretch is assistant education editor
of *Saturday Review*. *Saturday Review*. 51:116-17. N. 16, '68. Copyright 1968
Saturday Review, Inc. Reprinted with permission.

many years placed the needs of students at the bottom of the scale of priorities. From something so basic as poor living conditions, to aloofness of the faculty, to apparent indifference on the part of the administration, the elements of student life militated against a sense of cohesion and trust.

The faculty, too, suffered from alienation and poor morale. The decline in recent years of Columbia's standing regarding faculty salaries and graduate studies, the university's embarrassing involvement with the Strickman cigarette filter, and the administration's disregard of a number of faculty reports on university affairs, all contributed significantly. But the faculty never had nor sought a role in university governance. The centralized structure, where authority on all matters except curriculum resided with the president, had created "a wide and unbridged gulf between faculty and administration," the commission found. "That the faculty and the administration should be conceived to have disparate interests—that there should be need for a *tripartite* committee on discipline representing students, faculty, and administration, for example—strikes the outsider as both evidence and source of internal weakness."

The question of discipline, indeed, was a key factor in the deterioration of relations among the parties, and the report documents with care the "evasive improvisation" of the administration that cost it the trust and respect of the student body.

Columbia's disciplinary procedure provided for no student participation, no due process of any kind; but placed in the hands of the administration the final decision for meting out punishment. The history of this procedure is central to understanding the issue of amnesty, one of the primary demands of the students who held the buildings. In condemning the students, and particularly SDS, for failing to exhaust all peaceful means for influencing the university, the commission feels compelled to add, "We are not unmindful that the formal structure of Columbia's institutions, the apparent detachment of the faculty, and the record of the trustees and administration made those alternatives such discouraging prospects that no one should be very surprised that they were ignored."

But the report is not concerned simply with the mismanagement of administrative matters. In their examination of the causes of the disturbances, the commission members listened thoughtfully to the students' testimony of their aims. "The projected gymnasium in Morningside Park, which symbolized [to the students] the shortcomings of Columbia's attitude to her black neighbors" and "the University's relationship to the Institute for Defense Analysis [IDA], which symbolized complicity in the war in Vietnam" were real issues, contrary to the belief of the trustees and administration throughout the crisis. The failure of university officials to grasp this fact was but an instance, however, of its greater failure to respond to the changing political and social context in which it exists. These issues mattered greatly to the students, and the commission was wise enough to see beyond their disruptive manners to the substance of their concern.

In retelling the familiar chronology of the events of April 23 to 30, the commission has marshaled a mass of facts into a dramatic narrative. The whole story is here, with many details hitherto unknown. And beyond the facts are the agony and absurdity, the complexity and emotion. One sees the faculty working with a sense of guilt and desperation for a peaceful settlement that in retrospect can be seen as impossible, and the administration torn between its desire to end the whole business and bring in the police and its desire to avoid the irreparable breaches of trust that were not only inevitable, but had already been achieved. It is a tragic, foolish story told courageously and well.

Only one part is missing, and that is the role of the trustees. The commission mentions once "the lack of communication and understanding between the faculty and trustees" but does not "assign it any great importance." Yet the trustees are responsible for decisions such as affiliation with IDA, university expansion policy, and, most significantly of all, the appointment of the president. When the trustees are out of touch with their own institution, this surely is important. In today's society, when the university is taking on responsibilities so contrary to its former nature, perhaps it is time to rethink the role and structure of the board of trustees as well as the internal operations of the university.

For, finally, it is in the hands of the trustees whether Columbia makes triumph out of her trial. "The fabric of the University's life is now twisted and torn," writes the commission. "The violence has now yielded to bitterness and distrust. Only heroically open-minded and patient efforts can repair the injury."

LIVING WITH CRISIS: A VIEW FROM BERKELEY [2]

In 1965, I wrote an article on the Berkeley student movement. As I read it now, it is full of the shock and excitement of Berkeley then. Supporters of the student movement thought they were living in a revolutionary dawn; faculty and students together would overthrow a repressive and inefficient administration and build the university of the future. Opponents of the movement, on the other hand, believed that academic values could not be maintained in an atmosphere of shouting and slogans; some doubted that in an institution so shaken even the necessary minimum of order could be restored. Neither hopes nor fears were altogether ridiculous, but five years later the hopes are at best more sober and the fears more concrete.

Since the Free Speech Movement of winter 1964 the scene on and off the campus has changed past recognition. Violent student revolution has become worldwide, reflecting the division and near paralysis of reform, the discrediting of establishments, and also the bankruptcy of radical theory. In America the civil rights movement, the glow of Kennedy

[2] Article by Henry F. May, Margaret Byrne Professor of History at the University of California, Berkeley. Reprinted from *American Scholar*. 38:588-605 Autumn '69. Copyright © 1969 by the United Chapters of Phi Beta Kappa. By permission of the publishers.

and early Johnson reform seem very distant. The Right wins local triumphs, and the most serious struggle in Washington is between moderate and extreme conservatives. Above all, since about 1965 the Vietnam war, although it has played no direct part in the most recent Berkeley crises, has been the most powerful source of disaffection. The draft is the main fact in the lives of young men and their girl friends, a reason to stay on the campus and avoid graduation.

All these changes show their most extreme effects in California. Governor Reagan, supported against Pat Brown by many campus radicals, has made Berkeley a very profitable political issue and finally controls a majority of the Board of Regents. When these are irritated, they sometimes lash out in actions as ineffective and irrational as those of campus militants. Many citizens of California applaud them; others, bewildered by events, veer to Right or Left as violence seems to come from Left or Right.

A few faculty members leave Berkeley every year; most stay, divided between hopes and fears. If I ask almost any of my colleagues how he feels after reading the campus newspaper or going to a meeting of the Academic Senate, the answer is likely to reflect despair. If, however, I ask him how his graduate or undergraduate classes are going, his expression changes: "Let me tell you about a wonderful paper I got yesterday. A little nutty perhaps, but so bright, and so well researched. . . ."

The most obvious new development in Berkeley is the increase in violence. In 1964 peaceful sit-ins were shocking enough; between then and 1968 the movement confined itself to strikes and marches. In 1968-69 we have had four violent confrontations. Although my purpose in this article is to interpret and not to narrate, it is necessary to look briefly at each of these. Their differences and similarities say a lot about the Berkeley scene, and perhaps about wider matters.

The first outbreak of violence came in July 1968, in the form of a clash between the "street people" of Telegraph

Avenue and the police over an unauthorized meeting. ("Street people," which contrasts neatly with "straight people," is the current name for the unattached and sometimes bizarre youth who have flocked to Berkeley in increasing numbers since 1964.) There is no question that the area south of campus, fascinating to the young and in some aspects intriguing to their elders, has become an area of petty and not-so-petty crime, going well beyond marijuana and sex offenses, and that both the university and the Berkeley businessmen find it hard to live with. This clash arose over an unauthorized meeting; it did not involve the university administration or the summer students. Windows were smashed, rocks and at least one Molotov cocktail were thrown at police; bonfires were started. The public was horrified, but when the police overreacted, enforcing a curfew by indiscriminate attacks on anybody who happened to be in the wrong place at the wrong time, sympathy predictably shifted. The clash ended with a complete victory for the street people. Reversing itself, the city council permitted the closing of the avenue for a euphoric and highly untraditional Fourth of July celebration, to the intense anger of the police, who had been fighting to sustain an earlier and opposite decision.

The next crisis, in the fall, arose over a course in which Eldridge Cleaver was to give most of the lectures. His suitability for university teaching, although not his intelligence or importance, was questioned by some faculty. Nevertheless, the course was duly sanctioned by the new machinery for nondepartmental courses set up in the wake of the Free Speech Movement. The Regents, prompted by the Governor, forbade the granting of credit for the course and ruled that in future no guest lecturer could give more than one lecture in any course. This action seemed to the faculty to raise a dangerous question: were the Regents planning to assert powers, constitutionally theirs but delegated for at least half a century, to govern each of the nine campuses directly?

To a great many students, the Cleaver course became a symbol of two causes, experimental courses and racial equality. Naturally, the radical movement pounced on the issue, yet the resultant protests were a failure. A mild-mannered sit-in in Sproul Hall produced arrests. This was followed by a destructive and coercive sit-in in Moses Hall, modeled frankly on Columbia. This was dealt with by police with dispatch and also restraint; its leaders were arrested and punished also by campus authorities. There was almost no campus protest, the Governor praised the Chancellor, and many, some cheerfully and some sadly, concluded that the Berkeley student movement had committed suicide.

The winter quarter, however, put an end to any such hopes or fears. The new conflict arose over the issue of black studies which, in Berkeley as elsewhere, involves emotions of high intensity and shifts alignments. Berkeley, which had never had more than a handful of black students or faculty, had for several years felt guilty about this. The administration, with faculty support, had developed a program for special admissions on an increasing scale. When black militant students, supported by off-campus black groups, demanded a black-studies program, the administration had indicated approval in principle and appointed black administrators to develop a project. Some faculty members, especially those long concerned with closely related subjects, felt bypassed and many more had doubts about such matters as racial criteria for appointments or hints of special racial definitions of subject matter.

Well after it was clear that some action to increase black studies would be taken, and while the matter was proceeding through faculty committees in the time-honored and time-consuming manner, the Third World Liberation Front called a strike. The essence of its demands was a program for black, Chicano and Oriental studies, controlled by Third World faculty and students, with some connection to outside Third World communities. Somewhat half-heartedly, the considerable organized minority of teaching assistants called a separate strike of their own, combining a version of Third World demands with trade-union objectives. Most students, while generally sympathetic to minority studies, nonetheless failed to support the strike, and class attendance was almost normal. Frustrated and angry, black, Chicano and white militants resorted to three kinds of coercive action. The first, an attempt to break up large classes by threat of force, was overwhelmingly unpopular (at San Francisco State it had scored major successes). The second technique was mass picketing of the principal entrance to the campus, Sather Gate, sometimes in the form of actual shoulder-to-shoulder blocking of the entrance. (There are, of course, plenty of other ways to get on and off the campus, but some *anti*strike students and others insisted on their right to use Sather Gate, thus producing the sort of symbolic issue that seems most productive of emotion.) The third tactic was most dangerous: small groups of demonstrators, fifty to several hundred, would snake dance through the campus, visiting a different building each time, shouting slogans and obscenities, smashing rows of office windows with clubs, tossing rocks through library and classroom windows, or dumping library cards. There were many attempts at arson, and the largest classroom auditorium was gutted by an unexplained fire in the first night of the strike. These actions, far out of the control of a small campus police force on a large and open campus, led first to the summoning of considerable outside assistance by the campus administration, and then to the proclamation by the Governor with considerable fanfare of a state of extreme emergency. The practical effect of this was not only to bring hundreds of highway patrolmen to the campus but to turn over control of operations to the sheriff of Alameda County. Battles developed in which clubs and tear gas were used on one side and baskets of rocks and chunks of concrete on the other. Yet, until almost the end of this crisis, police were unable to control the situation: the snake dance still went on; windows were still broken, and life became nearly intolerable. Through it all, however, students and professors kept classes going, sometimes in situations that required considerable courage. Finally, the Academic Senate passed a resolution supporting an ethnic studies college in principle but granting none of the strikers' immediate demands, and the strike was called off.

Once more a period of calm seemed to arrive, and the shaken campus began to resume an air of near normality. In the spring quarter, however, all predictions were again nullified by the outbreak of the worst crisis so far over the least comprehensible issue, that of the People's Park.

Not Vietnam, not ethnic studies, but the disposition of a small piece of university-owned land produced the most alarming crisis Berkeley had seen. To solid citizens of Berkeley, to many faculty members, and to the administration the problem seemed simple: the university owned the land, it had long planned various uses for it, and now had decided to turn it into a soccer field. Squatter occupation would produce violations of laws concerning drugs, public decency, and sanitation. These fears were confirmed by the statements of some of the allies of the park developers. Moreover, as the struggle developed, command of the People's Park forces devolved on a familiar group of radical leaders who had led utterly different kinds of actions in the past.

To the other side, the issue was equally clear. The land had been long unused, and there was no evidence whatever that anybody wanted a soccer field. Students and street people, long urged to do something constructive, had planted grass and flowers and installed playground equipment, which was being used with enthusiasm by parents and children. The sudden decision to end all this by building a steel fence was part of a program of driving the hippies out of Berkeley, an objective that had indeed had articulate support from some Berkeley citizens.

Despite the explosive nature of the symbols of steel fences and flowers, this crisis might have been only middle-sized—say, another Cleaver affair—except for two facts. The first was a meeting in Sproul Plaza in which the student body president-elect was heard to urge the crowd to "take the park." (Exactly what he said, with what intent or effect, will be the subject of court action.) The crowd moved in the direction of the park. When they encountered police, some members of the crowd threw rocks and iron bars, a hydrant was opened, and one police car set on fire.

The second fact making this the worst of all our crises was the response of the police. Apparently somebody had decided that the police, this time, should "teach Berkeley a lesson." After immediately responding with tear gas to whatever threat existed (as usual, accounts differ radically), the police later in the afternoon of May 15 were issued shotguns charged both with bird shot and with lethal 00 buckshot. One man was killed and another blinded, a number were wounded, and students studying in a room in the library, far from the original encounter, were placed in danger of their lives when buckshot was fired through a window by police chasing demonstrators and apparently firing in the air. During the next few days police action made the university even more unsafe for peaceful pursuits than it had been made by militants in the previous episode. National Guardsmen ringed the campus with bayonets, making it at times impossible to move on or off, and indulged in crowd-control exercises in which large groups were moved at bayonet point. The noise of helicopters, constantly droning right overhead, rendered intellectual work almost impossible, and on at least one occasion CN gas was sprayed on a large area of the campus from the air. Under these circumstances, some professors who had insisted on sticking to routine in every previous episode met their classes off campus. Yet it was still a fact, and to me a moving one, that students resisted this near-shutdown by police as they had resisted other shutdown attempts by militants. Although some other campuses of the university were officially closed in protest, at Berkeley efforts to stop remaining classes were met once more with extreme hostility. Undergraduates sometimes called professors, reporting that they had tried to come to class but had been

stopped by bayonets or tear gas. Graduate students called
up to explain that their papers would be late because they
could not get into the library. The campus community had
never seemed so united.

In an effort to arouse Berkeley citizens and thus produce
pressure on the mayor and council against police action,
demonstrators used various nonviolent tactics in areas off
the campus (shop-ins, park-ins, et cetera). In reprisal, the
National Guard cordoned a large area of the principal
street, arresting 482 people who were there, including militants, bystanders, shoppers and one postman. These were all
taken to Santa Rita prison camp. Obviously knowing that
charges against them could not stand up, prison authorities
and police there treated those arrested with such brutality
that, after later investigation, prison authorities were punished by the thoroughly antiradical sheriff.

When emotions had tightened to a maximum, a protest
march was announced. This was expected to draw very large
numbers of people from widespread and diverse groups. The
police and guard were still in occupation, and still worse
violence seemed likely. The Academic Senate, the administration and the city council backed a last-minute compromise on the park issue involving leasing the land to the city
for some sort of park development. The march, past barbed-
wire barricades and first-aid stations manned by San Francisco medical students, turned into a bizarre, cheerful, entirely peaceful spring festival. By the end of the day flowers
were being twined in the barricades and even sported in the
helmets of smiling highway patrolmen. Hundreds of march
monitors, fifty official faculty observers, and many volunteers
of all sorts exhorted the crowds to avoid provocation. The
crisis passed, the fence remained, the campus turned with a
shudder to final examinations, and the Regents refused to
accept the compromise now backed by administration, students, faculty and the city government. With this and every
other issue unsettled, Berkeley in June 1969, once more began a new quarter with a semblance of academic calm.

From this abbreviated history, a few lessons immediately stand out. One is the unpredictability of events. In a divided and confused society, emotions are discharged by symbols, and only those immediately involved can understand why one symbol is effective and another not. Another is that in such a society all power is tenuous and shifting: neither the Regents, the administration, the faculty nor the students can altogether transcend the peculiar limits of time and mood. A third, and the only comforting conclusion, is the extreme toughness of serious intellectual values. In an effort to pursue these conclusions a little further, I will look first at power groups, then at types of problems.

Among groups, one might as well start with the students, and among them with the "tiny minority" of radicals, to whom conservatives always attribute semimagical powers of forcing "the vast majority" into subversive action. There is indeed a revolutionary minority in Berkeley, and it probably consists of a few hundred students and nonstudents. This minority is, as the recent SDS convention has shown, divided and subdivided among Maoists, Castroites, Black Panthers, and some more revolutionary than any of these. All know that revolution is not possible in the near future in the United States; indeed, some are so remote from actual politics that their usual behavior is academic and even decorous. Others, however, are quite frank in their belief that the only hope is to break down existing institutions by any means possible, and that the way to do this is to shift from one impossible demand to the next; any confrontation serves the ultimate purpose. These are aware that they are well known and intensely unpopular among the less radical students. Between each of our crises this year, representatives of the far Left have complained that the movement was dying. In February, shortly before the TWLF [Third World Liberation Front] strike (unexpected by most white radicals), Jerry Rubin, in the *New York Review of Books*, said he was

. . . depressed to see the old Berkeley audaciousness gone. . . . Three years ago, we were going to overthrow Washington from

Telegraph Avenue. Result: broken dreams for hundreds and hundreds of people. "Politico" has virtually become a term of insult in Berkeley today.

Meanwhile, the cops are smiling.

Rubin proved wrong this time: yet the demoralization of the Left is obvious. If it were not for the Governor, some of the Regents, and the police, Berkeley radicalism at present might be on its last legs.

The "vast," also known as the "silent," majority can be divided into two groups. The vaster and more silent consists of vocational students. Most engineers, many students of applied and some of pure science (although probably not most law students or members of the School of Social Welfare) belong in this category and take no part in campus political controversy. The other large group, made up mostly of graduate and undergraduate students in the liberal arts, consists of those who are to one degree or another disaffected. The number is hard to estimate; in the two major crises of the Free Speech Movement and the People's Park, perhaps five or six thousand were involved as voters, marchers or occasionally active sympathizers. These are the "youth of today" about whom so much is written. They find little to encourage them in the America of Nixon and Reagan; they detest the Vietnam war (and as a result cannot listen to any defense of American foreign policy) ; they believe passionately in personal freedom and approve, whether or not they participate in, such demonstrations of it as smoking marijuana, dressing unconventionally, and being open about one's sex life. These are the Berkeley students who used to swarm into the Peace Corps and VISTA and still volunteer in numbers to tutor ghetto children (or plant trees). They are concerned with contemporary art and literature and sometimes even with some of that of the past. Lacking intellectual discipline and a little more intolerant than they mean to be, they have a quick eye and ear for the phony and, in the long run, despite their belief in emotion and its expression, respect intellectual honesty. They can be triggered into political action quickly, but only by issues or symbols that appeal to their deepest feelings. These feelings are not primarily political, but are concerned with relations among individuals and no doubt, finally, with relations between them and their families.

The faculty had best be passed over rather quickly; their collective or political aspect is neither inspiring nor important. Repeating the motions of the great days of 1964 with less and less conviction, they go through the familiar routines of signing manifestos, caucusing, and even making speeches. What usually results is a resolution, carefully drawn up by negotiations among wily political opponents, condemning violence or the Regents, or deploring the situation. Understandably, few outsiders notice such resolutions, and most professors have ceased, except in moments of extreme tension, taking part in public affairs at all. If asked, many will explain this by the essential powerlessness of the faculty in the face of the Regents, but this is far too easy. The institution cannot operate without professors; they could, if they wanted to, enforce their essential demands. Their potential influence in the state and the nation is considerable. The real trouble lies in an unresolved inner conflict: while the training, the old loyalties and the emotions of most professors are liberal, their status is conservative. Most have moved from relative poverty to affluence; they are happy in their status and love their work; they do not want to rock the boat. Willing to condone almost any student action directed against the administration or the outside world, faculty members like other people move very quickly to the Right when their own interests—the classroom, the library, the laboratories—are menaced from the Left.

Most insist on maintaining, however, the fiction that they, unlike everybody else, are disinterested. Professors will not be effective in the present situation until they are willing to accept their privileged status more generously and honestly, and to speak for themselves, in terms of both group interests and deeply held, deeply traditional values.

About the administration, the most charitable thing to say is that it is tired. The current Berkeley campus administration is, like most administrations, unideological. Reacting to a truly desperate combination of pressures from militants, Regents, faculty and angry citizens, it has devoted itself almost entirely to keeping the university open. Roger Heyns, chancellor since 1965, has shown great—at times incredible—patience and astuteness as a negotiator. Doubtless these are indispensable qualities for his appalling assignment, but there are others. The administration is almost excessively unideological; it not only moves swiftly from condemning to applauding student power or educational experiment according to the tenor of the moment; it also leaves educational objectives entirely to a faculty too large and fragmented for action (yet tenacious of its powers). It is out of touch with the intellectual concerns of professors and the emotions of students. After all, the contacts of administrators with students are nearly all abrasive; their contact with faculty members often depressing. All that I have said of our administration could be said of all administrations of large universities in this country, and in some instances others could be criticized more harshly than ours. But the prevailing administrative style will not work much longer, even for its own modest purposes. To balance very long on a tightrope, one needs a sense of direction.

The Regents, who have constitutionally complete power over the university, have served it well during most of its first century (the centennial year has just, in awkward and gingerly manner, been celebrated). This appointive body, with its fourteen-year terms and its aloofness from current pressures, can be immensely useful as an intermediary between campus, legislature and people. One has to be a very faithful democrat to believe, looking at the history of either recent or remote crises, that the university would have been better under direct legislative or popular control. Yet it seems to most Californians unreasonable to suggest that the people who pay the bills should have nothing at all to say about what is done with their money. The present system gives them power ultimately to change the university by electing a new governor, just as the people of the nation can change the Supreme Court by changing the President.

At present, the majority of the Regents are heavily influenced by ex officio Regent Reagan, and their behavior is hardly helpful. Descending from Olympian clouds to meet each month on a different campus, they have intervened at times so heavy-handedly, for instance in both the Cleaver and the park crises, that the position of even the cautious and patient Heyns administration has been made almost if not quite intolerable. In their indignation at the reappointment of Herbert Marcuse at the San Diego campus, they resumed a power they had relinquished recently in the interests of decentralization: the right to approve or reject all tenure promotions and appointments. Most cases come up at about the same time of year. Thus they arrive together at two or three of the Regents' meetings. Each has already received prolonged and exhaustive investigation; almost every one has already been long delayed. In back of each is a restless individual, usually being courted by other universities. Since the Regents cannot possibly look into any but a very few, their resumption of this power can have at best little constructive and much destructive effect. Despite disclaimers, few faculty members believe the action was taken for any reason other than the possibility of intervention on political grounds. Political intervention in a tenure appointment, or even the suspicion of it, is one of the few acts that might unite faculty and students in the whole university and, indeed, the academic community of the nation.

Another group with important but limited power on the campus is the police. Although calling police onto the campus was unthinkable several years ago, few now would question that their presence in large numbers is sometimes necessary. As long as we have militants ready to resort to arson, vandalism and threats against teachers and students, to be without police is to give complete power to the most violent.

Liberals are at last beginning to think about this uncongenial problem. I have heard faculty members, indignantly liberal in 1964 and 1966, demanding sterner police action as they watched their office doors smashed or worried about their books or manuscripts. It is at present the case that once our small campus police force needs to call in outside help, command passes at once to the sheriff of Alameda County. Police actions in the last crisis, when they came nearer than militants ever have to shutting the campus down, make clear the dangers of this situation. Justifiably angry with those who habitually call them pigs, seriously concerned for their safety, many are also in the habit of considering all young men with long hair "creeps" and possible anarchists. Above all, few know what a university does, or what needs protecting. It is obvious that police excesses must be vigorously and tenaciously challenged, and their perpetrators punished. But this is not enough; liberals must turn their thoughts, however reluctantly, toward the detailed problems of police behavior. Unless, before our next crisis, there is some advance agreement on the command of police on campus, and on the limits of police action in various contingencies, any determined group of militants can bring on conditions approaching civil war and thereby shut the university down.

There is one more group with power—this time less limited although less direct. This is the people of California. Unfortunately, most members of the university community, particularly the faculty, are ignorant of the feelings and attitudes of most of their fellow citizens. Always to some degree, and at present still more acutely, academic liberals suffer from siege mentality. "They," the outsiders, are seen either solely in terms of possible danger or, worse, as people who need to be enlightened or educated. Although every issue of every more-or-less liberal newspaper urges its readers to understand students, or blacks, or radicals, nobody suggests trying to understand conservatives. Nobody suggests that the Right, like the Left, is complex and divided, that it is as ridiculous to consider every Reagan voter a Fascist as it is to consider every Third World supporter a Maoist. Nobody suggests that both sides of the generation conflict are painful; that it is natural for people to be disturbed if they think their children are turning to ideas and practices they fear and detest. A great many people in California are proud of the university and do not want it destroyed by anyone: the public was divided in the loyalty oath battle of the fifties and during the Free Speech Movement. If it is less divided now, that is partly the fault of the academy, and there is no possibility of improvement in the situation that does not restore serious discussion of *all* campus problems. Frankness, not bland or defensive counterpropaganda, is the chief need.

The groups stay the same; the issues shift and change. It may be that the real issues are not the local ones, but the unsolved problems that divide and afflict America and the world. Beneath or beyond even these issues, although it is unpopular to say so, lie the conflicts of students with their parents and their upbringing. On the surface, there are two kinds of recurrent conflicts around which our conflicting forces mass and shift.

The first involves student power. Since 1964 many liberals have blamed campus troubles on illiberal or arbitrary treatment of students. There is something in this; doubtless our young people are prevented from maturing by all sorts of forces. Sometimes liberals and radicals use obviously false analogies; giving grades to students or denying their right to devise their own education is compared to denying votes to Negroes, et cetera. Recently it has become obligatory for those who denounce campus troublemakers, from President Nixon down, to express also their sympathy for "legitimate demands of students to control their own lives" (the degree and manner of such control are seldom spelled out). In his smashingly successful speech to the Commonwealth Club after the People's Park crisis, Governor Reagan, after damning militants and defending the police, shifted the main attack to stuffy professors. Discussing the knowledge factory, research versus teaching and other familiar themes, he sounded at times almost like Paul Goodman. The Commonwealth Club gave him an ovation, but students have not as yet swung behind his banner.

It is customary, in discussing student power, to say that students today are more mature than students used to be. This may be so, since they are more troubled, but if maturity means knowing what one wants, I doubt it. One thing students *are* clear about is that they want their private lives free, and by now in most ways this objective is almost achieved. Clearly an academic institution cannot enforce the older generation's conception of proper behavior on 27,000 individuals in an urban setting. Yet the new thirteen demands of the People's Park proponents add up to more than most citizens of Berkeley are anywhere nearly willing to concede: an enclave in which laws regarding narcotics, sex and other matters are suspended, runaway children are welcome, and police power does not penetrate.

In terms of campus order, there has for long been too much tokenism and not enough experiment in actual student control of student concerns. There have been advisory student committees on rules, student officers speak at Academic Senate meetings and may shortly speak regularly at Regents' meetings; there are students on some committees and will be on others. In the strike of 1966 a group of the faculty demanded and secured the creation of a Student-Faculty Committee on Governance. This came up with a very long and complex document, the essence of which was student-faculty collaboration on all subjects, with the administration excluded. This report was largely ignored by everybody except the radical students, who denounced it, and the daily student paper, which gave it routine praise. Another manifesto by a relatively conservative group of professors, issued at the same time, was still more completely ignored. This urged experimentation in the direction of division rather than collaboration, with different spheres of competence recognized for faculty, students and administration, and students placed in genuine control, on an experimental basis, of political behavior and enforcement of free speech rules. Whatever the merits of these suggestions, regental aggressiveness and crisis mentality would make it difficult to implement them now.

As for student power in academic matters, it has proved very difficult, in Berkeley as elsewhere, to get clear student proposals for overall curricular changes. When students do generalize, they often demand at once immediate relevance to contemporary problems and complete individual freedom, two demands that are difficult seriously to combine. Students see, after all, only a small part of the university for a short time. This they see clearly and their *particular* suggestions are usually interesting. The university has recognized this through setting up machinery to legitimate, through faculty action, student-initiated courses. This has produced some dubious proposals ("theory and practice of meditation"), some controversial ones (lectures by Cleaver or Tom Hayden), some serious, demanding and well-conceived courses, some obvious free rides, and some straight chicanery. While difficult and sometimes abrasive, student-faculty conflict over this kind of issue seems to me entirely possible of solution. No such conflict, including that over the Cleaver course, has produced any of our most desperate confrontations. In the long run, students themselves reject courses, experimental or conventional, that lack content or quality. There are few graduates of universities who have never taken a bad course; perhaps to try and fail to organize a good one may be an educative experience. It may be that some further distinction can be devised between kinds of courses for which some curricular time is allotted and kinds that actually count toward degrees. It has also been suggested that the whole structure of courses and units be abolished in favor of infrequent but demanding examinations on larger subjects, following somewhat—one hopes not too closely—the European model. Meantime, if there is any subject on which students really want information and in which some sort of expert information exists (drugs and their effects, the sociology of sexual mores, contemporary religious practices), an urgent effort should be made to provide it on a serious level.

The second category of issues, often related to the first and to the underlying cultural conflict, is over the meaning and purpose of education. What is the university for? Thousands of students at Berkeley have little idea, and their elders are not providing very convincing answers. Today, as so often in the American past, a society that has always been anxious, suspicious, yet enormously concerned about education, is in the midst of an argument over its meaning.

Three main roles for the university are seriously presented, and none is new. The first, and often the strongest in America, is the civic or moral. Like Americans in the early Republic, Governor Reagan, Max Rafferty, the black militants, many education departments, and both the liberal and the conservative press are agreed that the job of the university is to instill correct principles in the young. All they disagree about is what these principles *are*. At the moment, no faction, radical or conservative, is having much success in indoctrination. Students at Berkeley have heard too many slogans, from the press and from the plaza. If they are somewhat more inclined to believe the radicals than the conservatives, this is because they find the society seriously unsatisfactory in terms of their own values and their own lives. Their deepest loyalties are to each other, to codes of behavior, to styles of life and not to programs: about programs they are accumulating a good deal of sad wisdom—perhaps too fast.

Thus the second role, proclaimed by many students and their friends off campus with real fervor, is self-expression. This again is familiar in America: it was the program of Transcendentalists and of the most radical progressives of the early twentieth century. In its present sometimes bizarre forms it shocks most middle-aged liberals: these, responsive to education for social justice, cannot accept meditation, encounter groups, Eastern religions and political existentialism.

The third purpose often proclaimed is still the disinterested search for truth. Like God, this is the object of faith
despite being seldom seen directly and obscured by traditional rhetoric. Yet most professors and I think most students
do believe in it to some degree. Real intellectual honesty
and, still more, real intellectual joy have remarkable capacity
to sustain themselves under difficulty. Our students usually
respond—sometimes reversing their own initial preferences
—to whatever approaches these standards.

Any solution to the conflict among these three purposes
must in a divided and complex society be radically pluralistic; none of the three can be dismissed. Certainly a vast
public university cannot ignore the acute problems of the
society that supports it. It is idle to deny that students—like
everybody—need to explore their own minds and personali-
ties. Some genuinely academic exercises, particularly those
involving serious and sympathetic criticism of student work,
can help in this task. Yet, I think whatever does not partake
to some extent of the pursuit of truth, whatever cannot be
judged at least in part by intellectual standards, is destructive of universities. It is where such standards have been
best maintained that we find even now our areas of strength.

This does not mean that the present system of courses,
units, grades, teaching assistants and degrees is sacred, or
that the object of the university must be for the largest possible number to move as far as possible toward the Ph.D. It
is extremely easy to confuse defense of academic standards
with defense of the status quo and especially of faculty privileges. It is very hard to apply standards of academic excel-
lence, free of cultural prejudice, to new subject matters, yet
the effort must be made. The study and appreciation of
mysticism or irrational feeling is clearly a part of the university's mission; but religious worship and encounter groups
must both remain, like sexual activity, extracurricular. As
for ethnic studies, it is obvious that whites need to know
more, think more, and even feel more about the worlds of
the Negro and of other minorities, and that these minorities

can honestly and legitimately approach some subjects from new and fruitful angles of vision. Although the debt of white Americans to racial minorities is real, it seems to me that a better rationale for minority studies is the genuine enrichment that can come to all from expanding the scope and variety of our understanding. No effort can be too great, few sacrifices too drastic, that will really help to overcome handicaps, get over barriers, or reduce failures of communication. Yet separate admissions, followed by separate curricula, separately taught and judged by separate standards, will not help; in the long run they can only be a fraud, and a racist fraud at that.

This review—and I really believe any attempt at an honest review—of the state of affairs at Berkeley can hardly lead to optimism. Any one of several familiar issues, for instance ethnic studies or tenure—or, more likely, another issue yet invisible—can result in crisis; any crisis can be escalated, if the moment and the symbols are right, into confrontation and violence. Certainly some faculty members will tire of the pressures and search for more peaceful scenes (whether or not they will find them is another matter). Yet I cannot but find some encouraging signs. First is the fact that students and faculty have learned to do excellent academic work even in crisis. Another perhaps is that faculty members have gone a bit beyond rhetoric: some have volunteered to observe police and militant actions in an effort to prevent bloodshed, and have learned something thereby. Again, the interest and even respect shown for opposite views by some speakers at the Berkeley City Council meeting during the park crisis was impressive; some hippies, blacks, merchants, professors, housewives know that the others are *there*.

It may be that in Berkeley we have begun to get over a set of illusions: the conservative illusion that firmness in punishing the "tiny minority" will end the trouble; the liberal illusion that academic reform or faculty-student committees will end conflict; the radical one that destruction of institutions will bring freedom. As in the profound and harrowing problems of the nation, there are no solutions in sight; solutions must wait on new alignments not easily arrived at. The best one can hope to do in a university that at all reflects the state of American society at present is to live through troubled times without quite losing sight of one's purpose. Is there any American community that has learned more about doing this than ours?

COLUMBIA: TO BE A REVOLUTIONARY OR NOT TO BE? [3]

It's been just a year since the Spring Revolution at Columbia, and many of us who were involved—as activists, observers, and reporters—are now able to look back at the eruptions with a peacetime perspective. During those months of April and May 1968, many people were enraged because formal educational activities of much of the university had come to a halt. But some of us learned more in those six weeks than we would have if the demonstrations had never taken place.

There was a special dimension to our education last spring. It had little to do with textbooks or traditional academic subjects; it dealt with politics, with power, with the way Real Life works. Through elementary and high school, we had grown up with the traditional fables that major American institutions—the government, the university—are delicately balanced structures designed to provide the greatest good for the greatest number, that they contain mechanisms to correct any major flaws that might develop. For many of us, that myth had begun to crumble even before we came to Columbia; the Vietnam war, perhaps more than any other factor, had made it clear how perverted American policy could become, how the safeguards and corrective mechanisms didn't always work.

[3] Article by Jerry L. Avorn, who edited the *Daily Spectator* at Columbia University during the uprising and was the principal author of *Up Against the Ivy Wall: A History of the Columbia Crisis* (Atheneum. '68). *Look*. 33:13-14. My. 13, '69. By permission of the editors. From the May 13, 1969 issue of *Look* Magazine. Copyright 1969 by Cowles Communications, Inc.

The war was not the only event that shaped our ideology of mistrust. We looked at the history of blacks in this country and saw that real change began to take place only after Martin Luther King was thrown into jail for leading "illegal" sit-ins. We looked at the way American cities had been left to rot and noticed that those in power became concerned enough to change things only after several summers of bloody rioting.

Against this historical background, spring came to Columbia last year. Earlier, students had presented President Kirk with a petition calling for the university to disaffiliate from a think tank doing weapons research for the Vietnam war. Kirk had never answered the petition. Construction continued on a gymnasium in nearby Harlem parkland, even though many people argued that Columbia had no right to gobble up the open space surrounding it without consulting the community. But these issues were only symbols of larger problems that underlay them: the university's growing bondage to Government- and military-related research, and its often heartless expansion into the surrounding black community. On a deeper level lay the broadest issues we were fighting: the Government's commitment to an evil and senseless war, and the racial prejudice that pollutes American life.

Soon after the occupation of the buildings at Columbia, I spoke to a middle-aged business executive about the revolt on campus. "I agree with what you kids want," he assured me, "but why can't you go about getting it in a *socially acceptable* way?" Leaders of the student movement have called this objection the Liberal Hang-up. It appears again and again in the report of the Cox Commission, the blue-ribbon panel set up last spring by the faculty to investigate the causes of the Columbia demonstrations. The reforms the students demanded were for the most part necessary and long overdue, the report conceded, and it was clear that they had little chance of accomplishing anything through ossified "legitimate channels." But, the report insisted, the students still should not have resorted to extralegal action to win their demands.

A great many young people today are infuriated by the priorities and values that govern American life. We'd like to believe that rational discourse is all that is necessary to right wrongs. But the world we see around us just doesn't bear that out. I was a big fan of the America that I found in my high school textbooks—any kid can become President, justice triumphs in the end—and I was bitterly disappointed when I saw how poorly it measured up to the truth. Something has gone wrong; one need only to walk through Harlem or read the casualty statistics to be aware of that. And to judge from some of the good and healthy changes that have come from the "illegitimate" protests of the early civil rights movement, the northern ghetto riots and the Columbia demonstrations, many of us wonder whether the best way to improve things is necessarily the most respectable. The university, like the nation, seems to be like a great, complex vending machine that has become rusted with age: the only way to make it work right is to kick it hard.

Some people argue that radical tactics are evil. I, too, am bothered by the violence and abrogation of free speech that have begun to tinge the leftmost edges of the student movement. And I am worried that civil disobedience is becoming the tactic of choice on many campuses when it should be used only as a last resort. I reject the notion of some ultra-Leftist students that one goal of campus protest should be the destruction of the university. But I confess that I'm more worried about the kind of damage done to a university by trustees who involve it institutionally in war research than I am about the damage done to it by students who take over its buildings for several days. So I cannot share the righteous indignation many of my elders feel about campus protest. The antiwar movement faced the same problem: Americans become more upset over burnt draft cards than over burnt babies.

It is interesting to see what has happened in the year since the Spring Revolution to the "unrealistic" demands that formed the backbone of the Columbia sit-ins. The students demanded that the university halt construction of its gym in Morningside Park. In March of 1969, Acting President Andrew Cordier, and the trustees concurred that it would be inappropriate to build a gym there if the community did not want one. The radicals had argued that the disciplinary structure of the university was authoritarian and unjust. That structure has, in response, been revamped. Discipline is no longer administered unilaterally by a dean; the accused student may appeal to a tribunal of students, professors and administrators. Even the most unthinkable demand of all—amnesty—has been all but granted, with the university belatedly dropping most criminal and disciplinary punishment pending against demonstrators. There has been another direct by-product of last spring's turmoil—the creation of a university senate, dominated by faculty and students, to make university policy. I know of no one familiar with Columbia who would maintain that these reforms would now be realities if the events of last spring had not happened.

Few of us saw last spring as the staunchest SDS ideologues did—as the opening shot in a national revolution. But it did serve the quasi-revolutionary function of shaking up the status quo so thoroughly that a wave of relatively peaceful change could take place. Maybe this is the greatest contribution of the radical and black militant movements: to act as a catalyst of social change by scaring hell out of those who are so sure that things are good enough as they are. Of course, the possibility remains that all of these "reforms" will, in the end, merely gloss over the basic problems that brought about the revolt. If reform turns out to be a veneer, then the future looks pretty dismal.

Those of us in my generation who are deeply committed to creative, constructive change face an existential choice between radical tactics and within-the-system reform. Some might still be willing to work through the accepted political channels—within the universities and in the world at large. But those who control that system of channels must first convince us that, if we do, genuine change is possible. Their record has not been good and shows little promise that it will change. If some of the most idealistic and capable members of my generation end up on the barricades instead of changing things from positions of legitimate power, it will be because of the Grayson Kirks of this world, not because of its Mark Rudds. Perhaps this is the real lesson of last spring at Columbia.

WHY SAN FRANCISCO STATE BLEW UP [4]

[Uneasy lies the head of San Francisco State College. While seven presidents have reigned during the past eight years, the Chancellor and trustees of California's statewide college system ruled the school. The huge (18,000 students) liberal arts college, a poor relation of the pampered university across the bay in Berkeley, has long been sickened by student unrest and faculty dissatisfaction. Last fall, when the Chancellor ordered President Robert R. Smith to suspend George Murray, a part-time instructor who preached a fiery Black Panther gospel, the latest crisis began. The Black Students Union and its ally, the Third World Liberation Front, called a student strike, pressing a list of nonnegotiable demands (mostly for an autonomous Black Studies Department). Black activists broke up classes, tried to shut down the school. Police and demonstrators clashed. President Smith resigned; Dr. Samuel I. Hayakawa took over and chose to hold the "hard line" urged by Governor Ronald Reagan. Bloody police-student battles ended only when the Christmas

[4] "Battle for a College—Why San Francisco State Blew Up" (two views): "We Needed a Revolution," article by Leo Litwak, novelist and associate professor of English at San Francisco State, and "An Arrogant Minority Victimized the College," by John H. Bunzel, chairman, Department of Political Science, San Francisco State. *Look*. 33:61-2+. My. 27, '69. By permission of the editors. From the May 27, 1969 issue of *Look* Magazine. Copyright 1969 by Cowles Communications, Inc. Mr. Litwak's article is reprinted by permission of the author and his agent, James Brown Associates, Inc. Copyright © 1969 by Leo Litwak.

vacation was called a week early. Then, in January, the American Federation of Teachers struck the college. Students and faculty both picketed. By March, the students and staff were back in their classrooms and the worst of recent college upheavals seemed over. Why did it happen? For answers by two members of the San Francisco State faculty, turn the page.—*Look* editorial note.]

We Needed a Revolution

Returning from Europe after World War II, I joined the swarm of GI's seeking academic careers. The college campus seemed a likely place to find peace and security. But it was every man for himself. We pursued our degrees in competition with others: our grades against theirs, our ability to charm professors against theirs. The curriculum was designed mainly to weed out the less worthy, and our intellectual life existed mostly beyond the academic walls.

After eighteen years, I was secure. I did my job. I had tenure, an adequate salary. I worked hard. Others made academic policy, but I didn't care. I was reconciled to the fact that my significant life was off-campus. I had no strong sentiments for my institution.

Then, last November, all this changed. The Black Students Union began a strike at San Francisco State College that ended my detachment and imperiled my security. The BSU came at us with nonnegotiable demands. It indicted the college as a racist institution, abused state and local officials as "racist pigs" and "slavemasters." Groups of militant blacks entered classrooms shouting," On strike! Shut it down!" They jostled professors, shoved students, ordered classes dismissed. Some smashed windows, broke lab equipment and set off fire alarms.

The objective of the strike was to close the college until the BSU demands were met. A coalition of other minority groups, called the Third World Liberation Front, joined the revolt and tacked on more demands.

I felt that the intrusion of the blacks into the classrooms was outrageous, that their bellicose demands were irrational and therefore frightening. They wanted an autonomous Black Studies Department and an Ethnic Studies School, with minority-group faculty and students having sole authority to hire, fire and determine policy. I listened to the BSU strike leaders and was repelled by their rhetoric. "Power to the people!" Wasn't that a Maoist line? "Racist pigs!" Did they mean our innocuous deans and administrators? The crowd chanted simple slogans that turned me off. "Shove the puppets against the wall!" If they reduced men to puppets, they might indeed be able to shove them against the wall. I decided to stay clear of the mess. While I resented the strikers, I shared some of their grievances. I might become involved and imperil my cozy academic status.

Plainclothesmen were guarding campus buildings. Blacks held class everywhere. A black youth with a West Indian accent warned, "Don't think about returning this campus to normal. Your education is going on right now. We black students are your teachers." The subject they taught was Power. "For too long we've politely requested what should always have been ours. No one has the power to *give* us freedom. And we don't *request* you people for our rights. We *demand* them." The students considered talks with the local administration useless. "You people have no power to give us what we demand. We been talking to you for two years, and we got nothing. We just get tricked. Now we will only talk to educate you, but our demands are nonnegotiable. This strike will be over when our demands are met."

The faculty was powerless. The Governor and state legislature gave power to the Board of Trustees and the Chancellor's office. Little reached the college president and less went to the council of deans and department chairmen. There was nothing left for the faculty and students. In our time of crisis, we discovered that the system allowed us no solutions.

A general faculty meeting remained in session for several weeks and passed seventy resolutions with no visible influence on the strike. Instead, we were accused of being soft on student radicals. Superintendent of Public Instruction Max Rafferty and Governor Ronald Reagan wanted these dissidents handled like a bunch of rowdies in an Old West saloon. Enough resolutions; enough talk; throw the bums out.

A small band of faculty militants called a short-lived strike against state interference, but a far larger group, while not joining that strike, had soured on the administration's unimaginative doctrine of "classes as usual." They wanted to suspend regular instruction, move out of the classrooms and onto the campus. I began to wonder why we couldn't use this scary energy for some new kind of educaton, rather than clamp a lid on it.

The majority of my colleagues, however, didn't want to surrender formal instruction. They asked, what about grades? What about teaching credentials? What about jobs that require a degree? Wasn't that what education was *really* about?

I decided, no. Not really. I questioned whether the contradiction between campus experience and community experience was any longer tolerable. I'd once welcomed the benign order of campus life. But did I want to continue paying the price for that security? I was subjected to educational policies that made no sense to me. I didn't feel there was anything sacred about our curriculum. On the contrary, it was my impression that most programs have no inherent justification but simply reflect campus politics. I agreed with those who wanted regular instruction suspended in favor of a different mode of encounter.

Only a minority of the faculty shared my view. There was considerable support for Professor S. I. Hayakawa, who announced that no student would interfere with the conduct of his classes. He urged strong police measures, and strong police measures were what we got.

Leaving a faculty meeting about that time, I heard screams. Two officers from the Tactical Squad hauled a BSU leader across the campus through hundreds of milling students. Both cops had revolvers out. One wheeled around to cover everyone, including me. Dozens of reporters and television crews were watching. A half dozen police found themselves in a tight spot. Suddenly, they lashed out. They beat a frail, bespectacled BSU leader to the ground. They swung their batons like baseball bats. They clobbered everyone in their way, including innocents. Soon I found myself aligned with colleagues trying to separate students and police. The Tac Squad photographer snapped my picture. Like it or not, I was involved.

The campus mayhem finally forced the faculty to suspend formal instruction, and the entire college was convoked to discuss the strike issues. Strike leaders confronted college faculty and administration on the stage of the main auditorium. All together—students and faculty—we faced the vital issues of our college.

The minority students presented a strong case in strong language. Could we be made to understand, they wondered, why they would never allow themselves to be absorbed into the traditional campus life while their people continued to suffer in the ghetto? They demanded an education that would enable them to serve their community. The existing curriculum was irrelevant to their purposes. They didn't balk at obscenity. They insulted their opposition and made open bids for audience sympathy. Our administrators responded to this passion with the tedious precision of accountants, citing the limitations of state codes, budgetary policy and a fiscal crisis.

The students, accusing the college administration of bad faith, brought the convocation to a premature end. Next, the trustees forced President Smith to resign and replaced him with Dr. Hayakawa, of the colorful tam-o'-shanter and hard line. Official California had chosen to ignore the basic dissatisfactions and possibilities for reform that lay beneath the rebels' furious rhetoric. The Governor—with popular support, it's true—wanted to restore the college of his Hollywood fantasies, a benign place for cheerleaders and absentminded professors.

Acting President Hayakawa declared all assemblies illegal unless authorized by him. Professors who did not hold classes as scheduled risked being fired. He announced that all necessary force would be employed to keep the campus open. He refused to negotiate with those he regarded as hooligans. Both sides chose *High Noon* as the kind of confrontation they preferred.

Six hundred cops assembled near the campus. Three thousand students gathered on the commons. Dr. Hayakawa piped from loudspeakers to everyone, "This is a warning. All innocent bystanders leave this vicinity. Go to your classes. Go to the library. Leave the troublemakers to the police. Those of you who want trouble, stay there; the police will see that you get it." For two weeks, there were daily confrontations. The script never changed. The cops approach; students taunt them; clods of turf and pinecones are flung. Suddenly, a cop let's go and flails away, and the movement spreads down the line. When they swing, they put their weight behind the sticks. I see them still flailing away after the kid is downed.

One of my colleagues, protesting a brutal arrest, was thrown down, handcuffed, led away wth a riot stick pressed to his throat. An officer squirted Mace in his eyes. Another came from behind—"How do you like this, you fancy-pants professor?"—and cut his head open with a blow from a riot stick that knocked him cold. The professor was charged with resisting and interfering with an arrest.

One of my students told me she was striking "because of the PIGS!" Her boyfriend had been photographing arrests behind the gym. A cop seized his camera and stripped the film. Another said, "No one's looking." They fractured his ribs, damaged a lung, thrust a riot stick under his genitals and hoisted up and down. They charged the boy with attempted murder. PIGS!

Hayakawa announced after a particularly bloody day: "This has been the most exciting day since my tenth birthday, when I rode a roller coaster for the first time." It was a callous statement. Yet it reflected what everyone experienced, a new energy that changed our connections to each other and to our institution. What a loss if we simply resumed teaching as before and didn't profit from these new connections. Should we simply repair broken windows, wash away strike slogans from building facades and plant flowers? Should we get back to Keats and California state history, and drama classes, and allow the performance of *Little Me* that had been interrupted by strike action? If students wished to participate in the fundamental design of my courses, why not? If my work could become relevant to my experience and theirs, perhaps teaching and learning could become more joyful.

Those of us who wanted to profit from the new energies on campus had no alternative but to join the American Federation of Teachers strike. We had no illusions that we could defeat the overwhelming power the state would muster against us. We were a minority of the faculty. Public sentiment strongly favored repressive measures. We were the villains; Hayakawa was the hero. But we felt that submitting to the old routines without any resistance would be degrading. We had everything to lose—rank, tenure, jobs, homes—yet we struck. We established a picket line around campus and marched through one of the wettest winters in San Francisco history. At times, we were frightened; often we were exhilarated. Yet we became united, with a new commitment to our institution.

The strike finally ended, but a volatile situation remains. The administration is still intransigent. But we are changing things in our classrooms. Students are collaborating in the design of courses. In some departments, we are moving away from the old hierarchical structure toward more democratic participation. Perhaps, through our strikes, we faculty and students have chosen a new and hopeful direction for higher education in America.

———

An Arrogant Minority Victimized the College

It has become a commonplace to say that what is happening on our campuses today cannot be separated from what is taking place in the rest of society. A college like San Francisco State cannot be divorced from the problems and tensions of San Francisco. In this case, everything is connected, much as the anklebone is connected to the leg bone and the leg bone to the hipbone.

But there is a deceptive simplicity in this argument. There are times when the anklebone can be examined and treated by itself, alone, for whatever ails it. The particular difficulties confronting our colleges and universities are both more or less than those afflicting our cities. They are also different—different because a college campus is not simply an extension of "downtown." It has a special way of life that is not found at Fifth and Market. And there are times when campus problems should be considered apart from what may be happening in the Fillmore or Haight-Ashbury.

"You don't approve of violence on the campus," one student militant told me. "But don't you realize that violence is going on all around us? There's violence in Vietnam and violence in the ghettos. Why should a college be protected, like some antiseptic ivory tower, from the real facts of life? And violence in this country is a fact." I found this a curious argument unless he was trying to make a case for violence as the recommended way of settling problems. I told him the main reason violence has no place in an academic community is that it corrupts and might easily destroy the community's basic values, purposes and procedures. He was not impressed, for his idea of a university was radically different from mine.

During the many months that San Francisco State has been gripped in a prolonged spasm, I have come to realize that this is an important dimension of the crisis. One's angle of vision, sense of priorities and personal commitment—all of these derive from the way one feels and thinks about a university community.

I opposed the recent teachers strike at the college, although I have been a strong trade-union supporter most of my life. But an effective strike should have solid backing, and that is precisely what the striking teachers did not have. A year or so ago, the union was specifically rejected as the faculty's bargaining agent, and during the strike, about two thirds of the faculty voted against it. Besides, I have some reservations about a teachers union treating a college in the same way an industrial trade union might treat an exploitive employer. Confrontations, strikes, withholding students' grades at the end of the semester—these tactics could do serious damage to an academic community if they became a permanent way of life.

There were even more serious reasons why I felt this was the wrong strike at the wrong time, and led by the wrong people. The president of the teachers union, in a letter sent to all his faculty colleagues, arbitrarily divided them into (his words) "friend versus enemy." Arrogantly and self-righteously, he pronounced the union's attitude: "You will not have the luxury of nice distinctions or Byzantine excuses," he told us, overlooking the fact that a community of scholars has a specific responsibility to make distinctions, nice or otherwise. "He who observes our picket line is a friend—anyone who plans to cross will be subject to moral force." I for one was subject to more than moral force. One night, someone slashed the tires of my car and my wife's and painted "fascist scab" all over them.

For me and most of the faculty, the significant question had been clear from the beginning of the strike: by what right did a small minority feel it could try to impose its ideology on the rest of us? These political moralists had little support from their colleagues. Yet they believed that rejection of their demand only confirmed their right to try to halt all teaching and suspend the academic program. The real danger lay in their desire to politicize the college, or, failing that, to shut it down. Demanding total freedom for themselves, they would deny it to the majority in the interest of a "higher" cause—namely, theirs.

San Francisco State has also been faced with a student strike that began last November when the Black Students Union and the Third World Liberation Front presented fifteen "nonnegotiable" demands. Some are reasonable (a Black Studies Department) and have been met; others are unreasonable and cannot be met ("That all Black Students wishing so, be admitted in the fall of 1969"). But the key term is *nonnegotiable*. There is no such thing as a nonnegotiable demand by anyone seriously interested in realistic, achievable goals. Reasonable men with differences have a better chance of accommodating each other if they can discuss concrete issues. The problem has been that too much talk by the militant black leadership has come through the end of a bullhorn. Explosively charged rhetoric has inflamed passions and generated emotional responses, obscuring the elements of reality and making it all the more difficult to examine reasonable proposals like the black-studies program.

"You're a racist pig who doesn't understand the black man's rage," I have been told many times this year. A liberal Democrat for more than twenty years, I was a member of the California Kennedy delegation at the Democratic convention in Chicago last year. To the extent that a white man (any white man) can say it, I think I do understand the rage of the black man in our society. And knowing myself, if I were black I suspect I would be bitter and militant too. But there is a problem with rage, whether it is directed at society or your wife or yourself. While it may help to ventilate grievances and provide psychic release, it too often erupts into dangerously violent behavior that is usually self-defeating and rarely solves the problems that produce the anguish. In a university environment, violence should never become a substitute for reason and persuasion. Democratic procedures, however imperfect, underpin those fragile understandings on which the academic community ultimately rests and depends.

At the beginning of this school year, the college vice president said, "I think you should know you're going to be a target this fall." As it turned out, he was right. My troubles started with a critical article I had written, "Black Studies at San Francisco State." I had been a strong supporter of a sound academic program in ethnic studies for four years or so. But I disagreed with the particular perspective of Nathan Hare, who has been our leading black militant in residence and who put together the proposal for Black Studies. Under his plan, teachers would work solely within "a black revolutionary nationalist framework." He has said, "I don't want any assimilationists," by which he means "Negroes." My article criticized this approach. In a recent public speech, Hare declared, "The Bible says there is a time for everything. I think this is a time for hate." I do not agree with that sentiment either, and I doubt that it can serve any useful purpose in a college program. But in the kind of polarized, combustible atmosphere that developed on campus, one either supported Mr. Hare's program in its entirety or was tagged an enemy.

One morning in October, a bomb was found against my office door. Fortunately, no one was hurt. But the bomb scares as well as real bombs, the destruction of property, arson, roving bands of vandals breaking into classes, guns on campus, intimidation and violence—these have all become a part of life at San Francisco State. And therein lies the real tragedy. In an academic community, ideas should triumph, not power, or some group's interests or demands, or the tactic of physical pressure or emotional duress.

At the beginning of the spring semester, I was singled out again. In my course on Community Power, some one hundred students showed up for the first meeting. About half of them had no legitimate interest in the course. I never got beyond my opening remarks when the room erupted into yells from twenty-five or more student radicals. One young man jumped to his feet time after time and declaimed quotations from Chairman Mao. Others kept up a machine-gun-like barrage of shouts that were shrill and more personal. Then the black students demanded to know why Stokely Carmichael or Huey Newton was not on the reading list. I said many other possible choices had been omitted too. The books on the list were racist, they charged. By what standards? "If you put it on the list, nine times out of ten it's a racist book," someone shouted back. I finally had to dismiss the class, but I told them I intended to teach the course in the way it had been taught for a number of years. At this point, a student said, "If we have to bring guns in here, you won't teach it. We'll teach you about community power." After several more such meetings, three students were suspended. One of the militant students told a reporter that they were determined to end the class. I was just as determined that they would not. And they did not.

It may well take five, perhaps ten years before this place recovers from its present grief. It may never really recover. We need time and money to move imaginatively and urgently on problems with which we are only beginning to grapple. If we are successful in our response to the revolution of rising expectations, then perhaps we will be able to thwart those who thrive on the expectation of rising revolutions.

But one thing is certain: San Francisco State will not survive if factions and power blocs continue claiming the right not merely to voice their dissent but to impose on everyone else the duty to listen and accept the truth of their claims. Reasoned inquiry will quickly give way to mindlessness and muscle, and the end result will be polarization and confrontation.

My colleague, Professor Philip Siegelman, says that those who occupy a bewildered and silent middle ground must be reminded of the menacing consequences of conscious or unconscious collaboration between the extremes of the Left and Right. The signs are everywhere. While colleges are being torn apart from the inside by the militants of the Left, the avenging furies of the Right are off campus, watching and waiting. The striking teachers and student radicals keep saying that what they have been doing is "saving" San Francisco State College and, along with it, higher education in California. What they in fact have *succeeded* in doing is to galvanize all of the conservative and reactionary forces in California so that today Governor Reagan's support and popularity have never been higher.

I have a tender regard for what a university is and the special values it represents. My idea of a university is very different from those who want to turn it into a political staging area or who insist that it become exclusively an instrument of social reconstruction. What these people miss, or refuse to understand, is that this is too narrow a view, that a university is *many* things. It is a place for people who want to teach and learn, where important research is done, where ideas are explored and exchanged, and where current fashions of social reform can be criticized. Those who claim that the university has some single or ultimate purpose would have us accept *their* set of goals and *their* plan of action. In short, they would betray knowledge for ideology. One of the major lessons to be learned from the crisis at San Francisco State is that academic freedom does not grant the right to teach the Truth but rather the right to *seek* the Truth.

DR. ABRAM ON EDUCATION [5]

Question: I'd like to ask you one main question: what do you think is wrong with education, and what can be done to improve it? Please don't limit yourself to higher education, because college students are coming to you from the lower levels of education.

Dr. Abram: For good or ill, this generation of college students were what they were—and are what they are—when they entered college this fall.

[5] Selections from a taped interview with Dr. Morris B. Abram by Ian Forman, education editor. Boston *Sunday Herald Traveler*. p 33. O. 12; p 28. O. 19, '69. Reprinted by permission. Dr. Abram, a lawyer by profession, was president of Brandeis University at the time.

When we talk about college students today, I want to make it perfectly clear that we are talking about our own children. Universities are merely the current habitations of our youth. This generation was not sired or raised by college administrators or faculties. For the most part, these young people were educated in the school systems of their home communities, and under laws and conditions we—their elders, their mothers and fathers and friends—either created or permitted to stand.

There is a filtering down of the simplistic propaganda that the radical student is using, and I say using, because he knows better. He's using it, it seems to me, as a form of hazing. When new students enter, they are subjected to this hazing-by-propaganda. For example, last September a freshman said to me, "At the Lemberg Center for the Study of Violence [at Brandeis], there are some students passing out propaganda, saying that the Center reports tell police how to suppress ghetto rebellions."

I told the student that it is my feeling the police do not create a political climate; they mirror it—and unfortunately this says something very disturbing about American society.

I said to him, "In my judgment, we need to give our police better training and better pay. We need to upgrade their selection and their status. We need better police. But right now, apparently, we don't disapprove of the kind of police we have to the point where we are willing to embark on the programs that will result in better police. And the Lemberg Center has been saying the same thing. Why don't you get the reports of the Lemberg Center and read them and answer your own questions?"

But you see, in effect, these students are victims of the hazing which does take place on the campus.

And I want to make an indictment. The university, which is the greatest research organ in the world, has failed to research the things which are most intimately connected with itself—mainly, the curriculum. Now we've all experimented with curricular changes. But you search the literature and you'll find that there's a scarcity of real honest-to-goodness controlled research of the same high standards that are important when you research everything else.

Take grading. I don't want to give up grading. I think grading is one of the greatest teaching instruments I know. I think it's one of the stimuli to learning that is needed. I think it's one of the ways that we tie knowledge together, into a whole. I think that the final examinations I had at Oxford, with the comprehensives, gave me a view of the politics, philosophy, and economics which I studied there which I would not have achieved had I not had to spend six months trying to put it together, so I could see the thing as a whole.

Well, some students say grading is tyranny—although not the goal-oriented ones, because they know that if they don't get the grades they may not get into the professional school they want. But you search the literature, and you see how much investigation has been done on testing and grading as an educational tool.

That, generally, is my view of the first question you asked me, and I would sum it up by saying that the reports which deal with disadvantaged children including those who have great difficulty in reading, seem to say that many learning problems are not really going to be remedied by the Head Start program, that by the end of the first two years of a child's life he has been so shaped and so bent that he either is educable or he isn't.

If that's true, this is a tremendous statement, because what it says is that the education process begins early and that the psychological values or qualities that were held by the mother and father determine so much. And, of course, many times the wrong that may be done to a child during this period is not done willfully—much of this treatment is merely circumstantial.

Question: You have complained before that undergraduate colleges are often dominated by the standards of graduate and professional schools—standards that are frequently un-

realistic, possibly unjustified and largely unreviewed. And
you've said many of the students' legitimate complaints
about college education stem from this situation.

If this is true, don't these same pressures work all the
way down the line—the college upon the high school, the
high school upon the junior high, and then upon grade
schools?

And all of this leads to a stifling effect upon creative intellectual activities; it tends to force schools into imparting
a body of knowledge, at a time when knowledge itself is
slippery, and how you treat it is more important than the
knowledge itself.

Do you agree? And if so, is there any way an institution
like Brandeis can help break this chain of intellectual op-
pression?

Dr. Abram: I don't agree. Look. Since, Benjamin Franklin
and Thomas Jefferson and Leonardo da Vinci and a few
exceptional characters in history, there have been few men
who might possess kaleidoscopic minds and have deep knowledge about many things. Jefferson was such a universal man.
He was a man of law, of letters, of diplomacy. He knew
about agriculture, architecture and music. In the case of
Benjamin Franklin, he probably knew much about these
subjects also—and he knew a lot about electricity, too.

What was it President Kennedy said when he welcomed
a group of Nobel Prize winners to the White House, "We
have gathered together under the roof of the White House
the greatest concentration of talent and intellect since
Thomas Jefferson dined here alone." That day's past. Nobody, in our complicated world, can really know the various
fields with any precision that a man of the seventeenth or
eighteenth century knew.

Now ours is a very precise world. Even a lawyer can't
really be a generalist. He knows the tax code or he knows
the real estate code.

So, consequently when people tell me—especially on a
college campus—that what education ought to be is a sensi-

tizing process, in which people are left to explore their emotional feelings, and have fast exchanges of sentiment, and to join in a sense of community, I say they're running away from reality.

This is a world in which people cannot be successful just by using words without knowledge behind them or generalities instead of particulars.

And it's becoming such a world more and more. Don't ask me if this is a better world than the world of Thomas Jefferson. I won't answer that except to say I think it is. I might have enjoyed living at another time—but only if I could have been able to avail myself of anesthesia, for instance, or penicillin.

I've just come back from a Franco-U.S. educators' conference in Paris. Everyone in Europe was, of course, excited about the moon shot. You know what the Europeans really admire? It isn't our moon shot. They think they had a part in that; they think Newton had a part in it, too. The Europeans admire the knowledge of the astronauts. They admire the astronauts' modesty and humility, too. As they pointed out, for the astronauts, precision counted. The Europeans were impressed because the astronauts never left anything to chance. They made history in an exacting society because they had mastered a particular and demanding field. I think the Europeans were paying the astronauts great compliments.

Now we live in a world in which the people who really are successful are going to have to have this kind of knowledge. I know that there's a revolution against precise knowledge. You must not study medieval history because medieval history is not relevant to modern history. Poppycock. It is relevant.

Since we cannot be the Jeffersons and we cannot be the Leonardo da Vincis, and we cannot be the Benjamin Franklins, we must have our universities do two things for a student: Give him some subjects which have academic importance, something of enduring significance—it may be philosophy, history, physics, poetry, a number of things—and enable him to pierce this subject of enduring significance deep enough so he learns how difficult learning is, and acquires the methods of piercing other fields. There are innumerable things I didn't learn in college. But the things I did learn in college helped me in developing the tools by which I learned other things.

Question: When you bring up this concept of piercing through the subject, you're dealing with ideas and the development of ideas. It's the lack of this that's turning kids off in the schools, don't you agree?

Dr. Abram: All I'm saying is that a good university or a good high school or a good grammar school should have teachers who should know what quality is.

Question: Do you feel that the current ideological and psychological onslaught by the young New Left, do you feel that in a strategic way it has jogged institutions like Brandeis or older ones out of a certain complacency?

Dr. Abram: I think it's made us investigate ourselves. It's made us think. Anything that makes you think is fine, but it's also had a very counterproductive effect, too.

Question: In what way has the campus revolution been counterproductive?

Dr. Abram: In the first place, take the cry of open admissions. At a time when there is tremendous pressure on the colleges and universities to admit more students, the places are simply not available—and one reason for this is that there is a backlash in the state legislatures. The state legislatures are simply not being generous, they are not opening up the facilities.

Question: Have people also reduced gifts to private universities like Brandeis?

Dr. Abram: We've had people who reduced their gifts; canceled expected legacies, yes, we have. I might add that last year, however, we raised more free money—unrestricted funds —than we've ever raised before, but I think we did it because we didn't give in to demands that clearly endangered academic standards.

Had we given in . . . people would have said Brandeis is nothing; it's an institution run by those who can muster the most pressure at the most sensitive point, at a given time.

I don't think people would have had any pride in Brandeis. And without pride, people don't want to give money. People want to feel they are an essential part of any cause or institution to which they contribute money, they want to identify with it.

Consequently, I would say that if you have disruption, bloodshed—which doesn't create a sense of pride; caving in to ridiculous demands, which doesn't create a sense of pride; the lowering of standards, which diminishes pride; this hurts higher education. My colleagues all over the country tell me that the student uproar has not been productive.

Question: We have this group of radical students which seems to be able from time to time to mobilize majority sentiment; you have an older generation with different values; we've had a year now where the situation has gone into a second year. Do you see any way out of the dilemma?

Dr. Abram: I think the remedy lies in all of those who have an interest in the University, and I include the Five Estates: trustees, students, faculty, administrators, and alumni. I think they should meet occasionally through their elected representatives and discuss their common problems. Then I think there is bound to emerge a sense of understanding of the possible and also of the order of priorities in the things which need improvement.

And if administrations will then, from those meetings, take the lessons and put into effect those which are possible, and if—and this is the big if—if you can extend the kind of understanding that would come out of such discussions to the broader community—and I don't yet know how to do that—I think we would have peace.

Question: You're saying, really that the administration and the trustees learn from the militants, the students and faculty, as well as the other way around.

Dr. Abram: You're right. And the conservatives learn; the liberals learn; the radicals learn. All the elements learn from each other. We emerged from our own meeting of the Five Estates with a lot more understanding and knowledge.

Let me put it this way: Our Five Estates meeting was the first effort of its type I know to define what a university is and you can't just make up that definition; that definition has to be made by a group; a group which has a rounded and total stake in the university.

There's one element further I do want to tell you. In the final analysis we've got to have order on the campus. And college students surely expect it. Those students who don't agree with the radicals, when are they going to be heard? When are they going to speak up? I learned something from Brandeis' Five Estates meeting. And I learned something from listening.

I think the moderate student says, "I'm here to get an education. I'm not here to learn these political issues; to become expert in debating with the radicals. I don't agree with the radicals. But I'm not going to spend the time reading the literature on all the issues that they raise day after day.

I'm going to learn history or biochemistry or mathematics or English, and I expect the administration to preserve an appropriate setting in which I can do these things. And I'm going to support the university with my feet by going to class and to the library. That's the way I vote."

I know that's what the moderate student is doing. He's with you. If you don't cave in. You can lose him, however, in many ways—especially if you cave in.

IV. BLACK STUDIES

EDITOR'S INTRODUCTION

The first three articles in this section appeal for a rational curriculum development calculated to meet the real needs of students both black and white. In the first selection Bayard Rustin contends that most black-studies programs ignore "the opportunity for a vastly expanded scholastic inquiry into the contribution of Negroes to the American experience" and appear to concentrate on protest as an end in itself. The second article discusses the risks of the cultural separation emphasized by some of the programs. In the third selection, the education editor of the *Saturday Review* provides a thoughtful survey of recent experiences on a number of campuses. Then Murray Kempton asks some searching questions on black studies and campus attitudes that suggest the problem is not as syllogistic as some would make it out to be. Black studies is a theme that also runs through Sections II and III of this volume.

ESCAPE INTO ISOLATION [1]

The confusion which the movement for programs in black studies has created on campus almost defies description. The extremes in absurdity were reached this past academic year at Cornell, where, on the one hand, enraged black students were demanding a program in black studies which included Course 300c, Physical Education: "Theory and practice in the use of small arms and hand combat. Discussion sessions in the proper use of force," and where, on the other hand, a masochistic and pusillanimous univer-

[1] From article "The Failure of Black Separatism," by Bayard Rustin, civil rights activist, director of the A. Philip Randolph Institute. *Harper's Magazine.* 240:25-32+. Ja. '70. Copyright © 1969, by Harper's Magazine, Inc. Reprinted from the January, 1970 issue of *Harper's Magazine* by permission of the author.

sity president placed his airplane at the disposal of two black
students so that they could go to New York City and pur-
chase, with $2,000 in university funds, some bongo drums
for Malcolm X Day. The foolishness of the students was
surpassed only by the public-relations' manipulativeness of
the president.

The real tragedy of the dispute over black studies is that
whatever truly creative opportunities such a program could
offer have been either ignored or destroyed. There is, first,
the opportunity for a vastly expanded scholastic inquiry
into the contribution of Negroes to the American experience. The history of the black man in America has been
scandalously distorted in the past, and as a field of study it
has been relegated to a second-class status, isolated from the
main themes of American history and omitted in the historical education of American youth. Yet now black students
are preparing to repeat the errors of their white predecessors.
They are proposing to study black history in isolation from
the mainstream of American history; they are demanding
separate black-studies programs that will not be open to
whites, who could benefit at least as much as they from a
knowledge of Negro history; and they hope to permit only
blacks (and perhaps some whites who toe the line) to teach
in these programs. Unwittingly they are conceding what
racist whites all along have professed to believe, namely, that
black history is irrelevant to American history.

In other ways black students have displayed contempt
for black studies as an academic discipline. Many of them,
in fact, view black studies as not an academic subject at all,
but as an ideological and political one. They propose to use
black-studies programs to create a mythologized history and
a system of assertive ideas that will facilitate the political
mobilization of the black community. In addition, they hope
to educate a cadre of activists whose present training is conceived of as a preparation for organizational work in the
ghetto. The Cornell students made this very clear when they
defined the purpose of black-studies programs as enabling

"black people to use the knowledge gained in the classroom and the community to formulate new ideologies and philosophies which will contribute to the development of the black nation."

Thus faculty members will be chosen on the basis of race, ideological purity, and political commitment—not academic competence. Under such conditions, few qualified black professors will want to teach in black-studies programs, not simply because their academic freedom will be curtailed by their obligation to adhere to the revolutionary "line" of the moment, but because their professional status will be threatened by their association with programs of such inferior quality.

Black students are also forsaking the opportunity to get an education. They appear to be giving little thought to the problem of teaching or learning those technical skills that all students must acquire if they are to be effective in their careers. We have here simply another example of the pursuit of symbolic victory where a real victory seems too difficult to achieve. It is easier for a student to alter his behavior and appearance than to improve the quality of his mind. If engineering requires too much concentration, then why not a course in soul music? If Plato is both "irrelevant" and difficult, the student can read Malcolm X instead. Class will be a soothing, comfortable experience, somewhat like watching television. Moreover, one's image will be militant and, therefore, acceptable by current college standards. Yet one will have learned nothing, and the fragile sense of security developed in the protective environment of college will be cracked when exposed to the reality of competition in the world.

Nelson Taylor, a young Negro graduate of Morehouse College, recently observed that many black students "feel it is useless to try to compete. In order to avoid this competition, they build themselves a little cave to hide in." This "little cave," he added, is black studies. Furthermore, black students are encouraged in this escapism by guilt-ridden New

Leftists and faculty members who despise themselves and
their advantaged lives and enjoy seeing young Negroes reject
"white middle-class values" and disrupt the university. They
are encouraged by university administrators who prefer political accommodation to an effort at serious education. But
beyond the momentary titillation some may experience from
being the center of attention, it is difficult to see how Negroes
can in the end benefit from being patronized and manipulated in this way. Ultimately, their only permanent satisfaction can come from the certainty that they have acquired the
technical and intellectual skills that will enable them upon
graduation to perform significant jobs competently and with
confidence. If they fail to acquire these skills, their frustration will persist and find expression in ever-newer forms of
antisocial and self-destructive behavior.

The conflict over black studies, as over other issues, raises
the question of the function in general served by black protest today. Some black demands, such as that for a larger
university enrollment of minority students, are entirely legitimate; but the major purpose of the protest through
which these demands are pressed would seem to be not so
much to pursue an end as to establish in the minds of the
protesters, as well as in the minds of whites, the reality of
their rebellion. Protest, therefore, becomes an end in itself
and not a means toward social change. In this sense, the
black rebellion is an enormously *expressive* phenomenon
which is releasing the pent-up resentments of generations of
oppressed Negroes. But expressiveness that is oblivious to
political reality and not structured by instrumental goals is
mere bombast.

WHAT KIND OF BLACK STUDIES? [2]

The aim of the black-studies program at Cornell University
is to sustain the culture of the black nation and to develop skills
which will be of service to that nation. . . . The black-studies
program will in essence be a cultural and education vehicle for

    [2] From article by John Hatch, free-lance writer. *New Statesman*, 77:756-7.
My. 30, '69. Reprinted by permission.

creating awareness, confidence, and determination in black people in order to achieve liberation, self-sufficiency, and nationhood. Tentative Course Outline, 300c Physical Education (Staff). Theory and practice in the use of small arms and hand-to-hand combat. Discussion sessions in the proper use of force.

These are the kind of demands which have been hurled at university presidents on American campuses right across the nation during the past academic year. Every spring, I visit a Texas consortium of universities. This year hardly any academic work was done, as three of the four campuses were rocked by black agitation. On one, one hundred black students stormed into the president's office with their demands; a few weeks later the Student Center and its bookshop were wrecked. When the top-drawer Ivy League colleges have encountered extreme demands such as those quoted from Cornell, it is clear that this is no wildcat campaign confined to the usual centers of dissent in California, nor simply an attempt to mobilize black students in their traditional bases of strength, the "predominantly Negro" colleges. It is a concentrated attack directed particularly at those campuses which have recently been deliberately recruiting black students.

It is easy to demolish the emotional, logic-chopping arguments used by these young black militants and the whites of the Students for a Democratic Society who egg them on. Some of the most distinguished black academics are doing so. Sir Arthur Lewis, now at Princeton, has warned that whatever changes come to American society

the problem of the black will essentially be the same . . . whether he is going to be mostly in the bottom jobs, or whether he will also get his 11-per-cent share of the top and the middle. And his chance at the top is going to depend on . . . getting the same kind of technical training that the whites are getting—not some segregated schooling specially adapted for him.

Martin Kilson, the leading young black political scientist, now at Harvard, has cautioned that the attempt to give black-studies departments autonomy could reduce the programs to "a kind of revivalist situation where the repetition of the experiences that each black kid has had will give him a sense of cathartic gain or of therapeutic value, but this will not be an intellectual process. It'll really be a kind of group therapy." Certainly, as those with experience in Negro education are all too aware, it is a myth to suppose that black students can be prised out of their endemic sense of inferiority at the university. This is inculcated at a very early age at primary school. It is cemented by the vicious circle of students badly taught at black colleges going as teachers into more black schools and colleges to pass on equally bad training to the next generation. If anyone, black or white, ever shows determination to dig up the roots of racial inequality in the United States he will start by revolutionizing the schools system. It is too late when the university is reached. ...

The black community as a whole is now standing on the touchline watching to see what the young black students make of their revolutionary slogans, their call to arms, their appeal to black nationalism. It is generally accepted that, for the time being at least, the integrationist, civil rights strategy has failed. When it came to the test it was seen that it was still the whites who determined who should be accepted or rejected. In any case, few Negro workers have been offered jobs as a result of civil rights campaigns; the increase in black student opportunities is more remote, individual appointments of middle-class Negroes still less relevant to ghetto life. But it should be realized that as the number of black students in white universities increases—and next year the Ivy League is increasing its black freshman intake by 89 per cent—for the first time substantial numbers come from the ghetto instead of from traditional middle-class homes. The demand for black studies and the violent tactics used or threatened reflect a conflict between ghetto and middle-class academic mores.

But if the objective of integration is rejected, what alternative remains? Harold Cruse (in *The Crisis of the Negro Intellectual* [Morrow, 1967]) has suggested that America is a pluralistic society composed of contending ethnic groups.

This concept explains the current attempt to identify a black nation capable of participating in America's international war. The creation of a historical mythology based on Africa's glorious past and the achievements of Negroes can help to build a black national identity; but surely the black leaders are mistaken in imitating the tactics of African anticolonial leaders. Africans rightly aimed at gaining control over the political instruments in colonial hands. They comprised 99 per cent of their populations; a minority of 11 per cent can hardly expect to win control of the state machine.

It seems to me, therefore, that most of today's militant black students are raising dangerously false expectations amongst their followers. But the strategy of which the black-studies demand forms the focus can have even more tragic consequences. If, as seems certain from the lack of trained teachers, they fall below comparable academic standards, black studies will become derisory, thus deepening the Negro students' sense of inferiority and the contempt of their white contemporaries. Those black intellectuals who have fought their way courageously to the top will be faced with the impossible choice of retaining their membership of their color-blind international fraternities and being derided as Uncle Tom traitors, or sacrificing all their efforts to join an irrational agitation which they know must distort many truths.

The most profound danger is the effect of this new strategy on the Negro community as a whole. The civil rights campaigns did turn black frustrations outward against reactionary whites. This was therapeutic. The most serious menace of American black nationalism is that it will again turn Negroes inward into the psychological quicksands of cultural separatism. As two black psychiatrists, Grier and Cobbs, put it . . . in *Black Rage* [Basic Books, 1968]: "the overriding experience of the black American has been grief and sorrow. . . . Depression and grief are hatred turned on the self."

As grief lifts and the sufferer moves toward health, the hatred he had turned on himself is redirected toward his tormentors, and the fury of his attack on the one who caused him pain is in direct proportion to the depth of his grief. When the mourner lashes out in anger, it is a relief to those who love him, for they know he has now returned to health.

The danger I fear is that the anger shown by today's black militants is directed not against white racists but against sympathetic administrators, like Cornell's Quaker president, James Perkins, or their own civil rights leaders, like Roy Wilkins of the NAACP. As their most extreme demands—for black studies taught by black professors from books written by black authors, for segregated departments, dormitories, refectories—seem to be cementing the ghetto walls inside the campus, that hatred may well be turned back within black society. And if, as seems almost certain, many of these studies are found to be spurious, to diminish opportunities for social and economic elevation, Negroes will again feel cheated. Then the frustrations will explode within the black community instead of against the roots of national discrimination.

There can be no doubt that there is a crucial need to fill the vacuum which has been traditionally left in the American heritage from ignorance or deliberate distortion of the facts of African history and Negro culture. The forty or so African programs are doing something, but too little, to fill this vacuum. Twenty-five million Americans have been denied their cultural legacy, whilst the rest have been led to despise them for its absence. But this is an all-American issue. It could only retard its solution for the Negroes to withdraw into cultural separatism, leaving the white majority to continue feeling contempt for them. It would also deny to the black community its strongest weapon. As our black psychiatrists shrewdly perceive: "If the white man challenges him, the black scholar must demolish him with truth. His sword is his science." Whatever political battles are waged, therefore, the Negro student must not be diverted from that form of education which can enable him both to gain influence in American society and to offer intellectual ammunition to the struggles of his community. For cultural separatism—or apartheid—can only stunt intellectual development and lead to introverted frustrations. If the present generation of black leaders seek a genuine educational program to attack the roots of racism, let them demand a rewriting of American history books, a revision of cultural teaching and a revolution in the education of black children from their first days at school. In this context black studies, or universal knowledge of the contribution of Negro culture to the American heritage, can help to undermine American racism; cultural separatism can only duplicate the tragedies of South African apartheid.

CAN THE UNIVERSITY SURVIVE THE BLACK CHALLENGE? [3]

The university, beset on the one side by those who would reform it, and on the other by those who would protect it, may well fall victim to its friends even if the campus revolutionaries fail to destroy it. The reformers would save the university by stimulating needed changes both in administration and curriculum, but their rhetoric is often so strident and their actions so violent that it is difficult to distinguish them from the revolutionaries who believe that society's institutions must be destroyed before they can be reshaped to serve humanity's ends. Small wonder then that the politicians, reflecting a confused and increasingly fearful public, are beginning to take action that violates the traditional autonomy of the university. And when this spring the nation was treated to pictures of black students filing out of Cornell's Willard Straight Hall, carrying guns and wearing bandoliers, it was clear that a new dimension had been added to campus ferment.

From Berkeley in 1964, to Columbia in 1968, and Harvard in 1969, campus activism has been predominantly white—even when black militants and their cause were included. But in the past year or two black activists have disassociated themselves progressively from white tactics and

[3] From article by James Cass, education editor. *Saturday Review*. 52:68-71+. Je. 21, '69. Copyright 1969 Saturday Review, Inc. Reprinted by permission.

goals. The more recent challenge to the university—at San Francisco State, Swarthmore, Brandeis, City College of New York, Cornell, and elsewhere—has been primarily black. And in a number of ways this black challenge poses a more fundamental threat to the university than its white counterpart, not only because of the potential violence inherent in racial confrontation, but because the black demands strike more basically at the traditional concept and function of the university.

This new challenge takes on special significance in the light of the recent announcement that the Ivy League and Seven Sister colleges, as well as other leading institutions, have accepted and enrolled a record number of black students for the next year. Several are more than doubling the total number on campus in a single year. The question immediately arises as to whether the larger number of black students presages a growing number of campus disruptions next year (it is difficult to tell at what point the critical mass will be reached on a particular campus), and whether the nation's leading institutions are making special provisions to deal with the issues raised by the militants.

Most of the colleges provide some kind of academic orientation program for black students and make tutoring available when necessary. Some offer more highly structured remedial programs, lighter academic programs during the first year or two, or prefreshman summer programs. Almost every institution, too, is planning some kind of black or Afro-American studies program for next fall. These range from scattered courses in black history and literature offered in existing departments, to full-fledged majors in black studies—either interdepartmental or in a separate department. With a rare exception or two, all are moving in response to black demands, but the sense of urgency and the degree of sophistication with which the task is approached vary widely. . . .

But it is unlikely that such modest innovations will prove more than palliatives. The sources of black student discontent are too pervasive and run far too deep.

Most black students, of course, do not want to pull down the academic house. Like the majority of their white brothers, they want to make it within the established structure of society. The university, for them, is the open door to success in the white world of affairs. But a substantial minority (one highly placed Cornell official estimates the number at one third of that university's 250 black students) reject the "white" education offered them, and demand radical change in the curriculum. And a far larger number are profoundly dissatisfied with the education they are receiving and the environment in which it is provided.

It is comforting for many whites to assume that the black militants are those disadvantaged students whose inadequate preparation or capacity for the intellectually strenuous competition of the university has led them to the brink of failure. Faced with academic disaster, they find it easier to rebel than to compete.

There is apparent justification for such an assumption. As the colleges have recruited black students more actively in recent years, they have found only a limited pool of students who can compete for admission on equal terms with whites. SAT scores for entering black students, for instance, average 100 to 150 points below the whites. The schools from which many are drawn are inferior, and when they attend predominantly white schools their records are often unimpressive. Admission directors have had to seek "other criteria" for selecting capable blacks. An increasing number of those who are admitted are, in standard admissions terms, marginal at best, and some are termed "high risk" students.

Given such a picture, it is easy to assume that it is the marginal and high risk students who are rebelling. Certainly the rebels do include some students—probably many—who are threatened by failure. But reports from numerous campuses belie the easy generalization. Although hard data are difficult to come by, a number of colleges report that the attrition rate for blacks is lower than for the student body as a whole, and at others only slightly higher. It is also clear that

substantial numbers of the militant leaders are not deprived
children of the ghetto, but sons and daughters of middle-class
professional men. They typically are succeeding in the classroom and sometimes are among the brightest and most academically capable students on campus. The reasons for their
discontent must be sought elsewhere.

When, four or five years ago, during the height of the civil-
rights/integration movement, a few bellwether institutions
such as Cornell and Wesleyan began to recruit black students
actively, the assumption was that capable blacks merely
needed to be encouraged to apply. Once enrolled, close acquaintance with white students and extended exposure to
white culture would lead automatically to assimilation. The
melting pot would function, in the new context, as it had in
the folklore of the past. A minimum of academic orientation
might be required for some of the black students, it was
thought, but no other preparation was needed—for blacks or
whites.

The realities proved more complex, despite some successes. Proximity accentuates differences as often as it fosters
assimilation. Not infrequently, as it turned out, it was distance that made the liberal heart grow fonder. Most students,
both white and black were unprepared by training or experience to reach across the lines of cultural difference and
accept each other easily and naturally. Social intercourse was
often awkward and uncomfortable; misunderstandings came
easily. Whites were only dimly aware of the degree to which
our culture is pervaded by assumptions of white superiority—
and the implicit acceptance of black inferiority—while blacks
were all too aware of the fact.

At the same time, for the more perceptive, familiarity
brought a clearer sense of what it means to be white and what
it means to be black in a white society. All men may be
brothers under the skin, but each brings his own cultural
heritage to the process of mutual accommodation—and it is
the black who is expected to do most of the accommodating.
After all, it is he, the minority, who is being invited to enjoy

the benefits of membership in the established society of the majority.

Doubtless many black students accepted admission to the promised land of the university with unrealistically high expectations. It embodied in a special way the American Dream of opportunity. A community devoted to learning and the life of the mind held new promise. But even here, black students soon found they were not free from the experience of prejudice—though it sometimes took a subtler form than elsewhere. (Repeated requests for identification by campus police, the sudden embarrassment of a professor when questions of race arose in class, even the graffiti on the rest room wall carried the message.) It wasn't long before the black students discovered that no matter how completely they made it in the classroom, they were still not accepted fully by large sectors of white society. They could never look forward to the day when they too would be "free, white, and twenty-one"—with all that the phrase implies.

Until very recently the black student's options were limited: he could reject the university and the opportunity it offered; he could deny his blackness and become as white in thought and action as his talents allowed; or he could follow the more difficult course of accepting the white man's offer of skills and knowledge, while fighting to retain his own sense of black identity.

A Dramatic Change

Two major factors made for dramatic change during the mid-1960s. First was the disenchantment of many of the younger leaders of the black community with the progress and promise of integration, and their increasing rejection of white society. Second was the gradual increase in numbers of black students on white campuses, to the point where a sense of group solidarity could develop. The message of the militant younger leaders had great appeal for these black students, despite repeated warnings against some of its excesses by many of the respected black leaders of the older generation. The heart of the message was that blacks have a valid culture of their own, separate from and, in some respects, superior to white culture; that to achieve their fullest human development blacks must become proud of their blackness ("black is beautiful"), and stop trying to become white men with black skins. The more extreme leaders added the corollary that to protect themselves and their culture, blacks must separate from the white society which will never understand or accept them until made to do so by force.

These two factors, group solidarity that comes from the increasing number of black students on campus, and the growing consciousness of race pride, reinforced each other to produce the distinctively black challenge to the university. As a result, a growing number of issues have been raised by blacks. They vary somewhat from one campus to another— each has its own local concerns—but there are certain basic demands that black students have made on the university in general.

First is the insistence that larger numbers of black students be accepted, with the necessary scholarship funds provided. Second is the demand for a black-studies department— with insistence upon varying degrees of autonomy and black control. Third is the demand for separate eating and living facilities, and the establishment of cultural centers for black students. Fourth, and in many ways most difficult, is reform of the curriculum to make it more relevant to the black experience.

How threatening these demands are to the university depends on how extreme their definition is on a given campus. Most of the better colleges in the country are already searching actively for qualified blacks. In many cases, black students on campus are working closely with the administration in seeking out potential applicants. But sometimes this is not enough.

Despite an active and apparently successful program for recruiting minority group students at the City College of New York, black and Puerto Rican students disrupted campus life for more than a month this past spring in support of their demands for enrollment of a larger number of deprived students. The college's SEEK (Search for Education, Elevation, and Knowledge) program had raised the percentage of black and Puerto Rican entrants from 15 to 24 per cent of the freshman class, but student activists insisted that a far larger number of students should be admitted from high schools in deprived neighborhoods, "without regard to grades."

City College has long been the brightest academic light in New York City's famed system of higher education. Admission has always been highly competitive, and the school has produced many of the city's business, political, and professional leaders. Therefore, when a faculty negotiating committee agreed to a plan for doubling the size of the freshman class by 1970, with half of the students selected on the traditional competitive basis, and the other half chosen for their academic potential rather than performance, the news sent shock waves throughout the city. Unfortunately, neither the agreement reached by respected members of the senior faculty, nor the thinking that led to it, was released to the press. As a result, it was reported, in sketchy fashion, in the midst of a heated primary mayoralty campaign and did not receive thoughtful consideration before political positions hardened.

Located within the borders of the black Harlem community, City College is subject to special pressures from the community as well as from its students. Nevertheless, the more optimistic observers claimed that if the negotiated agreement were approved, "elaborate" remedial and tutorial programs for the minority group students would avoid serious deterioration of the college's academic program. And they believed that the open enrollment policy would, over a period of time, raise the aspirations and motivations of students in high schools that traditionally have sent few of their graduates on to college. Less sanguine—and probably more realistic—observers, given the budget squeeze that the city colleges already face, foresaw only the destruction of a great institution. It would, they believed, become an all-black college, while the city's white students were absorbed by the other colleges of the city system—Hunter, Brooklyn, and Queens. . . .

There seems little doubt that the college, situated as it is, a captive of black Harlem, must reach out more actively than it has in the past to serve the surrounding community. Whether it and other urban institutions such as Columbia and Chicago can meet the demands being made upon them and still remain first-class institutions of higher learning, is far from clear.

Demands for a black-studies program are among the easiest for most institutions to accept in theory, but often present complex problems in practice. The history, literature, and music of black people, both in America and in Africa, are generally accepted as valid subjects for scholarly inquiry and study. The economics of poverty, racism, slavery, and the sociology of ghetto life are equally acceptable to most faculties. Some critics, to be sure, question whether the research base that now exists is sufficiently broad to justify extended study, or even whether the area offers enough substance to merit consideration as a separate discipline. But Yale is planning a major in Afro-American studies . . . and other leading colleges are moving rapidly toward establishment of interdepartmental "concentrations" that are expected to develop into majors in the near future.

On some campuses, however, students are demanding action-oriented programs that will take them into the inner city to study ghetto life at firsthand, and, in some cases, to provide information and organizational help for the residents. Some academicians believe that such activities should be extracurricular and that the study program should confine itself to scholarship. ("Why should we give them credit for organizing the ghetto?") But the students conceive of such practical training as an integral part of the black experience that the university should provide. ("There's already been so much talk and writing—if there's no action, it's just a lot more academic bull!") They are aware of how easy it is, on the white campus, to become divorced from the realities of black existence. They want to benefit from the knowledge and skills that the university offers, but they are determined not to lose the commitment to their own people. ("We want to remember that black people are starving in Newark.") It is too early to say how many black-studies programs will include an action component such as that planned for San Francisco State before disruption of the campus complicated the picture, but the demand is likely to endure.

The drive for separatism in study as well as eating and living facilities is more complicated. At some institutions students have demanded an exclusively black program (enrolling only black students and taught solely by black faculty) and separate living facilities that reflect their own culture. W. H. Ferry of the Center for the Study of Democratic Institutions has even suggested that the University of California create an all-black college because, "the tradition and practice of higher education is incorrigibly white and inevitably directed at white goals, and . . . such an educational apparatus, however benign its intentions, cannot possibly achieve an outlook or program that will meet permanently ignited black ambitions." Large numbers of black students, including many moderates, agree.

Although a few institutions have acceded to black demands for separate dormitories and eating facilities, few have seriously considered freeing black-studies programs from traditional faculty control, and most are reluctant to exclude white students who want to enroll. A number of the most eminent black leaders of the older generation have denounced the separatist movement as "Jim Crow in reverse," and contend that the psychological damage caused by segregation is no less great when it is voluntary rather than imposed. Last month, Kenneth Clark resigned as a trustee of Antioch College in protest against that institution's Afro-American Studies Institute which enrolls only blacks. And Roy Wilkins of the NAACP has threatened court action against any institution that uses public funds to set up racially exclusive programs. . . .

Other critics charge that whites stand in greater need of Afro-American studies than blacks. They contend that if such programs do become all black they inevitably will be academically inferior and, therefore, will defraud the students. And some claim that separatism will lead inevitably to closed programs—over which the university will have no control—that will be devoted primarily to training cadres of black revolutionaries.

Much of what the critics claim doubtless is true. Certainly the issues are complex. Some blacks on campus are true revolutionaries and violently hostile to all things white. They work actively to radicalize their more moderate brothers and don't hesitate to employ coercion when persuasion fails. They deny the validity of established society, and some are willing to destroy whenever necessity demands—or opportunity offers. But this is only part of the story—and today, still the lesser part.

The majority of black students want to make it within the white society, but they are no longer willing to do it solely on white terms. Some of these reformers indulge in abrasive rhetoric and violent action; in no other way, they contend, can they get the serious attention of the university (the experience of recent months provides some justification for their claims). The more moderate reformers are easier to hear—and to ignore—because their voices are calm and their actions nonviolent. But their message differs little, if at all, from that of the militants, and it challenges very basically the tradition of the university.

Like many white students, the black reformers reject the archaic nature of much of higher education—the competition for grades, the lecture system that became obsolete with the invention of printing, the vocational character of liberal studies that are designed for the production of scholar-apprentices rather than for the development of human beings, the failure to find new ways to organize knowledge in an age when no man can become expert in more than a narrow specialty. But even more fundamentally they challenge the university as the sole gateway to success in a white, middle-class society that talks constantly about the virtues of pluralism, but in practice demands a high degree of conformity to the dominant white values. Why, they ask, should we immerse ourselves exclusively in the culture of Western civilization when, over the centuries, it has rejected black people? They demand that the focus of university scholarship be broadened beyond its present parochial perspective so that it will have greater relevance for a society that is becoming increasingly aware of its pluralistic character.

Meanwhile, they are seeking ways "to make the university a fitting environment for black students," which will allow them to acquire the knowledge and skills they need, without losing their black identity. ("We don't want to come out as average graduates.") They want to emerge from their collegiate years not only with the intellectual skills required for success in the white world, but also with deeper knowledge of their own people and a continuing commitment to the black community. It is this desire that lies behind the demand for separate black study programs and living facilities. It is an insistence upon "an all-black experience" that will provide a "uniquely black psychological outlook and perspective" for students who continue to participate fully in the life of the white university.

The black challenge is not a temporary aberration in the life of the university, nor is it a simple one to deal with. Many of the demands being made on the academy today are unthinkable, but some of them, on reflection, deserve careful thought. They reflect youthful fantasies of romantic revolution and instant academic success as well as legitimate aspirations of minority groups. Demands that the university correct broad social inequities over which it has no control may be aimed primarily at producing disruption rather than reform, yet too often the academy has, itself, actively participated in perpetuating such inequities. A black-studies program made up exclusively of "soul" courses with strong emotional appeal and little substantive content is a denial of the realities of a world in which knowledge and skill are required of all. But a "black experience," parallel to the "white" education program, that not only provides the student with knowledge of his people, but also stimulates a continuing commitment to their welfare, can be preparation for another part of reality. It is obvious that the admission of large numbers of minority students who are not prepared to do college level work can only result in massive frustration and further alienation. Yet substantial numbers of "high risk" students who manifestly were not prepared for college, but did possess high motivation and received adequate help, have succeeded. . . .

One suggestion for radical change came last month from the retiring director of Upward Bound, Dr. Thomas A. Billings. He proposed an experimental university organized along racial lines rather than according to academic disciplines. His experience with Upward Bound, which has worked with notable success to stimulate poor but capable high school students to seek higher education, leads him to the conclusion that "race and ethnics . . . are inextricably bound up with what one learns." Therefore, he believes that we should experiment with an institution at which all students share classes in hard sciences and technology, which are "neutral" subjects; but that the humanities, which are not neutral, should be studied in separate colleges for blacks, American Indians, Mexican Americans, and other large minority groups. Such an arrangement, Dr. Billings believes, would offer opportunity for more sensitive response to the desires of minorities to explore their own heritage, and will result more readily in eventual integration.

The university's options remain open today. It is being asked to renew itself through reforms that have been demanded from many quarters. It is being asked also to assume a new role in society, to accommodate to the aspirations of minority groups whose members, in the past, have benefited from little more than token participation in the higher education enterprise. In order to do so it must learn to distinguish between the demands of the campus revolutionaries and those of the militant reformers. It must on occasion be willing to give thought to the unthinkable, for the alternatives are grim. The university is uniquely vulnerable to both the violence of campus revolutionaries and the vigilante action of its volunteer protectors. For higher education carried on behind barbed wire will prove to be no education at all.

MISBEHAVIOURAL SCIENCES [4]

The student rebellion brings out only infrequently the best in the young and all too frequently the worst in the middle-aged.

There is much talk about malice on both sides and not enough about simple confusion. Americans, particularly academics, do not have a firm enough sense of place. We have in general led lives so protected from historical disasters that we have trouble distinguishing the merely disturbing from the apocalyptic.

The faculty of City College of New York met . . . [April 1969] to consider the crisis presented to it by the occupation of a portion of its campus by 150 rebellious Negro students. As matters wore on, there were fewer than 200 persons present out of a teaching staff of 1,700. (These are, most of the time, scenes played by a very few actors.) It was a debate which never deviated from polemical abstraction. The radicals talked about the desperation of the oppressed; and at least one conservative expanded on the need to stand up to terror. Neither of these images of confrontation seemed to have much relation to the real faces of the Negro delegation arrayed before them.

These rebels had, to be sure, arranged themselves in patterns strongly influenced by Peter Brook; still, the disguises did not seem so impenetrable as to support impressions of

[4] From article by Murray Kempton, journalist. *Spectator* (London). 222:578. My. 2, '69. Reprinted by permission.

terror and desperation. One wishes that academics would look at people with some of the objectivity we hope they still bring to the laboratory. But the heads of departments continue to talk as though they are in the Winter Palace in Petrograd and dissident junior instructors continue to talk as though they are in the Sierra Maestra; and no debate can be of much use unless the parties have some sense of common ground.

It becomes clear very soon that most teachers at City College do not know the Negro students because they are not *their* students. Perhaps a thousand of the 11,000 day students at City College are Negro; and, of these, 800 are enrolled in SEEK, a program which aims at equipping the academically-deprived to be regular students. SEEK has its own teaching staff and curriculum; I cannot say for sure that SEEK enrollees are entirely cut off from the rest of the school; but I did notice that a SEEK student next to me was able to identify the only two Negro faculty members who spoke, and none of the white ones. The experience of these discussions sought to set anyone's teeth against words that are merely epithets; nevertheless it is rather hard to think of SEEK as anything but an educational ghetto.

Yet no speaker at the faculty meeting talked about SEEK, favorably or otherwise, as an educational experiment; there seemed to be an entire lack of functional interest in it. There seemed, indeed, among these persons of great intelligence, a general absence of functional interest in anything outside their own disciplines. The meeting opened with an aimless dispute about what power the faculty really had to render a decision, which ended when a young man in Black Panther beret assumed the microphone. "First this cat says that the faculty has no power," he commented, "and then this other dude comes along and says that the faculty has more power than the president."

There was a sudden passage of general laughter. The saddest thought was that the only moment of common response between these strangers had been in this brief occasion of shared confusion.

This is a trouble which comes to the college not, you decide, from interior promptings but from shouts in the street. There is very little in these deliberations to suggest that the essential indifference of men of goodwill is really changed. It is notable, for example, that even persons otherwise affronted by Negro demands accept the principle of separate departments of black studies, small as is their expectation that they will be useful.

After all, one City College professor of physics said, "It is their funeral. They will suffer or they will prosper; it will have very little effect on the rest of us." He was being facetious; but some of his feeling has to be seen as part of the readiness so many academics have to accept a program for which they have such small respect.

Black studies are a good deal cheaper than really intensive remedial education, just as the dole and slums are cheaper than corrective measures like the Job Corps. Even Harvard, wealthy as it is, agrees to give its Negro students control over their own black-studies program. After all, it is their funeral. Yet none of these institutions would grant its students any such power in any other department; men do not that easily give away anything they think worth having.

Despite the alarms, we may best be able to see the real future of these disturbances at Columbia, where the Students for a Democratic Society work desperately and futilely to be what they were a year ago. Columbia will not call the police again, and the revolution is wholly dependent on the counterrevolution's mistakes.

Last week SDS summoned the students of the New York high schools to come to Columbia's campus and protest against their exclusion from the chances of higher education; 2,000 were expected and only 200 came, to sit down decorously and briefly at the administration buildings and then to depart with an assurance from Dean Carl Hovde that he would call them back. SDS passed out leaflets for its mass meeting that night. "Confused? Bewildered? Come Anyway," the leaflet said. Even after this expression of the prevailing sense of futility, there were 500 students present; they gave no sense of knowing what to do.

And yet last spring's revolution seems, in rhetoric at least, to be this spring's conventional wisdom. Andrew Cordier, Columbia's acting president, reports on negotiations to persuade the Naval Reserve Officers' Training Corps to withdraw from the campus and announces plans to abandon classified defense program research. The Faculty of International Affairs passes a resolution condemning disruption on the campus after first resolving: "that this faculty commends the teaching staff, students and administration for their constructive efforts . . . to place this university in the forefront of American educational institutions in its programs of Afro-American studies, urban studies and in the governance and procedures of the university."

The abolition of military training, the severance of links with the defense establishment, some thought for the welfare of the people who live around Columbia, a place for the faculty and students in the government of the university: I do not argue the merits of these aspirations. It is enough that Columbia now boasts about its concern for them and that less than a year ago they were the demands of a rebellion vehemently condemned by all respectable institutions. SDS is fading away, the illusion of its danger and the usefulness of many of its nuisances alike unrecognized.

V. THE OVER THIRTY VIEW

EDITOR'S INTRODUCTION

As several articles in this section reveal, not all writers over thirty are as hostile to student activists as the latter seem to believe. In the first selection, Judge Charles E. Wyzanski, Jr., eloquently expresses the reasons for the students' revolt against the hypocrisy of their elders. In the next article Professor Sidney Hook, a noted spokesman of the anti-Communist Left, vigorously condemns the activists for what he regards as their ruthless intolerance of disagreement and contempt for the principles of academic freedom. Thus, one man sympathizes with their angry discontent, the other condemns their actions—both are rational men, but they are talking about two different things.

Viewing the age-old conflict between generations, the English novelist Philip Toynbee shows a deep understanding both of the philosophic basis of student unrest and of the elder generation's concern for stability. Concluding the section, Leo Rosten argues wryly and effectively first against the activists, and then against their older critics.

IN DEFENSE OF THE YOUNG [1]

It is rather strange that the generation gap is thought of as something to be regretted. In my book, conformity is generally more to be regretted, and a search for unity is already a denial of the diversity of human life. The creativity of God as he created Adam involved a gap. And indeed, it is

[1] Article "A Federal Judge Digs the Young: 'It Is Quite Right that the Young Should Talk About Us as Hypocrites. We Are,' " by Charles E. Wyzanski, Jr., chief judge of the United States District Court for Massachusetts; based on an address given at Lake Forest College, Illinois. *Saturday Review*. 51:14-16+. Jl. 20, '68. Copyright 1968 Saturday Review, Inc. Reprinted by permission of *Saturday Review* and the author.

the kind of challenge that comes from the electricity which crosses the gap that makes life meaningful.

Long ago, in a not very different spirit, the ancient Greek philosopher Heraclitus said, "That which opposes, also fits"; and while what he said may proleptically have had Freudian implications, it is ordinarily thought he was talking of a bow and arrow. I don't know whether the young are the arrow, but I am quite certain that there is no reason for anybody to regret the kind of challenge which comes from difference. Indeed, could there be a clearer indication of a static and decadent civilization than one in which each generation followed the pattern of the previous one?

We are, of course, well aware that this is no ordinary change from one generation to another. Indeed, what we are going through can be compared only with what happened at the end of the eighteenth century, with the American and French Revolutions; what happened in 1848, or nearly happened; what happened in 1917. We are in a great cataclysmic change, one of the most profound in world history, and lucky we are to live in this period.

Harold Howe II, [former] U.S. Commissioner of Education, talked recently about the possibility that the colleges were to blame, not the students, for what has been going on at Ohio State, Columbia, Boston University, in Paris and Italy. Wherever you are, you cannot pick up the morning paper without finding that the student revolt is spreading in every corner of the globe. In Paris, in Germany, with the attack on Axel Springer and his newspapers; in Italy, with its closed universities; at Barnard, where the New York *Times* exposed a single child and her parents to an invasion of privacy that it would have condemned editorially if anybody else had done it; at Boston University, where a courageous president told the students they were right about their demand for a larger representation of Negroes in the student body; at Radcliffe College, where students are seeking to be admitted to the board of trustees; at Columbia University, where one can see how justified students were in resenting a proposed gymnasium that would have a separate entrance for Harlem residents and which would be built on land leased at a ridiculously low price. Mr. Howe is right—perhaps the colleges should look at themselves as well as their students.

Certain aspects of the student revolt are much overrated by the commercial press and money-seeking exploiters: sex, drugs, and dress. Most people know what hypocrites the previous generation were. They did not have to wait for the biography of Strachey to know that Keynes and the Bloomsbury set, who determined the intellectual tone of the first quarter of the twentieth century, were hardly in the Sunday school copybook tradition. What Proust and Robert de Montesquiou represented, as we have recently been told in clear language, is that France was no different from Britain. And what person who lived as a young man between World War I and World War II wants to file a certificate as to the errors of Professor Kinsey?

We did not have to wait for the young generation in order to be aware that from the beginning of mankind premarital and postmarital sex have not been lived according to the graven tablets handed down to Moses. What is it that made sex such a dangerous activity in earlier years? Was it not conception and venereal disease? And are they not both, by technological advance, much altered in our society? What reason have we to be so certain, so terribly certain, that sexual chastity is the most desirable state at all stages of a man's and a woman's life? I don't believe it. Neither did the Greeks. Neither did the Asians. A particular Western sect, inspired by a religious leader without sexual experience, foisted that notion on the Western world. Is it not time to reconsider that idea?

And what of drugs? I make no case in behalf of marijuana, but who could tell how many more people have died on the roads in the last year as a result of marijuana than as a result of alcohol. Who could tell me more people have died as a result of marijuana than as a result of cancer caused by cigarette smoking? Is there anybody who doubts that the commercial motives of our society promote the sale of tobacco and the sale of alcohol, and that anybody who came from Mars or Venus or some remote place would find it absolutely impossible to decide on what basis we as a society had outlawed marijuana and not tobacco or alcohol? Have you any doubt in your own mind that it is merely habit and profit that make us of the older generation so content to live in a society where alcohol and tobacco freely circulate, and marijuana is outlawed?

Oh, we go to church, do we? Why? For social and commercial reasons and for consolation in time of trouble. But do we go with faith and conviction and discipline and self-denial? Which of us? From the day that Darwin and Huxley opened the doors and science walked into the church and we walked out, which of us has had that kind of faith which represents a deep commitment to that denial and sacrifice and discipline which are the essence of religion?

It is quite right that the young should talk about us as hypocrites. We are. And it is quite right that they should note that our hypocrisy is embedded in our materialism.

So we are critical of the young. Have they not far more reason to be critical of us? And what have we done to get them on the right path from the beginning? Most of us were quite content to have them undergo a permissive kind of education in which not merely the *quadrivium* and the *trivium,* but the whole core of humanistic learning was not part of their deep education. We allowed them pretty much, in their early primary and secondary stages, to have the kind of education from their schools and their peers which they wanted because we were not sufficiently convinced of our own beliefs. And they knew it.

We brought them up in a society in which we no longer believed in either the carrot or the stick. Nor did they. Our society afforded them as children, in their occupations as babysitters and otherwise, a salary rate sufficient to assure them a minor kind of affluence and independence. They walked as they pleased because they had the money, the very root of independence. Then, vastly and suddenly, and quite rightly, we expanded the total educational system so that we flooded the colleges and the universities of the nation at a rate at which nobody could possibly absorb.

Mark Hopkins at one end of the log and the student at the other? Doesn't it sound like a prehistoric fable? Which university student today is in a one-to-one relationship with anybody on the faculty? Which one has any kind of personal relationship in a large university? Was it not certain that men and women of any character would resent these institutions and seek some sort of outlet other than the formal ones in which they were treated like commuters in a subway train?

What is to be said about these young people, plus and minus? And those of us who sit where we hear both sides or many sides of the question know that truth is never or almost never all on one side. Let us give the young, first of all, credit for being right about their concern. They, at least, know that there can never be, in a growing society, a philosophy of consensus. They realize, to return to Heraclitus, that "strife is the source of all things." Growth implies discord as well as advance.

What the young care about is a deeper kind of democracy than some of us have been willing to accept. The French in their immortal division talked of liberty, equality, and fraternity. May one not say that in my generation the accent was heavy on the first? And we do not need to turn to Lord Acton to know that he who emphasizes liberty is he who is already privileged. Liberty means one thing if you are already in the top place and something very different if you are low on the scale.

Many know the classic remark of Mr. Justice Maule, phrased somewhat differently by Anatole France, when Justice Maule was faced by a divorce case in the nineteenth century. At that time in England you were free to get a divorce if you took a very lengthy expensive proceeding in the Probate, Divorce, and Admiralty Court. And there was before Justice Maule a poor man, poor of purse and poor of spirit,

who had not gotten a divorce but had married again. Justice
Maule said, "It is the glory of England that the law courts
are open alike to the rich and the poor." The glory of the law
which treats alike the rich and the poor is no glory. It is a
sham. And the society which pretends that it gives liberty to
all without being concerned with equality and fraternity is
a sham.

The young are quite right that equality and fraternity are
necessary for democracy and a kind of understanding of what
people are like. We in this country stand too close to know
how right the young are. If you look from a distance at what
goes on in the United States, there is much sense in the concern that the young have about our total order. It is no accident that the young and the Negro are allied, and this is not
pure sentimentalism. It is an awareness that in our civilization the litmus paper is black.

The young marched with the black, and now the young
are not wanted. The black do not want us, nor are they
wrong. One of the things that we must face up to, just as a
parent must face up to it with respect to a child, is that when
one is struggling for freedom and identity, sometimes one
must do it alone. The rejected, sympathetic, kindly person—
the parent or white man—does not understand; but it is his
fault. It is part of the process of growing up to grow on
your own.

There are those who don't like the phrase "black power."
It's a very correct phrase. Anyone who really studies democracy will find out that democracy is pluralistic in character.
It is those already in power who scorn the pressure groups.
But it is pressure groups—whether they be voter leagues
formed by women, labor unions formed by workers, black
organizations formed by colored people—that in the end
count and enter into the total social fabric. Democracy is a
struggle based not only on high ideals; it is power against
power. There is an overarch of principle, but the overarch
is to hold the ring firm while the contestants battle it out
within the limits authorized by the organized society.

The young are not wrong, either, in their wonder about the scope of violence. I tread on very dangerous ground here, and I beg indulgence as a quasi-historian and not as a judge. I ask you to reflect carefully on the Boston Tea Party, on John Brown and the raid on Harpers Ferry, on the sit-down strikes in 1937 in the plants of General Motors. Every one of these was a violent, unlawful act, plainly unlawful. In the light of history, was it plainly futile? There are occasions on which an honest man, when he looks at history, must say that through violence, regrettable as it is, justice of a social kind has worked itself out. Does that mean that I think that violence is right? Most certainly I answer ambiguously. I cannot know; none of us can know until long after this time has gone. But I warn those who think that violence is right because history, in the three instances that I have cited, and many others that one might mention, has shown that violence worked—I warn them that violence will lead to McCarthy I or McCarthy II. To which Senator's philosophy, if either, will this nation respond?

What I invite is caution. The young are right not to take too seriously our statement that they must always behave lawfully, but we who are older are also right to say, "We have lived through reaction, and we know what a price you will pay if you are wrong. And we remind you of the words of Charles Morgan that liberty is a room which can be defined only by the walls which enclose it." The young have a great responsibility. They cannot define liberty except in terms of limitation. Believe me, I do it every day!

The ultimate problem which the young face is whether they have the courage to be radical enough to face the implications of what they are doing. I fear not one bit what they have done so far, provided they go further.

In that wonderful play, even if it was a failure on Broadway, by Peter Ustinov, called *Halfway Up the Tree,* there was a British colonial officer who went abroad and left behind his wife and his two children. One was his son who went to Oxford and dressed like a hippie and was having a homosexual relationship with another fellow while they were carrying around a guitar which neither of them could play. The daughter was pregnant, by which of several men she wasn't sure. The colonial fellow returned—he was of my venerable age—and he wasn't disturbed by what his young had done, but he was a little concerned that the boy didn't know how to play the guitar and the girl didn't know how to keep house. If they had taken the first step, they must be prepared for the second. To show them how he felt about it, he went and lived up in a tree and took care of his own food needs and learned how to play the guitar. Well, it is all quite in point.

The young can be as radical as they like, but they must carry the consequence. It isn't enough to overthrow us. They have to establish themselves. It is one of the elements of life that there will be an establishment. They may not like ours —and I don't think they much care for the Communist one because they have seen how that works—but have they thought through what kind of establishment they want?

I am quite sure that one of the things they will have to do is rearrange the property structure of this nation. As any good lawyer will tell you, property is only an idea—*meum* and *teum*. *Meum* and *teum* are just a lawyer's idea. The things themselves are things. They don't belong to anybody except as we create the relationship.

There is no doubt that our social structure now works in a most undesirable way. Among the 80 per cent—and it is pretty nearly that—who have the benefits of our system, it works surprisingly well. Effort, at least if followed in paths of conformity, will in the long run yield affluence and security. Or at any rate, one will have an automobile! But if one is in the lowest 20 per cent, he is caught. He may proceed to gain a little, but the gap between him and the 80 per cent is not like the generation gap; it is like the gap between the underdeveloped and the developed nations—constantly growing and creating tensions and creating an envy which will surely lead to disaster.

I speak not in favor of a negative income tax, about which I understand far too little. Nor do I endorse a particular measure of any sort of redistribution or any particular kind of program of health, education, and welfare. I merely say to those who are young that it isn't enough to love your neighbor. You had better be concerned about how your neighbor will be in a position to love you.

What I have talked about doesn't get very close to specifics. But I do know something about what life presents. It presents a riddle that has no answer and never will. In [the German physicist] Erwin Schrödinger's phrase, it is a circle that always will have a gap.

Each generation is faced with a challenge of making some kind of sense out of its existence. In advance it knows from the Book of Job and the Book of Ecclesiastes and the Greek drama that there will be no right answer. But there will be forms of answer. There will be a style. As ancient Greece had the vision of *arete* (the noble warrior), as Dante and the medievalists had the vision of the great and universal Catholic Church, even as the Founding Fathers of the American Republic had the vision of the new order which they began, so for the young the question is to devise a style—not one that will be good *semper et ubique* [always and everywhere], but one for our place and our time, one that will be a challenge to the very best that is within our power of reach, and one that will make us realize, in Whitehead's immortal terms, that for us the only reality is the process.

STUDENT REVOLTS COULD DESTROY ACADEMIC FREEDOM [2]

One thing seems clear. In the crisis situations shaping up throughout the country, administrators are not going to enjoy a peaceful life. Their prospect of weathering the storms

[2] From article by Sidney Hook, head of the All-University Department of Philosophy, New York University, author of *Academic Freedom and Academic Anarchy* (Cowles. '70). *New York University Alumni News.* 13:3. My. '68. Reprinted by permission.

that will be synthetically contrived for them depends upon their ability and willingness to win the faculty for whatever plans and proposals they advance in the name of the university. For if they permit students or any other group to drive a wedge between them and the faculty, they will discover the sad fact of academic life that in such rifts the faculty will either play a neutral role or even assume a hostile one.

Not only on good educational grounds, therefore, but on prudential ones as well, the administration must draw the faculty into the formulation of institutional educational policy. I say this with reluctance because it means the proliferation of committee meetings, the dilution of scholarly interest, and even less time for students. But this is a small price to pay for academic freedom and peace.

In talking about academic freedom, nothing signifies the distance we have come in the space of my lifetime so much as the fact that we now are concerned with the academic freedom of *students*. For historical reasons I cannot now explore, academic freedom in the United States meant *Lehrfreiheit*, freedom to teach. *Lernfreiheit*, freedom to learn, has only recently been stressed. It does not mean the same as it meant under the German university system that presupposed the all-prescribed curriculum of studies of the *Gymnasium*. If academic freedom for students means freedom to learn, then two things should be obvious. There is no academic freedom to learn without *Lehrfreiheit* or academic freedom to teach. Where teachers have no freedom to teach, students have obviously no freedom to learn, although the converse is not true.

Second, students' freedom to learn was never so widely recognized, was never so pervasive in the United States as it is today—whether it be construed as the freedom to attend college or not, or the freedom to select the *kind* of college the student wishes to attend or his freedom of curricular choice *within* the kind of college he selects. Above all, if academic freedom for students means the freedom to doubt, challenge, contest and debate within the context of inquiry, American students are the freest in the world, and far freer than they were when I attended college.

I recall an incident when I was a student in a government class at CCNY. The teacher conducted the class by letting the students give reports on the themes of the course. All he contributed was to say "next" as each student concluded. But when in reporting on the Calhoun-Webster debates, I declared that it seemed to me that Calhoun had the better of the argument, that his logic was better than Webster's although his *cause* was worse, the instructor exploded and stopped me. After emotionally recounting his father's services in the Civil War, he turned wrathfully on me and shouted: "Young man! When you're not preaching sedition, you are preaching secession!" Whereupon he drove me from the class. (The "sedition" was a reference to an earlier report on Beard's economic interpretation of the Constitution that he had heard with grim disapproval.) And this was at CCNY in 1920! The incident wasn't typical, but that it could happen at all marks the profundity of the changes in attitudes toward students since then. . . .

Moral Premise

Of course, there is still a large group of potential college students who are deprived of freedom to learn because of poverty or prejudice or the absence of adequate educational facilities. And as citizens of a democratic society whose moral premise is that each individual has a right to that education that will permit him to achieve his maximum growth as a person, our duty is to work for, or support, whatever measures of reconstruction we deem necessary to remove the social obstacles to freedom of learning. It is perfectly legitimate to expect the university to study these problems and propose solutions to them. All universities worthy of the name already do. This is one thing. But to therefore conclude that these problems must become items not only on the agenda of study but for an agenda of action is quite another.

For it therewith transforms the university into a political action organization and diverts it from its essential task of discovery, teaching dialogue and criticism. Since there are profound differences about the social means necessary to achieve a society in which there will be a maximum freedom to learn, the university would become as partisan and biased as other political action groups urging their programs on the community. Its primary educational purpose or mission would be lost. It would be compelled to silence or misrepresent the position of those of its faculty who disagreed with its proposals and campaigns of action. Class and group conflicts would rend the fabric of the community of scholars in an unceasing struggle for power completely unrelated to the quest for truth.

Objectivity Imperiled

If the university is conceived as an agency of action to transform society in behalf of a cause, no matter how exalted, it loses its *relative* autonomy, imperils both its independence and objectivity, and subjects itself to retaliatory curbs and controls on the part of society on whose support and largesse it ultimately depends.

This is precisely the conception of a university that is basic to the whole strategy and tactics of the so-called Students for a Democratic Society. I say "so-called" because their actions show that they are no more believers in democracy than the leaders of the so-called Student Nonviolent Coordinating Committee [now the Student National Coordinating Committee] are believers in nonviolence. And indeed the leaders of the SDS make no bones about that fact. In manifesto after manifesto they have declared that they want to use the university as an instrument of revolution. To do so, they must destroy the university as it exists today.

I wish I had time to list some of the clever stratagems they have devised to focus their opposition. On every campus there are always some grievances. Instead of seeking peacefully to resolve them through existing channels of consultation and deliberation, the SDS seeks to inflame them. Where grievances don't exist, they can be created. In one piece of advice to chapter members, they were urged to sign up for certain courses in large numbers, and then denounce the university for its large classes!

Freedom of dissent, speech, protest is never the real issue. They are, of course, always legitimate. But the tactic of the SDS is to give dissent the immediate form of violent action. The measures necessarily adopted to counteract this lawless action then become the main issue, as if the original provocation hadn't occurred. Mario Savio admitted after the Berkeley affair [in 1964] that the issue of "free speech" was a "pretext" —the word was his—to arouse the students against the existing role of the university in society.

Seek to Destroy

One of the leaders of the SDS at Columbia is reported to have said: "As much as we would like to, we are not strong enough as yet to destroy the United States. But we are strong enough to destroy Columbia!" He is wrong about this, too— the only action that would destroy Columbia would be faculty support of the students!—but his intent is clear.

Actually, the only thing these groups, loosely associated with the New Left, are clear about is what they want to destroy, not what they would put in its stead. In a debate with Gore Vidal, Tom Hayden, one of the New Left leaders, was pointedly asked what his revolutionary program was. He replied: "We haven't any. First we will make the revolution, and *then* we will find out what for." This is truly the politics of absurdity.

The usual response present-day academic rebels make to this criticism is that the university today is nothing but an instrument to preserve the status quo, and therefore faithless to the ideals of a community of scholars. Even if this charge were true, even if the universities today were bulwarks of the status quo, this would warrant criticism and protest, not violent and lawless action in behalf of a contrary role, just as foreign to their true function. But it is decidedly *not* true!

There is no institution in the country in which dissent and criticism of official views, of tradition, of the conventional wisdom in all fields, is freer and more prevalent than in the university. The very freedom of dissent that students today enjoy in our universities is in large measure a consequence of the spirit of experiment, openness to new ideas, absence of conformity and readiness to undertake new initiatives found among them.

Arrogant Claim

The first casualty of the strategy of the campus rebels is academic freedom. It is manifest in their bold and arrogant claim that the university drop its research in whatever fields these students deem unfit for academic inquiry and investigation. This note was already sounded in Berkeley. It is focal at Columbia. It is a shameless attempt to usurp powers of decision that the faculty alone should have. After all, it is preposterous for callow and immature adolescents who presumably have come to the university to get an education to set themselves up as authorities on what research by their teachers is educationally permissible.

Unless checked, it will not be long before these students will be presuming to dictate the conclusions their teachers should reach, especially on controversial subjects. This is standard procedure in totalitarian countries in which official student organizations are the political arm of the ruling party. Already there are disquieting signs of this. At Cornell a few weeks ago—*before* the martyrdom of Dr. King—a group of Black Nationalist students invaded the offices of the chairman of the economics department and held him captive in order to get an apology from a teacher whose views on African affairs they disagreed with. Only yesterday, another group at Northwestern demanded that courses in "black literature" and "black art" be taught by teachers approved by the Negro students.

And there are spineless administrators and cowardly members of the faculty who are prepared to yield to this blackmail. Under the slogans of "student rights" and "participatory democracy" the most militant groups of students are moving to weaken and ultimately destroy the academic freedom of those who disagree with them.

Let us not delude ourselves. Even when these militant students fail to achieve their ultimate purpose, they succeed in demoralizing the university by deliberately forcing a confrontation upon the academic community that it is not prepared to face and the costs of which it is fearful of accepting. In forcing the hand of the academic community to meet force with force, the citadel of reason becomes a battlefield. . . .

There is always a small group—a strange mixture of purists and opportunists desirous of ingratiating themselves with students—who will *never* condemn the violence of students but only the violence required to stop it. These students succeed, even when they fail, in embittering relations between the administration and some sections of the faculty. They succeed, even when they fail, in antagonizing the larger community of which the university is a part, and in arousing a vigilante spirit that demands wholesale measures of repression and punishment that educators cannot properly accept.

How is it possible, one asks, for events of this character to happen? There have always been extremist and paranoidal tendencies in academic life, but they have been peripheral —individuals and small groups moving in eccentric intellectual orbits. But not until the last four or five years has the norm of social protest taken the form of direct action, have positions been expressed in such ultimatistic and intransigent terms, have extremist elements been strong enough to shut down great universities even for a limited time.

There are many and complex causes for this. But as I see it, the situation in the university is part of a larger phenomenon, viz., the climate of intellectual life in the country. I do not recall any other period in the last fifty years when intellectuals themselves have been so intolerant of each other, when differences over complex issues have been the occasion for denunciation rather than debate and analysis, when the use of violence—in the right cause, of course!—is taken for granted, when dissent is not distinguished from civil disobedience, and civil disobedience makes common cause with resistance, and readiness for insurrection. A few short years ago, anti-intellectualism was an epithet of derogation. Today it is an expression of revolutionary virility.

Fanaticism Rampant

In the fifties I wrote an essay on "The Ethics of Controversy," trying to suggest guidelines for controversy among principled democrats no matter how widely they differed on substantive issues. Today I would be talking into the wind for all the attention it would get. Fanaticism seems to be in the saddle. That it is a fanaticism of conscience, of self-proclaimed virtue, doesn't make it less dangerous. This past year has presented the spectacle of militant minorities in our colleges from one end of the country to another, preventing or trying to prevent representatives of positions they disapprove of from speaking to their fellow-students wishing to listen to them.

The spectacle shows that we have failed to make our students understand the very rudiments of democracy, that to tolerate active intolerance is to compound it. If we judge commitment by action, the simple truth is that the great body of our students is not firmly committed to democracy or to the liberal spirit without which democracy may become the rule of the mob.

I do not know any sure way or even a new way of combating the dominant mood of irrationalism, especially among students and even among younger members of the faculty whose political naïveté is often cynically exploited by their younger, yet politically more sophisticated, allies. What is of the first importance is to preserve, of course, the absolute intellectual integrity of our classrooms and laboratories, of our teaching and research against any attempt to curb it. We must defend it not only against the traditional enemies, who still exist even when they are dormant, but also against those who think they have the infallible remedies for the world's complex problems, and that all they need is sincerity as patent of authority. Fanatics don't lack sincerity. It is their long suit. They drip with sincerity—and when they have power, with blood—other people's blood.

We need more, however, than a defensive strategy, safeguarding the intellectual integrity of our vocation against those who threaten it. We need—and I know this sounds paradoxical—to counterpose to the revolt of the emotionally committed the revolt of the rationally committed. I do not want to identify this with the revolt of the moderates. There are some things one should not be moderate about. In the long run, the preservation of democracy depends upon a passion for freedom, for the logic and ethics of free discussion and inquiry, upon refusal to countenance the measures of violence that cut short the processes of intelligence upon which the possibility of shared values depends.

These are old truths but they bear repeating whenever they are denied. Even tautologies become important when counterposed to absurdities.

We as teachers must make our students more keenly aware of the centrality of the democratic process to a free society and of the centrality of intelligence to the democratic process. Democracy has our allegiance because of its cumulative fruits, but at any particular time the process is more important than any specific program or product. He who destroys the process because it does not guarantee some particular outcome is as foolish as someone who discards scientific method in medicine or engineering or any other discipline because of its failure to solve altogether or immediately a stubborn problem.

Courage Needed

There is one thing we cannot deny to the intransigent and fanatical enemies of democracy. That is courage. Intelligence is necessary to overcome foolishness. But it is not sufficient to tame fanaticism. Only courage can do that. A handful of men who are prepared to fight, to bleed, to suffer and, if need be, to die, will always triumph in a community where those whose freedom they threaten are afraid to use their *intelligence* to resist and to fight, and ultimately to take the same risks in action as those determined to destroy them.

Yes, there is always the danger that courage *alone* may lead us to actions that will make us similar to those who threaten us. But that is what we have intelligence for—to prevent that from happening! It is this union of courage and intelligence upon which the hope of democratic survival depends.

INTOLERABLE! [3]

If I write that the student eruption of 1968 is more like a religious than a political or economic movement, I use the word *religious* not to blame or to praise but simply as an attempt at definition. Religious founders and initiators have nearly always been young men: their elders have come along afterwards to institutionalize and intellectualize the burning message.

Consider the common reminder of religious zeal and youthful ardor in the following elements which unite nearly all the significant student phenomena of the past few months: (1) the return to absolute values, (2) the desire for personal purity, (3) hatred of "the world," (4) a metaphysical use of the word *real* (as in "real presence") by

[3] From article by Philip Toynbee, British novelist and journalist. *Observer* (London). p 21. Je. 23, '68. Reprinted by permission.

which an apparent reality is contrasted with a "more real" reality which can be perceived only by the initiates, (5) thus the inevitable élitism of "the saved," (6) combined with a firm rejection of empiricism amounting at times to a rejection of history, (7) the existence of holy writ, (8) the worship of a god or gods in human form.

This is an exaggeration, of course. Not all religions have included all these elements, nor do all the articulate student leaders subscribe to all these attitudes. But surely the resemblance is striking enough to be significant; and a more detailed examination of these religious elements may help to bridge the chasm of misunderstanding between "them" and "us."

1. The students seem to be absolutists in their strong tendency to demand a *total* reorganization of society on *totally* moral principles. Revisionists, social tinkerers, meliorists of all kinds are despised.

2. It appears that "the students"—I shall have to use this shorthand to describe the passionate and articulate minority of modern students—the students are more concerned with *being* something than with *doing* something; they usually refuse to describe in any detail the kind of world they want to create.

3. They reject *all* the available worlds—Communist or capitalist, social-democratic, racialist or feudal. Nor are they willing to make moral distinctions between them.

4. It is Marcuse's teaching that modern democratic capitalism is "really" a devastating form of authoritarianism. For although the people *seem* to prefer the status quo to any revolutionary alternative, their "real" natures demand a revolutionary change in the organization of society. Marcuse, and his student followers, know what the people "really" want better than the people themselves can know it.

5. Follows from (4).

6. The students are notably antihistorical in their apparent refusal to consider past patterns of revolution. They are aware that every past revolution has been "corrupted" to

a greater or a lesser degree—they might make an exception of Cuba—but this does not provide material for evolving a new set of social antipower mechanisms: it simply confirms (3).

7. To a greater or lesser extent the works of Marcuse, Fanon, Guevara, Mao, Debray and Reich have been treated as sacred texts.

8. Guevara—and Debray to a lesser extent—are the semi-divine heroes of student mythology.

Because we live in an antireligious world these descriptions have probably read like a series of sneers or denunciations. Yet I am, to the best of my ability, a religious man, and I believe that this student religion is both a noble and an interesting one. I cannot join it or share it, if only because I am fifty-two years old and religious faith in its pristine and undiluted form is not for people like myself. Nor do I write this with regret, for I think it proper that each of us should exercise the capacities and perceptions appropriate to his age, and that if we do this properly—I mean both vigorously and generously—then the tensions between the age-groups will be enlightening and fruitful. Few things cause more embarrassment than the spectacle of an old man trying to be one of the boys; except, perhaps, the spectacle of a young prig imitating the portentousness of his elders.

It is worth remembering—though easily forgotten by the no-longer-young—that to be young is not an attribute of the same order as to be tall, or to be white, or to be rich, or to be clever. For these are all, with a few rare exceptions, *permanent* characteristics: most people who are tall, white, rich or clever—or their opposites—remain so for the whole of their lives. Yet it is hard for the no-longer-young to keep in mind that the young who exasperated them ten, five or even two years ago are a different collection of individuals from the young who exasperate them today. And those young of ten years ago have long ago joined our own enormous ranks of the no-longer-young. The whole thing is more like a game of Oranges and Lemons than a contest between two unchanging teams. We chop off their heads, one by one, and when we have done so they join our side.

I know that this apparent cynicism and smugness is more infuriating to the young man than open denunciation and middle-aged fury. But it is one of the facts of life that the young cease to be young, and that their attitudes change when they do so. The alternative is a great deal more depressing—that cult of permanent youth which is either embarrassingly silly (Rupert Brooke) or a great deal worse (the fascist movements of the last half-century) . . . . To worship youth in all its aspects is surely the symptom of an aging and decrepit civilization.

There are two further points to be made. The middle-aged were once young, and the more they try to remember their own youth the more they will revive old feelings and attitudes which they once shared with those who are young today. But it is also the case that the young and the no-longer-young of today share something very important *in the present*—namely, the world as it is: the visible scene; the immediate problems. To be *fully* aware of how much I share with twenty-year-old students (a) by now experiencing the same period, (b) by having once been twenty myself, is already to take some of the high drama out of the age-war.

And this leads, of course, to the most important of all the unanswered questions: Is the apparent rebellion of the young in 1968 *a different sort of thing* from earlier rebellions?

The first thing to be said here is that the age-war is not a phenomenon of constant and unflickering intensity. All children have to free themselves from their parents, but it is not the case that this is always accompanied by violence, or even by hostility. Between the Romantic Movement of 1790 to 1820 and the twenties of our century the conflict between English generations was so mild as to be almost imperceptible. Between the beginning of the last war and about the year 1962 the age-war was again desultory, undramatic and fairly good-humored. It seems to have reached a point now where it is at least as violent as it was in the thirties, when I was young; and perhaps more violent than it has ever been before in European history. I think it more useful to say that the *extent* of the student revolt, combined with its new content, involves one of those Marxist changes of quantity into quality rather than the mere intensification of a perennial phenomenon.

In any case it is useless to "explain" this phenomenon by saying that the young have become more wicked and irresponsible, or more noble and generous than earlier generations. These battle-cries are pseudocausal explanations: in reality, partisan descriptions. Nor does it help much to suppose that the adult world of today is more horrible than any earlier adult world and that the young have simply responded with a deeper hatred. A comparison of historical periods in terms of relative hateability has never been much use to anyone.

All I can do is to put forward a few necessarily prejudiced suggestions of my own: and the first one is this—that for all our efforts to be fair and understanding to each other, neither side in the present age-war ought to fall over backwards in this attempt. My own vision of the world is the vision of someone who was born in 1916, and if I try too hard to see the world through the eyes of someone born thirty years later I shall end up by seeing nothing clearly at all. When I look at the present generation of students I look, I hope, with sympathy; I know, with interest. But I also look with the eyes of a middle-aged, middle-class Englishman.

From that vantage-point, wearing those blinkers, I would begin by saying that it is very rare indeed for the *cerebrations* of the young to be of any enduring interest. Nor do I find that the present hotchpotch of sacred texts makes coherent intellectual sense. Marcuse is a brilliant neo-Marxist and his denunciation of modern Western society has a prophetic eloquence as well as great sophistication of analysis and diagnosis. But his program is sketchy and dispiriting in the extreme, and his élitism would certainly lead to an intensification of that authoritarianism which he claims to destroy.

Guevara was a noble man, but his writing is exclusively concerned with the techniques of revolutionary wars in Latin America: the same is true of Debray. And it is hard indeed to see how Paris students will benefit from adopting the tactics suited to guerrillas in the Bolivian jungle. Fanon was concerned only with the identity and the problems of black men. Reich was an interesting and sympathetic psychologist with the simplistic view that nearly all the world's troubles could be cured by the abolition of sexual repression.

This does not "add up." But nor is it refuted or ridiculed by pointing out that it *is* a hotchpotch, and that no coherent program emerges from it. There are plenty of contradictions in primitive Christianity, and no coherent program emerged from *that*. And although the great majority of youthful minds are incompetent instruments of cogitation—effective cogitation depends on a body of effective experience—yet they are highly competent instruments for strong, enlightening and *informative* feeling. I don't believe that the feelings of the middle-aged are bound to atrophy: they sometimes become subtler, defter and more genuinely exploratory than they used to be. But the passions of the young have an unrepeatable intensity: a power to break through the familiar appearance of things and people; to seize hold of the world and squeeze it with an avidity which will never be recaptured.

What is more, there have been rare generations of the young who have arrived, through the passion of their vision and the happy opportunities of their epoch, in defining a new area of human sensibility. This was notably achieved by the first European Romantics. It was achieved, in the cruel forcing-house of the First World War, by the generation which was born at the turn of the century. There is no coherent body of romantic faith: the savage disillusionment, the kaleidoscopic shake-up which accompanied the first war cannot be formalized or easily defined. But the world was altered forever by each of those young generations.

What is needed for a young generation to be permanently effective is not a program, or even a cogent and self-sustaining argument. What is needed is powerful and novel articulation. I have not seen or heard of this yet, either from the young of today or from their immediate predecessors, but this may be because *my* eyes can't be focused to see it or *my* ears attuned to hear it. Or it may be because no such articulation has yet been achieved.

My own guess is that it *will* be achieved. I am certainly convinced that the young of 1968 are much better placed to make a permanent contribution to the social, intellectual and spiritual improvement of the race than any European or American generation of at least the past forty years. The religion of the present students is not a new one, but it has genuine sectarian fervor and a genuinely new and profoundly exciting collective aura. (Vague words indeed, but the thing itself is necessarily vague.) What they have achieved —apart from a few practical reforms—is a marvelously vivid reminder that our society is insufferable: that all societies have always been insufferable.

An episode in a television interview has stayed in my mind. Four very sympathetic students from the Hornsey College of Art had made cogent and persuasive complaints about the squalors and inadequacies of their college. An equally sympathetic middle-aged local councilor then explained that the college could receive a larger grant only at the expense of the local primary schools. There simply wasn't enough money to go round. The age-war was being politely fought on this occasion, but all its fundamental elements were there. "This is intolerable!" "I know it is, but . . . ." And it is the proper function of the middle-aged to say "but" —*but* there isn't enough money; *but* human nature cannot be changed overnight; *but* this policy has led to tyranny in the past; *but* a world without compromise would be a hellish conflict of rival fanaticisms. . . . And it is the function of the young to shout again, at the top of their lungs: "Nevertheless, this is *intolerable!*"

In Anouilh's *Antigone,* Creon patiently explains to the
heroine that in their hour of need the Thebans had required
him to accept political responsibilities, and he had known
that acceptance would involve him, step by step, in com-
promises and connivances. But he had said yes in spite of
that knowledge. *"Mais moi, je n'ai jamais dit oui!"* ["But *I*
never said yes!"], cries Antigone on a fine curtain of youthful
and religious passion. I know perfectly well that I belong
with the Creons. I suspect and dislike all simplifications; all
fanaticisms; all facile Utopianisms. I greatly value the
bourgeois and domestic virtues. I adore the Christian virtue
of prudence, with its marvelous humility and wit in the face
of noisier and nobler emotions. I am devoted to the subtle-
ties and ironies of common sense. But just because this is the
tendency of middle-age—with all the dangers of complacency
and blindness which are obviously involved in such a preference—it is all the more important that Antigone's voice
should be raised—and heard. *"Moi, je n'ai jamais dit oui."*

And this, of course, will appear to the young to be the
worst complacency of all—this fairly comfortable belief that
the young are right to shout "Intolerable!" and that the
middle-aged and elderly are right to answer "Yes, but . . . ."
Yet it is only the shouts of the young which have ever provided a true motive for change. It is only the reservations of
their elders which have prevented our Torquemadas and our
Robespierres from trying to purify the world by the stake
and the guillotine. The shouts of Cohn-Bendit, Rudi
Dutschke and the rest have evoked the usual drab and self-
righteous responses from the Professor Beloffs of our world
[Max Beloff is a professor of government and administration
at Oxford]. They have also compelled attention.

"Attention! Attention must be paid!" cried Willy Lo-
man's wife in *Death of a Salesman*; and this is the cry of all
religions at all times. The world is not all right: it is as bad
as Marcuse and Debray think it is. Nor will it be made all
right by a few minor reforms. The world is unbearably cruel,

oppressive, blind and vulgar. The young know this best, just as the middle-aged know that the world could be worse and that almost any social order is better than social chaos. If both sides in the age-war perform their functions properly their conflict may result in things becoming a little less unbearable than they are today.

TO AN ANGRY YOUNG MAN [4]

I have been getting lusty cheers and jeers for a rueful little paragraph I recently wrote about student riots. The most eloquent (and savage) letter ended: "Drop dead! ! !" Another diatribe was signed "Columbia Senior." I wish I knew where to send this reply to both:

Dear ?:

It will upset you to learn that I agree with many things you said. For instance. "Don't question our sincerity!" I don't. You are about as sincere as anyone can be. You are sincerely unhappy, sincerely frustrated and sincerely confused. You are also sincerely wrong about the few facts you cite, and sincerely illogical in the violent conclusions you reach. Besides, what does "sincerity" have to do with issues? Any insane asylum is full of sincere patients. Hitler was undoubtedly sincere. So are the followers of Voliva, who think the world is sincerely flat.

I sadly agree that your college courses have been "outrageously irrelevant to the times"—because your letter reveals that you could not pass a freshman exam in at least three fields in which you pass such sweeping judgments: economics, history, political theory.

You say, "Destroy a system that has not abolished unemployment, exploitation and war!" By the same reasoning, you should blow up all hospitals (and perhaps execute all doctors, biologists and researchers): they have not abolished disease.

[4] Article by Leo Rosten, author, special editorial advisor to *Look* Magazine. *Look*. 32:28. N. 12, '68. Copyright © by Leo Rosten.

Before you destroy a system, propose another that *will* solve (not hide, shift or disguise) unemployment, "exploitation," war. Anyone can promise Utopia—without specifying a program. Tom Hayden, idol of the New Left, has said: "First we'll make the revolution—then we'll find out what for." Would you employ a plumber who rips out all the pipes in your house before he learned how to repair a leak?

You say, "The mass media are not telling us the truth." Then how and from whom did *you* learn the "evils" you correctly deplore? After all, your information comes from one or another organ of—the mass media.

"This society is only interested in higher prices and profits!" You apparently do not understand this society, or *a* society, or the function of prices (and profits) in *any* economy. Has it never occurred to you that the marketplace is a polling booth? That buying is voting? That no economic system is possible without *some* form of pricing, without some measure of efficacy or worth? Has it never occurred to you that profits are a form of *proof* (that something gives satisfaction to those who pay for it)? Perhaps you should examine the public *uses* that we make of private profits— through taxation.

The countries that follow your platitude, "production for use," *without exception* produce far less for their people to enjoy, of much shoddier quality, at much higher prices (measured by the hours of work needed to buy something). Don't you know that "Socialist" countries are smuggling "capitalist" incentives into their systems? Has it not dawned on you that wherever and whenever there is no free market, there is no free thought, no free art, no free politics, no free life?

You rage against "a heartless country in which the poor get poorer." Alas, poor Yoricks: The *decline* in poverty in the United States is among the more astonishing and hopeful facts of human history. (In 1900, about 90 per cent of our population was poor; in 1920—50 per cent). You will cry that 15 per cent is outrageous. Agreed. The question is: How

best abolish it? (A negative income tax makes more sense
than anything your colleagues propose.)

"The middle class exploits the unemployed." Please examine that cliché. Would the middle class be worse off or
better off if all the unemployed magically disappeared? Obviously, *much* better off: Think of the enormous saving in
taxes, the enormous improvement in public services, the
enormous benefits from refocused energies now used to
ameliorate poverty's abominable toll.

You say your generation "wants to be understood." Well,
so does mine. How much have you tried to understand others?
You pillory us for injustices not of our making, frictions
not of our choice, dilemmas that history (or our forebears
or the sheer intractability of events) presented to us. You
say we "failed" because you face so many awful problems.
Will you then accept blame for all the problems that exist
(and they will) when you are twenty years older? And how
do you know that all problems are soluble? Or soluble swiftly? Or soluble peacefully? Or soluble, given the never-in-
finite resources, brains and experience any generation is
endowed with?

I say that *you* are failing *us*—in failing to learn and respect discomforting facts; in failing to learn how to *think* (it
is easier to complain); in using violence to shut down colleges; in shamefully denying the freedom of others to study
and to teach; in barbarously slandering and abusing and
shouting down those who disagree with you; in looting,
stealing and defiling; in failing to see how much more complicated social problems are than you blindly assume; in
acting out of an ignorance for which idealism is no excuse,
and a hysteria for which youth is no defense. "Understanding"? You don't even understand that when you call me a
"mother _____" you are projecting your unresolved inces-
tuous wishes on me. The technical name for such projection,
in advanced form, is paranoia.

Again and again, you say, "the American people want" or
"demand" or "insist." How do you know? *Every poll I have*

seen puts your position in a minority. You just say, "the American people demand"—then add whatever *you* prefer. This is intellectually sloppy at best, and corrupt at worst.

You want to "wreck this slow, inefficient democratic system." It took the human race centuries of thought and pain and suffering and hard experiment to devise it. Democracy is not a "state" but a process; it is a way of solving human problems, a way of hobbling power, a way of protecting every minority from the awful, fatal tyranny of either the few or the many.

Whatever its imperfections, democracy is the only system man has discovered that makes possible *change without violence.* Do you really prefer bloodshed to debate? Quick dictates to slow law? This democracy made possible a great revolution in the past thirty-five years (a profound transfer of power, a distribution of wealth, an improvement of living and health) without "liquidating" millions, without suppressing free speech, without the obscenities of dogma enforced by terror.

This "slow, inefficient" system protects people like me against people like you; and (though you don't realize it) protects innocents like you against those "reactionary . . . fascist forces" you fear: They, like you, prefer "action to talk." As for "security"—at what price? The most "secure" of human institutions is a prison; would you choose to live in one?

You want "a society in which the young speak their minds against the Establishment." Where have the young more freely, recklessly and intransigently attacked "the Establishment"? (*Every* political order has one.) Wherever "our heroes —Marx, Mao, Che" have prevailed, students, writers, teachers, scientists have been punished with hard labor or death— for what? For their opinions. Where but in "fake democracies" are mass demonstrations possible, or your bitter (and legitimate) dissent televised?

You rail against "leaders crazed with power," who "deceive the people." Your leaders are self-dramatizers who demand that power, which would craze them, and they deceive you in not telling you how they plan your "confrontations"—to force the police to use force, whose excesses I hate more than you do. *I,* unlike you, want no one put "up against the wall." No "cheap politician" more cynically deceived you than fanatical militants did—and will. Your support feeds their neurotic (because extremist) needs. Washington's " 'Non-Violent' Coordinating Committee" has engaged in gunfire for three days as I write this.

You say Marcuse "shows that capitalist freedom actually enslaves." (He doesn't "show"—he only *says*.) He certainly does not sound enslaved. And does mouthing fragments of nineteenth century ideology (Marx, Bakunin) really liberate? And is not Marcuse forty years "older than thirty," your cutoff on credibility? Incidentally, would you trust your life to a surgeon under thirty—who never finished medical school?

Your irrationality makes me wonder how you were ever admitted *into* Columbia. You confuse rhetoric with reasoning. Assertions are not facts. Passion is no substitute for knowledge. Slogans are not solutions. Your idealism takes no brains. And when you dismiss our differences with contempt, you become contemptible.

Very *sincerely* yours,
Leo Rosten

P.S. Please don't take any more courses in sociology, which seduces the immature into thinking they understand a problem if they discuss it in polysyllables. Jargon is not insight. Vocabulary is the opiate of radicals.

TO AN ANGRY *OLD* MAN [5]

I could massage your heartstrings or curl your hair, depending on your politics, by quoting from the torrential reaction (laudatory, furious, flattering, venomous) to my evangelical letter "To an Angry Young Man" . . . [see pre-

[5] Article by Leo Rosten, author, special editorial advisor to *Look* Magazine. *Look.* 33:14. Ap. 29, '69. Copyright © by Leo Rosten.

ceding article—Ed.]. Before it was printed, a friend urged me to soften my stand, saying, "It may play into the hands of the Right!" And of the sermon you are about to read, others may say, "It will play into the hands of the Left!"

Both positions seem to me indefensible. Surely, the validity of an idea has nothing to do with who agrees or disagrees with it. To censor the expression of your thinking because of whom it may please or displease is simply to let others do your thinking for you. I detest thought control. Here, *sans* apology, is my answer to some overheated letter writers from the Right.

Dear Mr. X:

Thank you for writing—and that's about all the thanks you'll get from me. You say, "Let's throw all these young rebels out of college!" Over my dead body. Free speech does not stop at the gates of a campus. On the contrary, it should find a special sanctuary there, for it is indispensable to the search for truth. A student has a perfect right to protest, picket, petition, dissent. When students riot, set fires, throw rocks, stop others from attending classes, use bullhorns to disrupt the peace—they are acting not as students but as hoodlums. Let the law attend to them—the swifter the better.

But *you* want students "thrown out" simply for protesting, which is what the Communists and Fascists do—from Russia to Spain, China to Cuba. *They* expel, intimidate or imprison those who question or complain. Don't emulate them.

You say, "Draft these college punks into the Army and let our GI's knock sense into their heads!" You horrify me, I don't want anyone to "knock sense" into anyone's head. To put the point sharply, I quote a great jurist: "Your freedom to move your fist ends at the point where my nose begins." I have a long nose.

As for the draft: I consider the present draft impractical, unnecessary and morally indefensible (it would take more than this page to explain why). The young have every right

to speak, petition and argue against it (this has nothing to do
with Vietnam)—peacefully.

"Why let these creeps wear stinking clothes and beards?
Line them up, hold them down, bathe them, shave them,
wash out their mouths with soap!!" I loathe your bullyboy
views more than their childish flight into dirtiness. Kooky
clothes break no laws (though courts *have* ruled on school-
board regulations governing dress, hair, etc.). Young slobs
pollute the nearby air—but the courts have not yet ruled on
that.

The defiant cultivation of filth is, of course, a clinical sign
of psychological disturbance. I feel sorry for the kids who
cannot know the psychological price they will pay for re-
gressing to the anal level. But your excessive response to the
dirty is as distasteful to me as their sad glorification of dis-
comfort disguised as "freedom."

You praise me for "speaking out for those students who
are not newsworthy because they don't riot" and add: "Defend our wonderful Establishment!" Well, the only Establishment I defend is the one called Reason. I find violence
abhorrent, fanaticism disgusting, and demagoguery unspeak-
able. The terrorist tactics of adolescents may parade as
"idealism," but they shatter that consensus of civility that is
the very heart of a civilization. Your blind veneration of the
status quo cannot help us solve problems that must and can
be solved—by intelligence, not force.

You ask, "What do students have to be so unhappy about
in our colleges?" A great deal: gargantuan classes and burst-
ing dormitories; professors who hate teaching because it interferes with their research; educator-bureaucrats who re-
ward the publication of trivia much more than dedication
to students and teaching; academic tenure, which encourages
some pedants to "goof off" in lectures and subsidizes others
to indulge their nonacademic hobbies.

But this does not mean we should turn our colleges over
to self-dramatizing militants whose most conspicuous talent
is a capacity to oversimplify problems whose complexity they

do not begin to comprehend. Rabble-rousers (Right *or* Left) are rabble-rousers, no matter what songs they sing, with what lumps in their throats, with whatever ambiguous dreams in their eyes. Nazi students also flaunted "rights" they held superior to the lawful processes of "hypocritical," "fake" democracy—and many of their professors, in Germany and Austria, cheered them on.

Rebels who think they should prevail *because* they dissent are deluded: Dissenters have no greater moral or political rights than nondissenters.

You ask, "What has basically bugged these hippies, anyway?" First, their parents, I suspect, who confused political liberalism with indecisiveness; who felt so guilty about discipline that they appeased temper tantrums and rewarded rage with concessions (forgetting that infants *want* boundaries placed on their freedom); who never gave their progeny a clear model of responsible conduct. I think many militant students are unconsciously searching for adults who will act as adults—without apology or ambivalence or guilt; adults who will not be bamboozled by adolescent irrationality; adults who respond with swift rebuffs to those challenges to authority that are, at bottom, a testing by the young of the moral *confidence* of their elders. Professor David Riesman says we are witnessing the rebellion of the first generation in history "who were picked up whenever they cried."

You say, "Why not show the young how wonderful our educational system is?" It is remarkable in what it has done (the greatest, widest mass education in history) and in what it *can* achieve. But I hold a very gloomy view about schools that can produce students (and teachers) who are so strikingly ignorant about (1) how this society actually works; (2) what the economic bases of a democracy must be; (3) what the irreplaceable foundations of freedom, and the inviolable limits of civil liberties, must be; (4) how conflicts between minorities and majorities must be managed. (Suppose that Ku Klux Klanners in Alabama occupied classrooms, asserted the right to appoint faculty, threatened to burn down buildings, and demanded total amnesty in advance?)

Immature students are mesmerized by utopian slogans that rest on fantasies; and they are ill-educated enough to mouth the obsolete clichés of anarchism, the "revolutionary" nostrums even Lenin called "infantile leftism," the grandiose "demands" that demonstrate a plain lack of sense and a massive ignorance of history. ("Student power" has simply ruined South and Central American universities.)

You ask, "Why doesn't anyone brand these troublemakers as the Communists they are?!" That organizers plan and foment trouble, going from campus to campus, is becoming clearer each day. That they are professed Communists is neither clear nor likely. Student incantations about Ho Chi Minh, Che and Mao are not so much evidence of communism as of naïveté. The young enjoy baiting their elders with shocking symbols, and ignore what Che, Ho and Mao stand for—total despotism over the mind. Dictatorship is no less vicious because it *claims* to seek "superior" freedom.

Students who are *not* Communists are, alas, employing Communist/Fascist tactics: "confrontations" designed to force the authorities to call in the police—and then to force the police to use force, which is decried (and televised) and used for propaganda purposes. They dare not reflect on what Mao has done to the Chinese "student cadres" he encouraged; or on what happens to students who criticize the Establishment in Moscow or Havana.

You say, "Professor Marcuse should not be allowed to teach at San Diego!" Dr. Marcuse has a right to say or write whatever he wants—however mushy, opaque, unsupported by data, insupportable in logic and ludicrous as economics it is. His competence and integrity as a teacher are for his colleagues—not you or me—to decide. And if San Diego has no professors who are able to punch holes in old Herbert's gaseous balloons, it should promptly hire some.

Incidentally, Marcuse, like you, wants to deny freedom of speech to "certain" people; you and he differ only on *whom* you want to confer the blessings of dictatorship: Marcuse has publicly said (at Rutgers, June, 1965) that since Negroes are "brainwashed," and presumably vote in a hypnotized manner, "I would prefer that they did not have the right to choose wrongly." Such thinking fills prisons and concentration camps.

Finally, to my angry old *and* young compatriots: If we cannot pursue knowledge with moderation and mutual respect in our colleges, then where on earth can we? "Society cannot exist," wrote Burke, "[without] a controlling power upon will. . . . The less of it there is within, the more there must be without . . . *Men of intemperate minds cannot be free. Their passions forge their fetters.*"

LEO ROSTEN

P.S. Once, after long and sober research, I estimated that 23.6 per cent of the human race are mad. I was wrong. I am now convinced that 32.6 per cent are.

VI. LAW AND ORDER

EDITOR'S INTRODUCTION

A careful reading of this section will indicate that there is much room, and much need, for dialogue between adult and adult, student and student, let alone student and administrator. J. Edgar Hoover, in addressing a law enforcement group, epitomizes the hard line and focuses on the disloyal and destructive elements in the youth movement. On the other hand, President Plimpton of Amherst, as does Judge Wyzanski in Section V, emphasizes that college students are right in finding much amiss in American society and in the actions of government at various levels. Every generation worth its salt deserves a chance to weigh the values of its elders. In between these two points of view we have the full letter of Father Hesburgh, president of the University of Notre Dame. As reported on February 18, 1969, in the New York *Times,* "The letter came three months after small groups of students obstructed access to on-campus recruiters from the Dow Chemical Company and the Central Intelligence Agency, and a week after some students forced their way into a campus building to show stag movies that had been withdrawn from a student-sponsored conference on legal aspects of pornography." Father Hesburgh's letter shows a sympathy to protest so long as it does not exceed the bounds of law, and even propriety. The statement of the American Civil Liberties Union offers a balanced judgment of the often conflicting claims of law and order on the one hand and the right to protest on the other. Following this, the New York City Board of Higher Education offers a statement that deals only with violent or otherwise disruptive protest. The next selection is the *Joint Statement on Rights and Freedoms of Students* drafted by a committee sponsored by five national associations. Finally, the Model

Code of the American Bar Association attempts to set the ground rules for both students and administrators. Model codes are not intended for universal adoption, but for adaptation by those concerned with promulgating standards.

FORWARD TO CHAOS—OR
THE NEW LEFT IN ACTION [1]

Almost like a whirlwind from nowhere, the student New Left has hit America!

In a few short months, the vocabulary of Americans has been expanded to include such expressions as "Yippies," the "Establishment," "murderous pigs" and "flower children." The initials, SDS, standing for Students for a Democratic Society, the New Left's most militant group, are known to virtually every radio listener, television viewer, and newspaper reader. The student New Left has come with a bang.

And quite a bang it was! At first a protest movement, growing largely out of the civil rights struggles, the New Left, with SDS in the vanguard, soon turned to extremism. The academic year just concluded saw the tragic fruits: campus riots, the ostentatious flaunting of guns on campus by students, the physical seizure of academic personnel and buildings, disrespect for individuals in position of authority, arson, theft and violence. Bombs ripped apart buildings. Institutions of higher learning—with long and distinguished records—were disrupted. Violence and extremism became the order of the day.

Just a few months ago this extremist mood on college and university campuses would have been unbelievable—that some young people would so detest their society and heritage that they would desecrate the American flag, burn their draft cards, throw bombs and attempt to destroy their schools. The nation little suspected such a maelstrom of disaffection.

[1] Article by J. Edgar Hoover, director of the Federal Bureau of Investigation. *Prosecutor.* 5:161-3. My.-Je. '69. Permission to reprint granted by the author and National District Attorneys Association.

Yet a basic reality of American life today is this: that there exists in this nation today a group of revolutionary young people, whose numbers total into the many thousands, who, for a variety of reasons, bitterly detest democratic principles and are intent on overthrowing our institutions of free society.

For that reason, it behooves Americans—especially you, as prosecutors—to be concerned about this new type of subversion in our midst. Who are these extremists? What do they really want? Why do they disavow their heritage and seek a revolution? How can a democratic society, dedicated to freedom, deal with these forces?

These are questions which we must face—*now*. The alternative can be disastrous.

Basic to understanding these student extremists is to be cognizant of some of the viewpoints which motivate their actions.

1. A belief that American society (scornfully called the Establishment) is corrupt, rotten and decadent and cannot (and should not) be saved, repaired or reformed.

In the eyes of these New Leftists, current society (our government, local, state and Federal; the military; private business; labor unions; educational institutions, college, secondary and primary; the professions) is "shot" through with dishonesty and hypocrisy. The older generation (over the age of thirty) has "sold" itself to the "system," and simply cannot be trusted. Adults say one thing and do another. The result is that young people are "enslaved," "coerced" and cannot control their lives.

"The culmination of such hypocrisy and cant" said one student, "is the feeling among young people that they are being manipulated and coerced into accepting a value system not their own." "Almost every institution in society seems determined to thwart a youth's ambition to realize his potentiality." "Youth everywhere are rejecting the institutions that have dominated their lives, while the adults are demanding ever more loudly that they had better 'come around.' " . . .

2. A rejection of the democratic processes of government, including our legal system and respect for the law, the efficacy of representative government and the ability of a free people to progress through peaceful reforms.

Nothing infuriates a hard-core New Leftist more than the assertion that a free people, through the orderly processes of a government of laws, can bring about a better life for its people. Nonsense, they say, liberalism is dead. "We reject the Mickey Mouse methods of liberal organizations—picketing the governor, letter writing, etc. . . . It is time to attack the legislators as the murdering pigs they are and to encourage all women to express their revolutionary anger—not by picketing, but by bombing a church or tearing apart a city."

The various political parties, government agencies, private businesses, the SDS militants say, are all part of the same old Establishment. Elections, they claim, are frauds. Regardless of the candidate, the power structure won't be changed. Don't bother to vote. Don't trust the law or its officials. "Millions now perceive the futility of the electoral process and the decay of representative government." The only hope, they say, is to *reject the system.* "I maintain," said one student, "that the appropriate strategy is a radical one, to be distinguished from a liberal one. . . . This means that you do not work inside the system."

3. The rise of a mood of nihilism (and anarchism) in which the extremist student develops intense personal hatred and vindictiveness toward society and all those who, in his opinion, uphold and support it.

Here arises one of the most tragic—and dangerous—aspects of the current New Left extremist movement. These students, alienated from current society, find that there is little (in terms of power and influence) which they can do to impede or interfere with that society's operations or existence. Hence, they feel frustrated, hostile, and bitter. "Having rejected, not merely this or that law, but the entire structure of authority in the country where they happened to be born," writes a New Left author, "they are nevertheless powerless at present to overthrow the government which they reject. Their perspective must therefore be to live for an indefinite future under the nominal authority *of a government to which they no longer feel legally or morally bound.*" (underscoring added)

Hence, their chief aim is to destroy, to tear down, to pull apart the Establishment they so bitterly detest. They have absolutely no respect for the institutions of our society or the representatives of these institutions (such as officials of the government, the military, colleges and universities). They speak in violent, threatening and defiling terms. Their hatred of *you*—as a member of the Establishment—is intense, deep and abiding. The law enforcement officer, the judge, the prosecutor, any official in our court system—all become special targets of attack. Out of this personal hatred and alienation can come violence, crime and evil deeds. This is a mood of retribution, revenge and revolt.

4. These student extremists have become infected with an incipient totalitarianism which makes them, in their own eyes, the custodians of the truth and therefore others are wrong, stupid and/or evil.

It is sometimes downright frightening—and often amusing—to see the arrogance, smug righteousness and self-anointed infallibility which New Leftists can exude.

If you are always right, if you know all the truth, why have discussions and dialogue?

Education in capitalist America is a lie [says a New Leftist article]. It should be ruined before it is allowed to further ruin the lives of millions of people here at home and the oppressed of the world. Schools should either serve the people or be destroyed.

Or this comment. "If you keep as your central demand *that students have a right to control everything involving them,* that this demand isn't negotiable and you'll disrupt

until they give in, then you have a certain amount of leverage." (underscoring added)

In this mood of arrogance, they make preposterous and
exaggerated demands. They want frequently, for example,
to stipulate the academic courses a college offers, to determine the qualifications of professors and to abolish grades.
They know (without experience or specialized training)
how to run a university, a business or the government!

In this arrogance, many have rejected history—and its
many lessons. A dangerous anti-intellectualism is developing
which pokes fun at Western civilization and its values of
decency, fair play and tolerance. These extremists prefer to
play a game of campus power rather than maintain academic
standards; to demand instant solutions to problems rather
than really work for a better society.

*5. More and more the feeling is growing that violence
pays—that the way to goad, disrupt and harass the hated
Establishment is through the application of violence.*

All through the New Left movement, and especially the
SDS, is an escalating mentality of violence. At SDS's 1968
national convention in Michigan, a workshop on sabotage
and explosives was held. How can a Molotov cocktail bomb
be manufactured? Where can an explosive charge be placed
in a building to achieve maximum damage?

A leaflet entitled *What Must We Do Now? An Argument
for Sabotage as the Next Logical Step Toward Obstruction
and Disruption of the U. S. War Machine* has been widely
circulated among New Left circles. Among its admonitions:

> Furthermore, simply continually breaking windows and strew-
> ing parking lots with broken glass and bent carpet tacks are rela-
> tively minor but effective methods of harassing Selective Service
> employees.
> Is there anyone who doubts that a small homemade incendiary
> device with a timing mechanism planted in a broom closet at the
> induction center could result in fire and smoke damage to the
> entire building, thus making it unusable for weeks or months?

This whole concept of violence as the way to effect change
in society means—very tragically for our country—a rejection

of reason and dialogue, the tools of a democratic society. "Dialogue is a slow thing," commented one student. "I won't wait for dialogue to do it. . . . We should decide whether we should use some other way of stopping the [Vietnam] war."

Campus violence will continue as long as its instigators believe that it is helping their cause. "Force is becoming a popular student tactic," writes one college editor, "because students are learning that it works." Moreover, if perpetrators of violence are constantly given amnesty (as they always want) or if the laws are not enforced, the cause of democratic society will suffer. Firm steps within the law are needed to meet this challenge.

6. A primary aim of the extremist New Left is REVOLUTION, meaning the development inside the United States of a movement which has as its purpose the overthrow of the hated Establishment and its replacement (by what the New Left has not clearly defined).

How can a revolution be brought about in twentieth century America? Can students alone change the basic power structure of the nation or must they seek allies, as among the workers? What about the revolutions of Fidel Castro and Mao Tse-tung? What lessons do they hold? What about Karl Marx? How relevant are his teachings on revolution?

These questions are being debated with great seriousness in New Left circles today. Yes, says one spokesman, "revolution is possible in an advanced industrial society," while another points out that making a revolution is not a game but something deadly serious:

In our groping toward making a revolution, it is difficult for us not to play at it some of the time, because when we look at other revolutions, all we can see is that which is most readily visible: the guerrillas, the takeover of towns and cities, the waving of flags and shouting of slogans. . . . But . . . there aren't any pictures of Lenin writing and thinking, talking and analyzing. And those are the pictures we need to see.

Silly as these discussions may sound, they evidence a deep current of disaffection from our democratic principles and values. The very existence of such sentiments should be a matter of urgent concern. Moreover, another danger lurks. These young people, in this bitter mood of alienation, can become—and are becoming—revolutionary tinder in the hands of the real masters of revolution, the Old Left.

7. *The New Left is increasingly falling under the control of Marxist-Leninist influences which have created problems of internal dissension, but have also sharpened most considerably the movement's threat to our internal security.*

Marxist influence is growing within the New Left. The Old Left (the Communist Party, USA, pro-Moscow; Progressive Labor Party [PLP], pro-Red China; Socialist Workers Party, Trotskyite) has always had considerable inroads in the New Left, though many New Leftists detest its bureaucracy, discipline and ideological dogmatism.

The recent SDS national convention in Chicago (June 1969), for example, reflected the PLP's great strength—which led to SDS's split. The PLP wanted, among other things, an alliance between the students and the workers. Being Marxist, the PLP insists that the class struggle must be the basis of any revolution.

Yet, even the non-PLP forces in SDS find the attraction of Marxism almost irresistible. After all, it was Marx who laid down the so-called scientific rules for conducting a revolution. How can you circumvent Marx's influence if you are planning a revolution? Here is the dilemma of the New Left. Is it possible to have a revolution without Marx? The answer: it would be most difficult.

No wonder large segments of SDS and the New Left are drifting more and more to the Marxist principles of the Old Left, whether they be Communist Party, USA, or Progressive Labor Party.

The dreary answer is that the New Left, starting with great promise and idealism, has been so compromised, maneuvered and betrayed by Marxist and extremist elements that it has degenerated into a fanatic rabble of divisive voices hostile to the beliefs of a free people. It is marching forward to chaos!

Americans should know more about the New Left and what these young people aim to achieve, their viewpoints, their tactics, what threat they pose to our country. In recent months, more evidence is accumulating of tactical coopera-tion in riotous situations between SDS-New Left extremism and black power extremism. The cooperation of these New Leftists (mostly white students) and groups such as the Black Panther Party could bode great evil for the future.

The adult generation should do everything possible to maintain a dialogue with our youth—to know what they are thinking. Many young people have legitimate complaints. Our society is not perfect. We need to listen to their ideas about the problems facing us. We have a capable, intelligent and sophisticated young generation and we should listen to them.

LETTER TO NOTRE DAME FACULTY AND STUDENTS [2]

Dear Notre Dame Faculty and Students:

This letter has been on my mind for weeks. It is both time and overtime that it be written. I have outlined the core of it to the Student Life Council, have discussed the text with the Chairman of the Board of Trustees, the Vice Presidents Council, all the Deans of the University, and the Chairmen of the Faculty Senate and the Student Life Coun-cil. This letter does not relate directly to what happened here last weekend, although those events made it seem even more necessary to get this letter written. I have tried to write calmly, in the wee hours of the morning when at last there is quiet and pause for reflection.

My hope is that these ideas will have deep personal res-onances in our own community, although the central prob-

    [2] Letter dated February 17, 1969, to the Notre Dame faculty and students, by the Rev. Theodore M. Hesburgh, C.S.C., president, University of Notre Dame, long active in the field of civil rights. Text supplied by the office of President Hesburgh. University of Notre Dame, Notre Dame, Ind. 46556.

lem they address exists everywhere in the university world today and, by instant communication, feeds upon itself. It is not enough to label it the alienation of youth from our society. God knows there is enough and more than enough in our often nonglorious civilization to be alienated from, be you young, middle-aged, or old.

The central problem to me is what we do about it and in what manner, if we are interested in healing rather than destroying our world. Youth especially has much to offer—idealism, generosity, dedication, and service. The last thing a shaken society needs is more shaking. The last thing a noisy, turbulent, and disintegrating community needs is more noise, turbulence, and disintegration. Understanding and analysis of social ills cannot be conducted in a boiler factory. Compassion has a quiet way of service. Complicated social mechanisms, out-of-joint, are not adjusted with sledge hammers.

The university cannot cure all our ills today, but it can make a valiant beginning by bringing all its intellectual and moral powers to bear upon them: all the idealism and generosity of its young people, all the wisdom and intelligence of its oldsters, all the expertise and competence of those who are in their middle years. But it must do all this as a university does, within its proper style and capability, no longer an ivory tower, but not the Red Cross either.

Now to the heart of my message. You recall my letter of November 25, 1968. It was written after an accident, or happening if you will. It seemed best to me at the time not to waste time in personal recriminations or heavy-handed discipline, but to profit from the occasion to invite this whole university community, especially its central councils of faculty, administration, and students, to declare themselves and to state their convictions regarding protests that were peaceful and those that threatened the life of the community by disrupting the normal operations of the university and infringing upon the rights of others.

I now have statements from the Academic Council, the Faculty Senate, the Student Life Council, some College Councils, the Alumni Board, and a whole spate of letters from individual faculty members and a few students. . . . In general, the reaction was practically unanimous that this community recognizes the validity of protest in our day—sometimes even the necessity—regarding the current burning issues of our society: war and peace, especially Vietnam; civil rights, especially of minority groups; the stance of the university vis-à-vis moral issues of great public concern; the operation of the University as university. There was also practical unanimity that the university could not continue to exist as an open society, dedicated to the discussion of all issues of importance, if protests were of such a nature that the normal operations of the University were in any way impeded, or if the rights of any member of this community were abrogated, peacefully or nonpeacefully. I believe that I now have a clear mandate from this university community to see that: (1) our lines of communication between all segments of the community are kept as open as possible, with all legitimate means of communicating dissent assured, expanded, and protected; (2) civility and rationality are maintained as the most reasonable means of dissent within the academic community; and (3) violation of others' rights or obstruction of the life of the university are outlawed as illegitimate means of dissent in this kind of open society. Violence was especially deplored as a violation of everything that the university community stands for.

Now comes my duty of stating, clearly and unequivocally, what happens *if*. I'll try to make it as simple as possible to avoid misunderstanding by anyone. May I begin by saying that all of this is hypothetical and I personally hope it never happens here at Notre Dame. But, if it does, anyone or any group that substitutes force for rational persuasion, be it violent or nonviolent, will be given fifteen minutes of meditation to cease and desist. They will be told that they are, by their actions, going counter to the overwhelming conviction of this community as to what is proper here. If they do not within that time period cease and desist, they will be asked for their identity cards. Those who produce these will be suspended from this community as not understanding what this community is. Those who do not have or will not produce identity cards will be assumed not to be members of the community and will be charged with trespassing and disturbing the peace on private property and treated accordingly by the law. The judgment regarding the impeding of normal university operations or the violation of the rights of other members of the community will be made by the Dean of Students. Recourse for certification of this fact for students so accused is to the tripartite Disciplinary Board established by the Student Life Council. Faculty members have recourse to the procedures outlined in the Faculty Manual. Judgment of the matter will be delivered within five days following the fact, for justice deferred is justice denied to all concerned.

After notification of suspension, or trespass in the case of noncommunity members, if there is not then within five minutes a movement to cease and desist, students will be notified of expulsion from this community and the law will deal with them as nonstudents.

Lest there be any possible misunderstanding, it should be noted that law enforcement in this procedure is not directed at students. They receive academic sanctions in the second instance of recalcitrance and, only after three clear opportunities to remain in student status, if they still insist on resisting the will of the community, are they then expelled and become nonstudents to be treated as other nonstudents, or outsiders.

There seems to be a current myth that university members are not responsible to the law, and that somehow the law is the enemy, particularly those whom society has constituted to uphold and enforce the law. I would like to insist here that all of us are responsible to the duly constituted laws of this university community and to all of the laws of the land. There is no other guarantee of civilization versus the jungle or mob rule, here or elsewhere.

If someone invades your home, do you dialogue with him or call the law? Without the law, the university is a sitting duck for any small group from outside or inside that wishes to destroy it, to incapacitate it, to terrorize it at whim. The argument goes—or has gone—invoke the law and you lose the university community. My only response is that without the law you may well lose the university—and beyond that—the larger society that supports it and that is most deeply wounded when law is no longer respected, bringing an end of everyone's most cherished rights.

I have studied at some length the new politics of confrontation. The rhythm is simple: (1) find a cause, any cause, silly or not; (2) in the name of the cause, get a few determined people to abuse the rights and privileges of the community so as to force a confrontation at any cost of boorishness or incivility; (3) once this has occurred, justified or not, orderly or not, yell police brutality—if it does not happen, provoke it by foul language, physical abuse, whatever, and then count on a larger measure of sympathy from the up-to-now apathetic or passive members of the community. Then call for amnesty, the head of the president on a platter, the complete submission to any and all demands. One beleaguered president has said that these people want to be martyrs thrown to toothless lions. He added, "Who wants to dialogue when they are going for the jugular vein?"

So it has gone, and it is generally well orchestrated. Again, my only question: must it be so? Must universities be subjected, willy-nilly, to such intimidation and victimization whatever their good will in the matter? Somewhere a stand must be made.

I only ask that when the stand is made necessary by those who would destroy the community and all its basic yearning for great and calm educational opportunity, let them carry the blame and the penalty. No one wants the forces of law on this or any other campus, but if some necessitate it, as a last and dismal alternative to anarchy and mob tyranny, let them shoulder the blame instead of receiving the sympathy of a community they would hold at bay. The only alternative I can imagine is turning the majority of the community loose on them, and then you have two mobs. I know of no one who would opt for this alternative—always lurking in the wings. We can have a thousand resolutions as to what kind of a society we want, but when lawlessness is afoot, and all authority is flouted, faculty, administration, and student, then we invoke the normal societal forces of law or we allow the university to die beneath our hapless and hopeless gaze. I have no intention of presiding over such a spectacle: too many people have given too much of themselves and their lives to this university to let this happen here. Without being melodramatic, if this conviction makes this my last will and testament to Notre Dame, so be it.

May I now say in all sincerity that I never want to see any student expelled from this community because, in many ways, this is always an educative failure. Even so, I must likewise be committed to the survival of the university community as one of man's best hopes in these troubled times. I know of no other way of insuring both ends than to say of every member of this community, faculty and students, that we are all ready and prepared and anxious to respond to every intellectual and moral concern in the world today, in every way proper to the university. At the same time, we cannot allow a small minority to impose their will on the majority who have spoken regarding the university's style of life; we cannot allow a few to substitute force of any kind for persuasion to accept their personal idea of what is right or proper. We only insist on the rights of all, minority and majority, the climate of civility and rationality, and a preponderant moral abhorrence of violence or inhuman forms of persuasion that violate our style of life and the nature of the university. It is, unfortunately, possible to cut oneself off from this community, even though the vast majority of our members would regret seeing it happen. However, should this occur, the community as a whole has indicated that it will vote and stand for the maintenance of this community's deepest values, since this is the price we all pay for the survival of the university community in the face of anyone and everyone who would destroy or denature it today, for whatever purposes.

May I now confess that since last November I have been bombarded mightily by the hawks and the doves—almost equally. I have resisted both and continue to recognize the right to protest—through every legitimate channel—and to resist as well those who would unthinkingly trifle with the survival of the university as one of the few open societies left to mankind today. There is no divine assurance that the university will survive as we have known and cherished it—but we do commit ourselves to make the effort and count on this community, in this place, to uphold the efforts that you have inspired by your clear expression of community concern. Thanks to all who have declared themselves, even to those who have slightly disagreed, but are substantially concerned as well.

As long as the great majority of this community is concerned and involved in maintaining what it believes deeply to be its identity and commitment, no force within it, however determined or organized, can really destroy it. If any community as a whole does not believe this, or is not committed to it, it does not deserve to survive and it probably will not. I hope we will. To this, I commit myself with the presumption that the great majority of you are with me in this concern and commitment.

I truly believe that we are about to witness a revulsion on the part of legislatures, state and national, benefactors, parents, alumni, and the general public for much that is happening in higher education today. If I read the signs of the times correctly, this may well lead to a suppression of the liberty and autonomy that are the lifeblood of a university community. It may well lead to a rebirth of fascism, unless we ourselves are ready to take a stand for what is right for us. History is not consoling in this regard. We rule ourselves or others rule us, in a way that destroys the university as we have known and loved it.

Devotedly yours in Notre Dame,
T. M. HESBURGH, C.S.C.

LETTER TO PRESIDENT NIXON [3]

My dear Mr. President:

The faculty and students of Amherst College have just experienced an extraordinary two days. Our usual educational activities were replaced by debate, discussion and meditation which have given shape to our beliefs about the nature of higher education and the governance of educational institutions. It is clear that we have much to do to set our own house in order. We are convinced, and have shown during these days, that changes, even fundamental ones, can take place without physical duress. It will require all our care and energy in the months ahead to combine change with continuity, to provide students with a real and regular role in influencing their education and the college's government, and to honor both intellectual discipline and creativity. We have as a college emerged from these two days with a renewed sense of the urgency and seriousness with which we must attend to our primary purpose.

We have also as a college embraced a new sense of urgency of another kind. We believe that we must speak out to make clear that much of the turmoil among young people and among those who are dedicated to humane and reasoned changes will continue. It will continue until you and the other political leaders of our country address more effectively, massively, and persistently the major social and foreign problems of our society. Part of this turmoil in universities derives from the distance separating the American dream from

[3] Letter dated April 29, 1969, addressed to President Nixon by Calvin H. Plimpton, president of Amherst College. Text supplied by President Plimpton. Amherst College. Amherst, Mass. 01002. Reprinted by permission.

the American reality. Institutions dedicated to the nurture, husbanding, and growth of critical intelligence, and to inquiry into basic problems cannot but open people's eyes to the shoddiness of many aspects of our society.

In yesterday's New York *Times* it is reported that five officers in your Cabinet "seemed to agree that the disorder was caused by a small minority of students." Our conviction is that such a view is seriously in error if it is taken to mean that no legitimate and important reasons exist for the anger and sense of impotence felt by many students and faculty. The pervasive and insistent disquiet on many campuses throughout the nation indicates that unrest results, not from a conspiracy by a few, but from a shared sense that the nation has no adequate plans for meeting the crises of our society. To name only one issue of special concern to the students: since the Kerner Commission's report [on civil disorders], there has been no decisive response to its recommendations.

We do not say that all the problems faced by colleges and universities are a reflection of the malaise of the larger society. That is not true. But we do say that until political leadership addresses itself to the major problems of our society—the huge expenditure of national resources for military purposes, the inequities practiced by the present draft system, the critical needs of America's 23 million poor, the unequal division of our life on racial issues—until this happens, the concern and energy of those who know the need for change will seek outlets for their frustration.

We realize that in writing this letter we have taken the unusual step of speaking publicly for our community on pressing issues of the moment. We do this out of an urgent concern to question the widely held view that university unrest is merely an internal problem or at most fomented by outside influences. More, we believe that if political leaders act on this mistaken assumption, their actions will serve only to widen the separations within the university and between the universities and society at large. If, however, this important element in student unrest is understood, it would be possible for you, Mr. President, to redirect youthful energy toward those more idealistic, creative and generous actions which reflect a concern for others. Your influence can provide that hope which encourages those visions to which young men so gladly dedicate themselves, and we will support those efforts.

I send this letter to you on behalf of an overwhelming majority of Amherst students, faculty and administration who attended the closing meeting of our days of inquiry tonight. Copies of this letter with the signatures of all those who wish to subscribe will follow as soon as possible.

Respectfully yours,
CALVIN PLIMPTON

STATEMENT ON CAMPUS DEMONSTRATIONS [4]

Recent demonstrations, strikes, sit-ins and other outbreaks on college campuses in various parts of the United States are evidence of a serious malaise in American academic life as well as in the society at large. Their causes are complex and involve other groups in the university besides the students, so that they cannot simply be dismissed as due to immaturity, alienation, irresponsibility or conspiracy. On many campuses there have been grave violations of the principles of sound academic governance by administrations which have denied students reasonable participation in matters of university policy in which their interests have been clearly involved, by faculties which have been indifferent to the needs and aspirations of students, and by students who by various actions have interfered with the processes of teaching, learning and the right to free speech. The values of academic freedom associated with these processes are as relevant in moments of stress as in normal times, and cannot be suspended for however worthy a cause without doing serious or irreparable damage to them.

[4] Press release issued by the American Civil Liberties Union on June 25, 1968. The Union. 156 Fifth Ave. New York 10010. '68. 4p. mimeo. Reprinted by permission.

In some cases the police have been called in under circumstances reflecting a complete breakdown in the internal discipline of the university. The invitation of civil authorities onto the campus endangers the autonomy of the institution, and should be resorted to only when *all* other avenues have failed and then preferably under strict procedural rules laid down and agreed to by administration, faculty and students. In view of the brutality of some police actions the formulation of such rules appears to be a matter of urgent priority. While any group sufficiently bent on disruption can presumably force an intervention of this kind, such groups generally represent a small minority among the students and would not be likely to succeed in large-scale actions on campuses where there was a manifest unity of interest among faculty, students and administration.

The manner in which demonstrations have been conducted, at least in some notorious cases, must be condemned as disproportionate to the grievances of the students and as categorically in violation of basic principles of academic freedom. The fact that significant reforms may be won by violent action does not justify the resort to violence, even if such action seems plausible to some in a society marked by violence both internally and in its external actions, and even if an apparent justification after the fact seems to be provided by a violent response, for example a police action. The so-called politics of confrontation invites, and is intended to invite, such a response, but in so far as it seeks its ends by means which infringe on the liberties of others it is out of keeping with the principles by which and the purposes for which the university exists.

It must be admitted that an examination of the conditions which have triggered demonstrations shows that in a majority of cases students have had a prima facie justification for their concern, if not for their manner of expressing it. They have protested against compulsory ROTC (Tuskegee), the suspension of politically active students (Stanford), the neglect of Negro students (Northwestern), alleged mistreatment of controversial faculty members (Roosevelt), the use of slum parkland for a university facility and the university's ties with defense-related research (Columbia). The list could be prolonged. These causes are of unequal weight and have sometimes been used, even by students without political or ideological commitments, as excuses for the expression of more fundamental hostilities, reflecting among other things a widespread frustration and disillusionment with the foreign and domestic policies of the present Government. But the fact that local pretexts have been so easily come by is no more to be overlooked than the problems of war and race which have set the stage for so many of these episodes.

The internal condition pointed to by the frequency and intensity of these disturbances can best be represented as a progressive neglect of certain principles (full and open communication between all elements within the university—trustees, president, administration, faculty, and students—and a rigorous priority of academic and human considerations over financial and organizational ones) together with a change in the nature of the student body and its relations with faculty and administration, a change of which the latter groups have hardly been aware. Three aspects of this change, familiar enough in isolation but rarely considered together, are the demographic shift to a younger population, the extension of the period of formal training and therefore of dependence, and the lowering of the age of social maturity. The passivity of many faculties has allowed most of the power in the university to pass into the hands of the administration, and the administration has been only too ready to accept this power and to exercise it in an essentially managerial way, with little regard for the characteristic intellectual and social realities of academic life. It is a significant fact that many university administrators are as much at home on the boards of large corporations and in the upper echelons of the bureaucracy as they are on their own campuses. Activist students have played a useful role in helping to draw attention to the imbalance of power within the university, as

well as to the increasing identification of the university with
a social order of which it should properly be the critic and
conscience. At the same time it seems short-sighted, in the
attempt to modify this social order, to seek to destroy the only
institution capable of playing such a role effectively.

The American Civil Liberties Union, attaching great importance as it does to the preservation of a strong and viable
university system as one of the underlying conditions for civil
liberties in general, is concerned that the meaning of these
events should not be lost sight of through concentration of
attention on their more dramatic features. The Union's interest in the principles of academic governance and organization is of long standing. But the time is overdue for a
review of the structure and internal relations of the university on every campus, in order to secure the full involvement
and cooperation of all concerned groups in the formulation
and execution of academic policy at all levels.

RULES ON CAMPUS CONDUCT [5]

The tradition of the university as a sanctuary of academic freedom and center of informed discussion is an hon-
ored one, to be guarded vigilantly. The basic significance
of that sanctuary lies in the protection of intellectual freedoms: the rights of professors to teach, of scholars to engage
in the advancement of knowledge, of students to learn and
to express their views, free from external pressures or interference.

These freedoms can flourish only in an atmosphere of
mutual respect, civility and trust among teachers and students, only when members of the university community are
willing to accept self-restraint and reciprocity as the condition upon which they share in its intellectual autonomy.

Academic freedom and the sanctuary of the university
campus extend to all who share these aims and responsibili-

[5] Resolution and new rules of campus conduct adopted by the New York
City Board of Higher Education, June 23, 1969. Text from New York *Times*.
p 28. Je. 24, '69.

ties. They cannot be invoked by those who would subordinate intellectual freedom to political ends, or who violate the norms of conduct established to protect that freedom. Against such offenders the university has the right, and indeed the obligation, to defend itself.

I. Rules

1. A member of the academic community shall not intentionally obstruct and/or forcibly prevent others from the exercise of their rights. Nor shall he interfere with the institution's educational processes or facilities, or the rights of those who wish to avail themselves of any of the institution's instructional, personal, administrative, recreational and community services.

2. Individuals are liable for failure to comply with lawful directions issued by representatives of the university/college when they are acting in their official capacities. Members of the academic community are required to show their identification cards when requested to do so by an official of the college.

3. Unauthorized occupancy of university/college facilities or blocking access to or from such areas is prohibited. Permission from appropriate college authorities must be obtained for removal, relocation and use of university/college equipment and/or supplies.

4. Theft from or damage to university/college premises or property, or theft of or damage to property of any person on university/college premises is prohibited.

5. Each member of the academic community or an invited guest has the right to advocate his position without having to fear abuse, physical, verbal or otherwise from others supporting conflicting points of view. Members of the academic community and other persons on the college grounds shall not use language or take actions reasonably likely to provoke or encourage physical violence by demonstrators, those demonstrated against or spectators.

6. Action may be taken against any and all persons who have no legitimate reason for their presence on any campus within the university/college, or whose presence on any such campus obstructs and/or forcibly prevents others from the exercise of their rights or interferes with the institution's educational processes or facilities, or the rights of those who wish to avail themselves of any of the institution's instructional, personal, administrative, recreational and community services.

7. Disorderly or indecent conduct on university/college-owned or controlled property is prohibited.

8. No individual shall have in his possession a rifle, shotgun or firearm or knowingly have in his possession any other dangerous instrument or material that can be used to inflict bodily harm on an individual or damage upon a building or the grounds of the university/college without the written authorization of such educational institution. Nor shall any individual have in his possession any other instrument or material which can be used and is intended to inflict bodily harm on an individual or damage upon a building or the grounds of the university/college.

II. Penalties

1. Any student engaging in any manner in conduct prohibited under substantive Rules 1 to 8 shall be subject to the following range of sanctions as hereafter defined in the attached appendix: admonition, warning, censure, disciplinary probation, restitution, suspension, expulsion, ejection and/or arrest by the civil authorities.

2. Any tenured or nontenured faculty member or tenured or nontenured member of the administrative or custodial staff engaging in any manner in conduct prohibited under substantive Rules 1 to 8 shall be subject to the following range of penalties: warning, censure, restitution, fine not exceeding those permitted by law or by the bylaws of the Board of Higher Education or suspension with/without pay pending a hearing before an appropriate college authority,

dismissal after a hearing, ejection and/or arrest by the civil authorities.

In addition, . . . a tenured faculty member, or tenured member of the administrative or custodial staff engaging in any manner in conduct prohibited under substantive Rules 1 to 8 shall be entitled to be treated in accordance with applicable provisions of the Education Law or Civil Service Law.

3. Any visitor, licensee or invitee engaging in any manner in conduct prohibited under substantive Rules 1 to 8 shall be subject to ejection and/or arrest by the civil authorities.

Appendix

Sanctions defined:

A. Admonition—An oral statement to the offender that he has violated university rules.

B. Warning—Notice to the offender, orally or in writing, that continuation or repetition of the wrongful conduct, within a period of time stated in the warning, may be cause for more severe disciplinary action.

C. Censure—Written reprimand for violation of specified regulation, including the possibility of more severe disciplinary sanction in the event of conviction for the violation of any university regulation within a period stated in the letter of reprimand.

D. Disciplinary Probation—Exclusion from participation in privileges or extracurricular university activities as set forth in the notice of disciplinary probation for a specified period of time.

E. Restitution—Reimbursement for damage to or misappropriation of property. Reimbursement may take the form of appropriate service to repair or otherwise compensate for damages.

F. Suspension—Exclusion from classes and other privileges or activities as set forth in the notice of suspension for a definite period of time.

G. Expulsion—Termination of student status for an indefinite period. The conditions of readmission, if any is permitted, shall be stated in the order of expulsion.

H. Complaint to civil authorities.

I. Ejection.

JOINT STATEMENT ON RIGHTS AND FREEDOMS OF STUDENTS [6]

In June, 1967, a joint committee, comprised of representatives from the American Association of University Professors, U. S. National Student Association, Association of American Colleges, National Association of Student Personnel Administrators, and National Association of Women Deans and Counselors, met in Washington, D.C., and drafted the Joint Statement on Rights and Freedoms of Students published below.

The multilateral approach which produced this document was also applied to the complicated matter of interpretation, implementation, and enforcement, with the drafting committee recommending (a) joint efforts to promote acceptance of the new standards on the institutional level, (b) the establishment of machinery to facilitate continuing joint interpretation, (c) joint consultation before setting up any machinery for mediating disputes or investigating complaints, and (d) joint approaches to regional accrediting agencies to seek embodiment of the new principles in standards for accreditation.

Since its formulation, the Joint Statement has been endorsed by each of its five national sponsors, as well as by a number of other professional bodies. The endorsers are listed below:

U.S. National Student Association
Association of American Colleges

[6] Text from *College Law Bulletin.* p 43-6. F. '70.

American Association of University Professors

National Association of Student Personnel Administrators

National Association of Women Deans and Counselors

American Association for Higher Education

Jesuit Education Association

American College Personnel Association

Executive Committee, College and University Department, National Catholic Education Association

Commission on Student Personnel, American Association of Junior Colleges

Preamble

Academic institutions exist for the transmission of knowledge, the pursuit of truth, the development of students, and the general well-being of society. Free inquiry and free expression are indispensable to the attainment of these goals. As members of the academic community, students should be encouraged to develop the capacity for critical judgment and to engage in a sustained and independent search for truth. Institutional procedures for achieving these purposes may vary from campus to campus, but the minimal standards of academic freedom of students outlined below are essential to any community of scholars.

Freedom to teach and freedom to learn are inseparable facets of academic freedom. The freedom to learn depends upon appropriate opportunities and conditions in the classroom, on the campus, and in the larger community. Students should exercise their freedom with responsibility.

The responsibility to secure and to respect general conditions conducive to the freedom to learn is shared by all members of the academic community. Each college and university has a duty to develop policies and procedures which provide and safeguard this freedom. Such policies and procedures should be developed at each institution within the framework of general standards and with the broadest possible participation of the members of the academic community. The purpose of this statement is to enumerate the essential provisions for student freedom to learn.

I. Freedom of Access to Higher Education

The admissions policies of each college and university are a matter of institutional choice provided that each college and university makes clear the characteristics and expectations of students which it considers relevant to success in the institution's program. While church-related institutions may give admission preference to students of their own persuasion, such a preference should be clearly and publicly stated. Under no circumstances should a student be barred from admission to a particular institution on the basis of race. Thus, within the limits of its facilities, each college and university should be open to all students who are qualified according to its admission standards. The facilities and services of a college should be open to all of its enrolled students, and institutions should use their influence to secure equal access for all students to public facilities in the local community.

II. In the Classroom

The professor in the classroom and in conference should encourage free discussion, inquiry, and expression. Student performance should be evaluated solely on an academic basis, not on opinions or conduct in matters unrelated to academic standards.

A. Protection of Freedom of Expression

Students should be free to take reasoned exception to the data or views offered in any course of study and to reserve judgment about matters of opinion, but they are responsible for learning the content of any course of study for which they are enrolled.

B. Protection Against Improper Academic Evaluation

Students should have protection through orderly procedures against prejudiced or capricious academic evaluation.

At the same time, they are responsible for maintaining standards of academic performance established for each course in which they are enrolled.

C. *Protection Against Improper Disclosure*

Information about student views, beliefs, and political associations which professors acquire in the course of their work as instructors, advisers, and counselors should be considered confidential. Protection against improper disclosure is a serious professional obligation. Judgments of ability and character may be provided under appropriate circumstances, normally with the knowledge or consent of the student.

III. *Student Records*

Institutions should have a carefully considered policy as to the information which should be part of a student's permanent educational record and as to the conditions of its disclosure. To minimize the risk of improper disclosure, academic and disciplinary records should be separate, and the conditions of access to each should be set forth in an explicit policy statement. Transcripts of academic records should contain only information about academic status. Information from disciplinary or counseling files should not be available to unauthorized persons on campus, or to any person off campus without the express consent of the student involved except under legal compulsion or in cases where the safety of persons or property is involved. No records should be kept which reflect the political activities or beliefs of students. Provisions should also be made for periodic routine destruction of noncurrent disciplinary records. Administrative staff and faculty members should respect confidential information about students which they acquire in the course of their work.

IV. *Student Affairs*

In student affairs, certain standards must be maintained if the freedom of students is to be preserved.

A. *Freedom of Association*

Students bring to the campus a variety of interests previously acquired and develop many new interests as members of the academic community. They should be free to organize and join associations to promote their common interests.

1. The membership, policies, and actions of a student organization usually will be determined by vote of only those persons who hold bona fide membership in the college or university community.

2. Affiliation with an extramural organization should not of itself disqualify a student organization from institutional recognition.

3. If campus advisers are required, each organization should be free to choose its own adviser, and institutional recognition should not be withheld or withdrawn solely because of the inability of a student organization to secure an adviser. Campus advisers may advise organizations in the exercise of responsibility, but they should not have the authority to control the policy of such organizations.

4. Student organizations may be required to submit a statement of purpose, criteria for membership, rules of procedures, and a current list of officers. They should not be required to submit a membership list as a condition of institutional recognition.

5. Campus organizations, including those affiliated with an extramural organization, should be open to all students without respect to race, creed, or national origin, except for religious qualifications which may be required by organizations whose aims are primarily sectarian.

B. *Freedom of Inquiry and Expression*

1. Students and student organization should be free to examine and discuss all questions of interest to them, and to express opinions publicly and privately. They should always be free to support causes by orderly means which do not disrupt the regular and essential operation of the institution.

At the same time, it should be made clear to the academic and the larger community that in their public expressions or demonstrations students or student organizations speak only for themselves.

2. Students should be allowed to invite and to hear any person of their own choosing. Those routine procedures required by an institution before a guest speaker is invited to appear on campus should be designed only to insure that there is orderly scheduling of facilities and adequate preparation for the event, and that the occasion is conducted in a manner appropriate to an academic community. The institutional control of campus facilities should not be used as a device of censorship. It should be made clear to the academic and large community that sponsorship of guest speakers does not necessarily imply approval or endorsement of the views expressed, either by the sponsoring group or the institution.

C. *Student Participation in Institutional Government*

As constituents of the academic community, students should be free, individually and collectively, to express their views on issues of institutional policy and on matters of general interest to the student body. The student body should have clearly defined means to participate in the formulation and application of institutional policy affecting academic and student affairs. The role of the student government and both its general and specific responsibilities should be made explicit, and the actions of the student government within the areas of its jurisdiction should be reviewed only through orderly and prescribed procedures.

D. *Student Publications*

Student publications and the student press are a valuable aid in establishing and maintaining an atmosphere of free and responsible discussion and of intellectual exploration on the campus. They are a means of bringing student concerns to the attention of the faculty and the institutional authorities and of formulating student opinion on various issues on the campus and in the world at large.

Whenever possible the student newspaper should be an independent corporation financially and legally separate from the university. Where financial and legal autonomy is not possible, the institution, as the publisher of student publications, may have to bear the legal responsibility for the contents of the publications. In the delegation of editorial responsibility to students the institution must provide sufficient editorial freedom and financial autonomy for the student publications to maintain their integrity of purpose as vehicles for free inquiry and free expression in an academic community.

Institutional authorities, in consultation with students and faculty, have a responsibility to provide written clarification of the role of the student publications, the standards to be used in their evaluation, and the limitations on external control of their operation. At the same time, the editorial freedom of student editors and managers entails corollary responsibilities to be governed by the canons of responsible journalism, such as the avoidance of libel, indecency, undocumented allegations, attacks on personal integrity, and the techniques of harassment and innuendo. As safeguards for the editorial freedom of student publications the following provisions are necessary:

1. The student press should be free of censorship and advance approval of copy, and its editors and managers should be free to develop their own editorial policies and news coverage.

2. Editors and managers of student publications should be protected from arbitrary suspension and removal because of student, faculty, administrative, or public disapproval of editorial policy or content. Only for proper and stated causes should editors and managers be subject to removal and then by orderly and prescribed procedures. The agency responsible for the appointment of editors and managers should be the agency responsible for their removal.

3. All university published and financed student publications should explicitly state on the editorial page that the

opinions there expressed are not necessarily those of the college, university, or student body.

V. Off-Campus Freedom of Students

A. Exercise of Rights of Citizenship

College and university students are both citizens and members of the academic community. As citizens, students should enjoy the same freedom of speech, peaceful assembly and right of petition that other citizens enjoy and, as members of the academic community, they are subject to the obligations which accrue to them by virtue of this membership. Faculty members and administrative officials should insure that institutional powers are not employed to inhibit such intellectual and personal development of students as is often promoted by their exercise of the rights of citizenship both on and off campus.

B. Institutional Authority and Civil Penalties

Activities of students may upon occasion result in violation of law. In such cases, institutional officials should be prepared to apprise students of sources of legal counsel and may offer other assistance. Students who violate the law may incur penalties prescribed by civil authorities, but institutional authority should never be used merely to duplicate the function of general laws. Only where the institution's interests as an academic community are distinct and clearly involved should the special authority of the institution be asserted. The student who incidentally violates institutional regulations in the course of his off-campus activity, such as those relating to class attendance, should be subject to no greater penalty than would normally be imposed. Institutional action should be independent of community pressure.

VI. Procedural Standards in Disciplinary Proceedings

In developing responsible student conduct, disciplinary proceedings play a role substantially secondary to example, counseling, guidance, and admonition. At the same time, educational institutions have a duty and the corollary disciplinary powers to protect their educational purpose through the setting of standards of scholarship and conduct for the students who attend them and through the regulation of the use of institutional facilities. In the exceptional circumstances when the preferred means fail to resolve problems of student conduct, proper procedural safeguards should be observed to protect the student from the unfair imposition of serious penalties.

The administration of discipline should guarantee procedural fairness to an accused student. Practices in disciplinary cases may vary in formality with the gravity of the offense and the sanctions which may be applied. They should also take into account the presence or absence of an honor code, and the degree to which the institutional officials have direct acquaintance with student life in general and with the involved student and the circumstances of the case in particular. The jurisdictions of faculty or student judicial bodies, the disciplinary responsibilities of institutional officials and the regular disciplinary procedures, including the student's right to appeal a decision, should be clearly formulated and communicated in advance. Minor penalties may be assessed informally under prescribed procedures.

In all situations, procedural fair play requires that the student be informed of the nature of the charges against him, that he be given a fair opportunity to refute them, that the institution may not be arbitrary in its actions, and that there be provision for appeal of a decision. The following are recommended as proper safeguards in such proceedings when there are no honor codes offering comparable guarantees.

A. *Standards of Conduct Expected of Students*

The institution has an obligation to clarify those standards of behavior which it considers essential to its educational mission and its community life. These general behavioral expectations and the resultant specific regulations should represent a reasonable regulation of student conduct, but the student should be as free as possible from imposed limitations that have no direct relevance to his education. Offenses should be as clearly defined as possible and interpreted in a manner consistent with the aforementioned principles of relevancy and reasonableness. Disciplinary proceedings should be instituted only for violations of standards of conduct formulated with significant student participation and published in advance through such means as a student handbook or a generally available body of institutional regulations.

B. *Investigation of Student Conduct*

1. Except under extreme emergency circumstances, premises occupied by students and the personal possessions of students should not be searched unless appropriate authorization has been obtained. For premises such as residence halls controlled by the institution, an appropriate and responsible authority should be designated to whom application should be made before a search is conducted. The application should specify the reasons for the search and the objects or information sought. The student should be present, if possible, during the search. For premises not controlled by the institution, the ordinary requirements for lawful search should be followed.

2. Students detected or arrested in the course of serious violations of institutional regulations, or infractions of ordinary law, should be informed of their rights. No form of harassment should be used by institutional representatives to coerce admissions of guilt or information about conduct of other suspected persons.

C. *Status of Student Pending Final Action*

Pending action on the charges, the status of a student should not be altered, or his right to be present on the campus and to attend classes suspended, except for reasons relating to his physical or emotional safety and well-being, or for reasons relating to the safety and well-being of students, faculty, or university property.

D. *Hearing Committee Procedures*

When the misconduct may result in serious penalties and if the student questions the fairness of disciplinary action taken against him, he should be granted, on request, the privilege of a hearing before a regularly constituted hearing committee. The following suggested hearing committee procedures satisfy the requirements of procedural due process in situations requiring a high degree of formality.

1. The hearing committee should include faculty members or students, or, if regularly included or requested by the accused, both faculty and student members. No member of the hearing committee who is otherwise interested in the particular case should sit in judgment during the proceeding.

2. The student should be informed, in writing, of the reasons for the proposed disciplinary action with sufficient particulars, and in sufficient time, to insure opportunity to prepare for the hearing.

3. The student appearing before the hearing committee should have the right to be assisted in his defense by an adviser of his choice.

4. The burden of proof should rest upon the officials bringing the charge.

5. The student should be given an opportunity to testify and to present evidence and witnesses. He should have an opportunity to hear and question adverse witnesses. In no case should the committee consider statements against him unless he has been advised of their content and of the names of those who made them, and unless he has been given an opportunity to rebut unfavorable inferences which might otherwise be drawn.

6. All matters upon which the decision may be based must be introduced into evidence at the proceeding before the hearing committee. The decision should be based solely

upon such matters. Improperly acquired evidence should not be admitted.

7. In the absence of a transcript, there should be both a digest and a verbatim record, such as a tape recording, of the hearing.

8. The decision of the hearing committee should be final, subject only to the student's right of appeal to the president or ultimately to the governing board of the institution.

MODEL CODE FOR STUDENT RIGHTS, RESPONSIBILITIES & CONDUCT [7]

Short Title

§ 1. These rules shall be known as the ——— ——— [insert name of institution] Code of Conduct.

Bill of Rights

§ 2. The following enumeration of rights shall not be construed to deny or disparage others retained by students in their capacity as members of the student body or as citizens of the community at large:

A. Free inquiry, expression and assembly are guaranteed to all students.

B. Students are free to pursue their educational goals; appropriate opportunities for learning in the classroom and on the campus shall be provided by the institution.

C. The right of students to be secure in their persons, living quarters, papers and effects against unreasonable searches and seizures is guaranteed.

D. No disciplinary sanctions may be imposed upon any student without notice to the accused of the nature and cause of the charges, and a fair hearing which shall include confrontation of witnesses against him and the assistance of a person of his own choosing.

E. A student accused of violating institutional regulations

---

[7] Model code issued by the Law Student Division of the American Bar Association, May 31, 1969. Copyright © 1969 American Bar Association. 1155 E 60th St. Chicago 60637. Reprinted by permission. (For a legal commentary on this code write to the publishers.)

is entitled, upon request, to a hearing before a judicial body composed solely of students.

Definitions

§ 3. When used in this Code

(1) The term *institution* means ——— ——— [insert name of college or university] and, collectively, those responsible for its control and operation.

(2) The term *student* includes all persons taking courses at the institution both full-time and part-time pursuing undergraduate, graduate or extension studies.

(3) The term *instructor* means any person hired by the institution to conduct classroom activities. In certain situations a person may be both "student" and "instructor." Determination of his status in a particular situation shall be determined by the surrounding facts.

(4) The term *legal compulsion* means a judicial or legislative order which requires some action by the person to whom it is directed.

(5) The term *organization* means a number of persons who have complied with the formal requirements of institution recognition as provided in § 11.

(6) The term *group* means a number of persons who have not yet complied with the formal requirements for becoming an organization.

(7) The term *student press* means either an organization whose primary purpose is to publish and distribute any publication on campus or a regular publication of an organization.

(8) The term *shall* is used in the imperative sense.

(9) The term *may* is used in the permissive sense.

(10) All other terms have their natural meaning unless the context dictates otherwise.

Access to Higher Education

§ 4. Within the limits of its facilities, the institution shall be open to all applicants who are qualified according to its admission requirements.

A. The institution shall make clear the characteristics and expectations of students which it considers relevant to its programs.

B. Under no circumstances may an applicant be denied admission because of race or ethnic background.

C. (Optional) Religious preferences for applicants shall be clearly and publicly stated.

Classroom Expression

§ 5. Discussion and expression of all views relevant to the subject matter is permitted in the classroom subject only to the responsibility of the instructor to maintain order.

A. Students are responsible for learning the content of any course for which they are enrolled.

B. Requirements of participation in classroom discussion and submission of written exercises are not inconsistent with this Section.

§ 6. Academic Evaluation of student performance shall be neither prejudicial nor capricious.

§ 7. Information about student views, beliefs, and political associations acquired by professors in the course of their work as instructors, advisers, and counselors, is confidential and is not to be disclosed to others unless under legal compulsion.

A. Questions relating to intellectual or skills capacity are not subject to this section except that disclosure must be accompanied by notice to the student.

Campus Expression

§ 8. Discussion and expression of all views is permitted within the institution subject only to requirements for the maintenance of order.

A. Support of any cause by orderly means which do not disrupt the operation of the institution is permitted.

§ 9. Students, groups, and campus organizations may invite and hear any person of their own choosing subject only to the requirements for use of institutional facilities (§ 14, *infra*)

Campus Organizations

§ 10. Organizations and groups may be established within the institution for any legal purpose. Affiliation with an extramural organization shall not, in itself, disqualify the institution branch or chapter from institution privileges.

§ 11.

A. A group shall become an organization when formally recognized by the institution. All groups that meet the following requirements shall be recognized:

1. Submission of a list of officers and copies of the constitution and by-laws to the appropriate institution official or body. All changes and amendments shall be submitted within one week after they become effective.

2. Where there is affiliation with an extramural organization, that organization's constitution and by-laws shall be filed with the appropriate institution official or body. All amendments shall be submitted within a reasonable time after they become effective.

3. All sources of outside funds shall be disclosed.

B. Upon recognition of an organization, the institution shall make clear that said recognition infers neither approval or disapproval of the aims, objectives and policies of the organization.

C. Groups of a continuing nature must institute proceedings for formal recognition if they are to continue receiving the benefits of § 14, 16, and 17.

D. Any organization which engages in illegal activities, on or off campus, may have sanctions imposed against it, including withdrawal of institution recognition for a period not exceeding one year.

E. Any group which engages in illegal activities on campus may have sanctions imposed against it, including withdrawal of institution recognition for a period not exceeding one year.

§ 12. Membership in all institution-related organizations, within the limits of their facilities, shall be open to any member of the institution community who is willing to subscribe to the stated aims and meet the stated obligations of the organization.

§ 13. Membership lists are confidential and solely for the use of the organization except that names and addresses of officers may be required as a condition of access to institution funds.

§ 14. Institution facilities shall be assigned to organizations, groups, and individuals within the institution community for regular business meetings, for social programs, and for programs open to the public.

A. Reasonable conditions may be imposed to regulate the timeliness of requests, to determine the appropriateness of the space assigned, to regulate time and use, and to insure proper maintenance.

B. Preference may be given to programs designed for audiences consisting primarily of members of the institutional community.

C. Allocation of space shall be made based on priority of requests and the demonstrated needs of the organization, group, or individual.

D. The institution may delegate the assignment function to an administrative official.

D. (Alternate Provision) The institution may delegate the assignment function to a student committee on organizations.

E. Charges may be imposed for any unusual costs for use of facilities.

F. Physical abuse of assigned facilities shall result in reasonable limitations on future allocation of space to offending parties and restitution for damages.

G. The individual, group, or organization requesting space must inform the institution of the general purpose of any meeting open to persons other than members and the names of outside speakers.

§ 15. The authority to allocate institutional funds derived from student fees for use by organizations shall be delegated to a body in which student participation in the decisional process is assured.

A. Approval of requests for funds is conditioned upon submission of budgets to, and approval by, this body.

B. Financial accountability is required for all allocated funds, including statement of income and expenses on a regular basis. Otherwise, organizations shall have independent control over the expenditure of allocated funds.

C. (Optional) Any organization seeking access to institutional funds shall choose a faculty member to be a consultant on institution relations. Such a person may not have a veto power.

§ 16. No individual, group, or organization may use the institution name without the express authorization of the institution except to identify the institutional affiliation. Institution approval or disapproval of any policy may not be stated or implied by any individual, group, or organization.

Publications

§ 17. A student, group, or organization may distribute written material on campus without prior approval providing such distribution does not disrupt the operations of the institution.

§ 18. The student press is to be free of censorship. The editors and managers shall not be arbitrarily suspended because of student, faculty, administration, alumni, or community disapproval of editorial policy or content. Similar freedom is assured oral statements of views on an institution-controlled and student-operated radio or television station.

A. This editorial freedom entails a corollary obligation under the canons of responsible journalism and applicable regulations of the Federal Communications Commission.

§ 19. All student communications shall explicitly state on the editorial page or in broadcast that the opinions expressed are not necessarily those of the institution or its student body.

Institutional Government

§ 20. All constituents of the institutional community are free, individually and collectively, to express their views on issues of institutional policy and on matters of interest to the student body. Clearly defined means shall be provided for student expression on all institutional policies affecting academic and student affairs.

§ 21. The role of student government and its responsibilities shall be made explicit. There should be no review of student government actions except where review procedures are agreed upon in advance.

§ 22. Where the institution owns and operates residence halls, the students shall have final authority to make all decisions affecting their personal lives including the imposition of sanctions for violations of stated norms of conduct, except that the institution may impose minimal standards to insure compliance with all Federal, state, and local laws.

§ 23. On questions of educational policy, students are entitled to a participatory function.

> A. Faculty-student committees shall be created to consider questions of policy affecting student life.
>
> B. Students shall be designated as members of standing and special committees concerned with institutional policy affecting academic and student affairs, including those concerned with curriculum, discipline, admissions, and allocation of student funds.
>
> C. (Optional) There shall be an ombudsman who shall hear and investigate complaints and recommend appropriate remedial action.

Protest

§ 24. The right of peaceful protest is granted within the institutional community. The institution retains the right to assure the safety of individuals, the protection of property, and the continuity of the educational process.

§ 25. Orderly picketing and other forms of peaceful protest are permitted on institution premises.

A. Interference with ingress to and egress from institution facilities, interruption of classes, or damage to property exceeds permissible limits.

B. Even though remedies are available through local enforcement bodies, the institution may choose to impose its own disciplinary sanctions.

§ 26. Orderly picketing and orderly demonstrations are permitted in public areas within institution buildings subject to the requirements of noninterference in § 25A.

§ 27. Every student has the right to be interviewed on campus by any legal organization desiring to recruit at the institution.

A. Any student, group, or organization may protest against any such organization provided that protest does not interfere with any other student's right to have such an interview.

Violation of Law and University Discipline

§ 28. If a student is charged with, or convicted of, an off-campus violation of law, the matter is of no disciplinary concern to institution unless the student is incarcerated and unable to comply with academic requirements, except,

A. The institution may impose sanctions for grave misconduct demonstrating flagrant disregard for the rights of others. In such cases, expulsion is not permitted until the student has been adjudged guilty in a court of law, and;

B. Once a student is adjudged guilty in a court of law the institution may impose sanctions if it considers the the misconduct to be so grave as to demonstrate flagrant disregard for the rights of others.

§ 29. Under § 28A, the institution shall reinstate the student if he is acquitted or the charges are withdrawn.

§ 30. The institution may institute its own proceedings against a student who violates a law on campus which is also a violation of a published institution regulation.

Privacy

§ 31. Students have the same rights of privacy as any other
citizen and surrender none of those rights by becoming members of the academic community. These rights of privacy
extend to residence hall living. Nothing in the institutional
relationship or residence hall contract may expressly or im-
pliedly give the institution or residence hall officials authority to consent to a search of a student's room by police or
other government officials.

§ 32. The institution is neither arbiter or enforcer of student
morals. No inquiry is permitted into the activities of students away from the campus where their behavior is subject
to regulation and control by public authorities. Social
morality on campus, not in violation of law, is of no disciplinary concern to the institution.

§ 33. When the institution seeks access to a student room
in a residence hall to determine compliance with provisions
of applicable multiple dwelling unit laws or for improvement or repairs, the occupant shall be notified of such action
not less than twenty-four hours in advance. There may be
entry without notice in emergencies where imminent danger
to life, safety, health, or property is reasonably feared.

§ 34. The institution may conduct a search of a student
room in a residence hall to determine compliance with Federal, state and local criminal law where there is probable
cause to believe that a violation has occurred or is taking
place. "Probable cause" exists where the facts and circumstances within the knowledge of the institution and of which
it has reasonably trustworthy information are sufficient in
themselves to warrant a man of reasonable caution in the
belief that an offense has been or is being committed.

Student Records

§ 35. The privacy and confidentiality of all student records
shall be preserved. Official student academic records, supporting documents, and other student files shall be maintained only by full-time members of the institution staff em-

ployed for that purpose. Separate files shall be maintained of the following; academic records, supporting documents, and general educational records; records of discipline proceedings; medical and psychiatric records; financial aid records.

§ 36. No entry may be made on a student's academic record and no document may be placed in his file without actual notice to the students. Publication of grades and announcement of honors constitute notice.

§ 37. Access to his records and files is guaranteed every student subject only to reasonable regulation as to time, place, and supervision.

A. A student may challenge the accuracy of any entry or the presence of any item by bringing the equivalent of an equitable action against the appropriate person before the judicial body to which the student would be responsible under § 52.

§ 38. No record may be made in relation to any of the following matters except upon the express written request of the student:

A. Race;

B. Religion; (omit if § 48C is enacted)

C. Political or social views; and

D. Membership in any organization other than honorary and professional organizations directly related to the educational process.

§ 39. No information in any student file may be released to anyone except with the prior written consent of the student concerned or as stated below;

A. Members of the faculty with administrative assignments may have access for internal educational purposes as well as routinely necessary administrative and statistical purposes.

B. The following data may be given any inquirer; school or division of enrollment, periods of enrollment, and degrees awarded, honors, major field, and date.

C. If an inquiry is made in person or by mail, the following information may be given in addition to that in Subsection B: address and telephone number, date of birth, and confirmation of signature.

D. Properly identified officials from Federal, state and local government agencies may be given the following information upon express request in addition to that in Subsections B and C: name and address of parent or guardian if student is a minor, and any information required under legal compulsion.

E. Unless under legal compulsion, personal access to a student's file shall be denied to any person making an inquiry.

§ 40. Upon graduation or withdrawal from the institution, the records and files of former students shall continue to be subject to the provisions of this Code of Conduct.

Sanctions

§ 41. The following sanctions may be imposed upon students:

A. *Admonition*: An oral statement to a student that he is violating or has violated institution rules.

B. *Warning*: Notice, orally or in writing, that continuation or repetition of conduct found wrongful, within a period of time stated in the warning, may be cause for more severe disciplinary action.

C. *Censure*: A written reprimand for violation of specified regulations, including the possibility of more severe disciplinary sanctions in the event of the finding of a violation of any institution regulation within a stated period of time.

D. *Disciplinary probation*: Exclusion from participation in privileged or extracurricular institution activities as set forth in the notice for a period of time not exceeding one school year.

E. *Restitution*: Reimbursement for damage to or misappropriation of property. This may take the form of appropriate service or other compensation.

F. *Suspension*: Exclusion from classes and other privileges or activities as set forth in the notice for a definite period of time not to exceed two years.

G. *Expulsion*: Termination of student status for an indefinite period. The conditions of readmission, if any, shall be stated in the order of expulsion.

§ 42. No sanctions may be imposed for violations of rules and regulations for which there is not actual or constructive notice.

Proscribed Conduct

§ 43. Generally, institutional discipline shall be limited to conduct which adversely affects the institutional community's pursuit of its educational objectives. The following misconduct is subject to disciplinary action:

A. All forms of dishonesty including cheating, plagiarism, knowingly furnishing false information to the institution, and forgery, alteration or use of institution documents or instruments of identification with intent to defraud.

B. Intentional disruption or obstruction of teaching, research, administration, disciplinary proceedings or other institution activities.

C. Physical abuse of any person on institution premises or at institution sponsored or supervised functions.

D. Theft from or damage to institution premises or damage to property of a member of the institutional community on institution premises.

E. Failure to comply with directions of institution officials acting in performance of their duties.

F. Violation of published institutional regulations including those relating to entry and use of institutional facilities, the rules in this Code of Conduct, and any other regulations which may be enacted.

G. Violation of published rules governing residence halls.
H. Violation of law on institutional premises or residence halls in a way that affects the institutional community's pursuit of its proper educational purposes.

Procedural Standards in Discipline Proceedings

§ 44. Any academic or administrative official, faculty member or student may file charges against any student for misconduct. In extraordinary circumstances the student may be suspended pending consideration of the case. Such suspension shall not exceed a reasonable time.

§ 45. The institution may make a preliminary investigation to determine if the charges can be disposed of informally by mutual consent without the initiation of disciplinary proceedings.

§ 45. (Alternate) The institution may make a preliminary investigation to determine if the charges can be disposed of informally by mutual consent without the initiation of disciplinary proceedings. Such disposal will be final and there shall be no subsequent proceedings or appeals.

§ 46. All charges shall be presented to the accused student in written form and he shall respond within seven school days. The time may be extended for such response. A time shall be set for a hearing which shall not be less than seven or more than fifteen school days after the student's response.

§ 47. A calendar of the hearings in a disciplinary proceeding shall be fixed after consultation with the parties. The institution shall have discretion to alter the calendar for good cause.

§ 48. Hearings shall be conducted in such manner as to do substantial justice.

A. Hearings shall be private if requested by the accused student. In hearings involving more than one student, severance shall be allowed upon request.
B. An accused student has the right to be represented by counsel or an adviser who may come from within or without the institution.

C. Any party to the proceedings may request the privilege of presenting witnesses subject to the right of cross-examination by the other parties.

D. Production of records and other exhibits may be required.

§ 49. In the absence of a transcript, there shall be both a digest and a verbatim record, such as a tape recording, of the hearing in cases that may result in the imposition of the sanctions of restitution, suspension, and expulsion as defined in § 41.

§ 50. No recommendation for the imposition of sanctions may be based solely upon the failure of the accused student to answer the charges or appear at the hearing. In such a case, the evidence in support of the charges shall be presented and considered.

§ 51. An appeal from a decision by the initial hearing board may be made by any party to the appropriate appeal board within ten days of the decision.

A. An appeal shall be limited to a review of the full report of the hearing board for the purpose of determining whether it acted fairly in light of the charges and evidence presented.

B. An appeal may not result in a more severe sanction for the accused student.

C. An appeal by the institution, in which the decision is reversed, shall be remanded to the initial hearing board for a determination of the appropriate sanction.

Judicial Authority

§ 52. Appropriate judicial bodies shall be formed to handle all questions of student discipline. The initial hearing board shall be composed solely of students and any appeal board shall have voting student representation.

§ 53. The judicial bodies may formulate procedural rules which are not inconsistent with the provision of this Code.

§ 54. The judicial bodies may give advisory opinions, at their sole discretion, on issues not before any judicial body and where no violation of institutional regulations has taken place. Such opinions shall not be binding on the party making the request nor . . . used as precedent in future proceedings.

§ 55. A judicial body may be designated as arbiter of disputes within the institutional community. All parties must agree to arbitration and agree to be bound by the decision with no right of appeal.

VII. EPILOGUE

EDITOR'S INTRODUCTION

Spring 1970 added a new and somber chapter to the record of campus strife. The immediate and underlying causes of the killing of four students at Kent State University on May 4, 1970, have yet to be determined, but *Time* has captured the mystery and tragedy of the unexplainable in a way which makes one want to believe that people do not die in vain. The *Newsweek* and *Wall Street Journal* articles that follow summarize the fever pitch of campus activity following President Nixon's decision to send American troops into Cambodia and the National Guard's lethal volley at Kent State. Polarization not only was a campus issue but spread to the Potomac, as evidenced by Secretary of the Interior Hickel's revealing letter to President Nixon, here reproduced in full. The deaths at Jackson State College, Mississippi, and at Augusta, Georgia (not a campus incident but one with menacing implications for students on black campuses) will have repercussions not yet felt. Whitney M. Young, Jr., supplied the documentation to prove a point: "If repression of blacks is tolerated, then repression of whites will follow." The last item unfolds a new development on the campus—not intracampus politics, but university involvement in the political process.

It is difficult to evaluate events and how they mesh; this epilogue is certainly not an ending, but a new beginning for the academic world.

KENT STATE: MARTYRDOM THAT SHOOK THE COUNTRY [1]

It took half a century to transform Kent State from an obscure teachers college into the second largest university in

[1] From article in *Time*. 95:12-14. My. 18, '70. Reprinted by permission from *Time*, the Weekly Newsmagazine; Copyright Time Inc. 1970.

Ohio, with 21,000 students and an impressive array of modern buildings on its main campus. But it took less than ten terrifying seconds last week to convert the traditionally conformist campus into a bloodstained symbol of the rising student rebellion against the Nixon Administration and the war in Southeast Asia. When National Guardsmen fired indiscriminately into a crowd of unarmed civilians, killing four students, the bullets wounded the nation.

Paradoxically, the turn toward violence at Kent State was not inspired by the war or politics. The first rocks thrown in anger were hurled through the muggy Friday night of May 1 by beery students who could not resist the urge to dance on a Kent street. Hundreds of students were drinking at the bull-and-beer spots that flourish in most college towns. Spirits were light. A crowd swarmed into the warm night, blocking busy North Water Street, responding to the rock beat.

One irate motorist gunned his car's engine as if to drive through the dancers. Some students climbed atop the car, jumped on it, then led a chant: "One-two-three-four, we don't want your ——— war!" A drunk on a balcony hurled a bottle into the street and suddenly the mood turned ugly. Students smashed the car's windows, set fires in trash cans, began to bash storefronts. Police were called. Kent Mayor LeRoy Satrom had ordered a curfew, but few students were aware of it. Police stormed into bars after midnight, turning up the lights, shouting "Get out!" Some 2,000 more students, many of whom had been watching the Knicks-Lakers basketball game on TV, were forced into the street. Police and sheriff's deputies pushed the youths back toward the campus, then fired tear gas to disperse them.

Saturday began quietly. Black student leaders, who had been demanding the admission next year of 5,000 more blacks to Kent State (it now has about 600), and leaders of the mounting antiwar sentiment on campus talked of joining forces. They got administrative approval to hold a rally that evening on the ten-acre Commons at the center of the campus. There, despite the presence of faculty members and student marshals, militant war protesters managed to take complete charge of a crowd of about 800, many still smarting from the conflict of the night before. They disrupted a dance in one university hall, then attacked the one-story Army ROTC building facing the Commons. They smashed windows and threw lighted railroad flares inside. The building caught fire. When firemen arrived, students threw rocks at them and cut their hoses with machetes until police interceded with tear gas. Without bothering to consult Kent State authorities, Mayor Satrom asked for help from the National Guard. Governor James Rhodes, still engaged in his tough—and ultimately unsuccessful—campaign for the Senate nomination, quickly ordered Guardsmen transferred from points of tension in a Teamster strike elsewhere in Ohio.

Within an hour, about 500 Guardsmen, already weary from three nights of duty, arrived with fully loaded M-1 semiautomatic rifles, pistols and tear gas. They were in time to help police block the students from charging into the downtown area. Students reacted by dousing trees with gasoline, then setting them afire. Order was restored before midnight. On Sunday, Governor Rhodes arrived in Kent. He made no attempt to seek the advice of Kent State President Robert I. White and told newsmen that campus troublemakers were "worse than Brown Shirts and Communists and vigilantes—they're the worst type of people that we harbor in America." He refused to close the campus, as Portage County Prosecutor Ronald Kane pleaded; instead he declared a state of emergency and banned all demonstrations on the campus. Late that night, about 500 students defied the order and staged a sitdown on one of Kent's busiest intersections. Guardsmen, their number now grown to 900, moved into the face of a rock barrage to arrest 150 students.

On Monday, the campus seemed to calm down. In the bright sunshine, tired young Guardsmen flirted with leggy coeds under the tall oaks and maples. Classes continued throughout the morning. But the ban against mass assemblies was still in effect, and some students decided to test it again.

"We just couldn't believe they could tell us to leave," said one. "This is *our* campus." At high noon, youngsters began ringing the school's Victory Bell, normally used to celebrate a football triumph but rarely heard of late. About 1,000 students, some nervous but many joking, gathered on the Commons. Another 2,000 ringed the walks and buildings to watch.

From their staging area near the burned-out ROTC building, officers in two Jeeps rolled across the grass to address the students with bullhorns: "Evacuate the Commons area. You have no right to assemble." Back came shouts of "Pigs off campus! We don't want your war." The Jeeps pulled back. Two skirmish lines of Guardsmen, wearing helmets and gas masks, stepped away from the staging area and began firing teargas canisters at the crowd. The Guardsmen moved about 100 yards toward the assembly and fired gas again. A few students picked up canisters and threw them back, but they fell short of the troops. The mists of stinging gas split the crowd. Some students fled toward Johnson Hall, a men's dormitory, and were blocked by the L-shaped building. Others ran between Johnson and nearby Taylor Hall.

A formation of fewer than 100 Guardsmen—a mixed group including men from the 107th Armored Cavalry Regiment based in neighboring Ravenna, and others from a Wooster company of the 145th Infantry Regiment—pursued fleeing students between the two buildings. The troopers soon found themselves facing a fence and flanked by rock-throwing students, who rarely got close enough to hit anyone. Occasionally one managed to toss a gas canister back near the troops, while delighted spectators, watching from the hilltop, windows of buildings and the roof of another men's dorm, cheered. Many demonstrators were laughing.

Then the outnumbered and partially encircled contingent of Guardsmen ran out of tear gas. Suddenly they seemed frightened. They began retreating up the hill toward Taylor Hall, most of them walking backward to keep their eyes on the threatening students below. The crowd on the hilltop consisted almost entirely of onlookers rather than rock throwers. The tight circle of retreating Guardsmen contained officers and noncoms from both regiments, but no single designated leader. With them in civilian clothes was Brigadier General Robert Canterbury, the ranking officer on the campus, who said later: "I was there—but I was not in command of any unit." ...

When the compact formation reached the top of the hill, some Guardsmen knelt quickly and aimed at the students who were hurling rocks from below. A handful of demonstrators kept moving toward the troops. Other Guardsmen stood behind the kneeling troops, pointing their rifles down the hill. A few aimed over the students' heads. Several witnesses later claimed that an officer brought his baton down in a sweeping signal. Said Jim Minard, a sophomore from Warren, Ohio: "I was harassing this officer. I threw a stone at him, and he pointed a .45-caliber pistol at me. He was brandishing a swagger stick. He turned away. He was holding his baton in the air, and the moment he dropped it, they fired." Within seconds, a sickening staccato of rifle fire signaled the transformation of a once-placid campus into the site of an historic American tragedy.

Like a Firing Squad

"They are shooting blanks—they are shooting blanks," thought Kent State Journalism Professor Charles Brill, who nevertheless crouched behind a pillar. "Then I heard a chipping sound and a ping, and I thought, 'My God, this is for real.'" An Army veteran who saw action in Korea, Brill was certain that the Guardsmen had not fired randomly out of individual panic. "They were organized," he said. "It was not scattered. They all waited and they all pointed their rifles at the same time. It looked like a firing squad." The shooting stopped—as if on signal. Minutes later, the Guardsmen assumed parade-rest positions, apparently to signal the crowd that the fusillade would not be resumed unless the Guardsmen were threatened again. "I felt like I'd just had an order to clean up a latrine," recalled one Guardsmen in the firing unit. "You do what you're told to do."

The campus was suddenly still. Horrified students flung themselves to the ground, ran for cover behind buildings and parked cars, or just stood stunned. Then screams broke out. "My God, they're killing us!" one girl cried. They were. A river of blood ran from the head of one boy, saturating his school books. One youth held a cloth against the abdomen of another, futilely trying to check the bleeding. Guardsmen made no move to help the victims. The troops were still both frightened and threatening. After ambulances had taken away the dead and wounded, more students gathered. Geology Professor Glenn Frank, an ex-Marine, ran up to talk to officers. He came back sobbing. "If we don't get out of here right now," he reported, "the Guard is going to clear us out any way they can—they mean *any* way."

In that brief volley, four young people—none of whom was a protest leader or even a radical—were killed. Ten students were wounded, three seriously. . . .

Flimsy Excuse

Multiple investigations at Federal and state levels are under way to determine why anyone was killed at Kent State. Far worse disorders have been controlled at other campuses without fatalities. Many of the students had obviously committed lawless acts during that long weekend. Apparently they thought that they could do so with impunity.

General Canterbury and his superior, Ohio Adjutant General Sylvester Del Corso, at first sought refuge in a flimsy excuse for uncontrolled gunfire. They said that their men had been fired upon by a sniper. By the end of the week, even Del Corso conceded that there was no evidence of any such attack.

A more plausible explanation was fear that bordered on panic. "Each man made the judgment on his own that his life was in danger," said Canterbury. "I felt that I could have been killed out there." A number of the men believed that the crowd was going to engulf them, perhaps take away their loaded weapons and turn the M-1's on the troopers. Some had been hurt by thrown objects—but none seriously enough to require hospitalization. Though the units had served in riot situations before, most of the lower-ranking enlisted men had no war experience. . . . Some of the younger men had enlisted in the Guard to avoid regular military service and the hazards of Vietnam. Said the wife of one Guardsman: "My husband is no murderer. He was afraid. He was sure that they were going to be overrun by those kids. He was under orders—that's why he did it. He said so."

Whose orders? At week's end there was still no answer. Canterbury insisted that "no one gave an order." That statement strains credibility. By Canterbury's own count, 16 or 17 men fired 35 rounds. They started at virtually the same moment and stopped at the same moment. Many civilian spectators at the scene and some officials seeking to reconstruct the event are convinced that an order was given. And someone made the initial mistake of ordering live ammunition distributed to all the men and permitting them to load their rifles—a procedure that is contrary to regular Army practice in civil disturbances. Once weapons are loaded, says one Pentagon officer, "you have effectively lost control of that unit. You have given them the license to fire." The Ohio Guard officers contend that loaded weapons have a deterrent value. No doubt. But no one informed the demonstrators that the troops had live ammunition. Nor were any warning shots fired. Those facts, together with the totally inadequate tactical leadership of the group that felt it was entrapped, raise serious doubts about the Guards' professionalism—and about the wisdom of the decision to employ them.

THE REBELLION OF THE CAMPUS [2]

It was just three weeks ago [in April 1970] that the Vietnam Moratorium Committee shut its central office in Wash-

[2] From article in *Newsweek*. 75.28-30. My. 9, '70. Copyright Newsweek, Inc. 1970. Reprinted by permission.

ington, declaring that the era of the mass peace demonstration was over. Yet here on the fifty-two acres of the Ellipse, across the street from the White House South Grounds, 75,000 hot and restless young people stood in the . . . sun . . . [on May 9, 1970], bearing witness to the furious campus reaction across the country to Richard Nixon's Cambodian intervention and to the shooting of four students at Ohio's Kent State University.

If the demonstration finally went down as a peaceful anticlimax, it was only because the week's activities on a thousand campuses had seemed so uncompromising. More than twenty universities were racked by riots. The National Guard was called out in Illinois, Maryland, New Mexico, Wisconsin and Kentucky as well as at Kent State in Ohio. More than two hundred colleges and universities shut down for at least one day in protest against the United States action in Cambodia and the Kent State affair, and at least eight (including Princeton) closed for the rest of the semester. In California, faced with incendiary anger from one end of his state college and university system to the other, Governor Ronald Reagan stole the radicals' thunder by shutting down all twenty-eight four-year campuses for four days—incidentally breaking a sixteen-month-old vow to keep the schools open "at the point of a bayonet if necessary."

At many colleges around the country, the faculty broke precedent to take a formal stand with the students in opposition to Government policy. Indeed, out of the emotions and pressures of the week, a new campus-based political movement seemed to be emerging. . . .

In several places, the antiwar demonstrations moved off the campus. There were rallies or marches in Columbus, Austin and Los Angeles, to cite a few, and in Chicago protesters staged the biggest peace demonstration in memory. Adults joined young people at many of the demonstrations. The one main group missing was the blacks, who stayed aloof from the turmoil all week long. "A black kid got killed at Greensboro a year ago and nobody got upset," said a black student at North Carolina A&T College in Greensboro. "Now some white kids get killed at Kent State and everybody wants to march."

So amiable was the gathering on the Ellipse in Washington that the main worry of city officials throughout the long afternoon was the heat. Mayor Walter Washington shipped three truckloads of salt tablets to the demonstrators, and worried whether the fifteen water fountains would suffice for the huge throng. The young people not only survived but flourished, turning the Ellipse into an instant Woodstock while antiwar speakers (among them, Dr. Benjamin Spock) took their turns at the microphone.

Many factors contributed to the relaxed tone. The Administration apparently helped itself considerably by setting up a battery of telephones through which the demonstrators could arrange informal talks with sub-Cabinet members of all Government branches. Informal seminars took place in the offices of the Department of Health, Education, and Welfare, twelve blocks from the Ellipse, and HEW Secretary Robert Finch met with several groups of demonstrators—whose size ranged from fewer than twelve to more than one hundred. Still, the peacefulness of the demonstration was not entirely a matter of amiability. "The people here understand that we are surrounded by fully armed troops," said one Washington University freshman, "and that if we started anything we'd be destroyed."

The Government's security preparations were indeed complete—and sensibly unobtrusive. About 5,600 Federal troops were poised on the perimeter of the demonstration grounds, but they were all tucked out of sight inside huge Government buildings. A barricade of buses surrounded the White House, and behind them stood ranks of helmeted police. But the only police visible to the demonstrators were those directing traffic.

After the rally broke up, a minority of hard-core activists tried to start trouble near Lafayette Park, just north of the White House and nearby on Pennsylvania Avenue. The crowds were dispersed with tear gas, as were other knots of "trashers" who broke windows later along Connecticut Avenue. The incidents were relatively minor, but more than one hundred were arrested that night.

The big Washington demonstration was the climax of the most turbulent week on the campus since the protest era began. At the University of Maryland, normally a placid temple to beer and football, a mild springtime protest against the Cambodian invasion managed to pump itself up into a two-day riot that brought 350 state and local police swarming on campus, injured 63 and resulted in 25 arrests. Just when it seemed quieted down, the whole thing erupted again, and this time 80 National Guardsmen were called in. More than 75 persons were injured and 157 arrested. "It's easy to say it was the police's fault," said one graduate student. "There was an awful lot of tear gassing and screaming by officers. But it wasn't all one-sided. The police were getting called names, and stuff was thrown at them."

One of the week's uglier battles took place on the scarred campus of the University of Wisconsin. "We're gonna open up a second front in Madison, Wisconsin," shouted one speaker at a smoldering student rally. "Are you ready to bleed?"

In seemingly automatic response, hundreds of students began moving up the hill toward the Army Mathematics Research Center, part of what one student called "the war machine on campus." Police had surrounded the building and as the students approached they let fly with tear-gas canisters. Half a dozen times the students re-formed and probed the police and National Guard lines. A student was knocked unconscious by a gas canister; a cop was felled by a thrown rock. As the battle dragged out another day, the police began firing the canisters as missiles, and their beatings of random students became willful. Two helicopters hovered and roared over the campus, spotlighting small groups of students. A youth named Terry Johnson approached a group of guardsmen at the Social Science building. "Don't you guys see?" he said. "We bomb and we bomb and we bomb, and we kill and we kill and we kill. *Stop it."* A Madison policeman backed him against the wall until an unmarked car arrived to haul him away.

Before it was over, scores of Wisconsin students were injured and the faculty voted to shut down the university for a week. Perhaps the most important casualty was University of Wisconsin President Fred Harvey Harrington—one of the eight university presidents who went to Washington to consult with Mr. Nixon—who took one look at his shattered campus in Madison and announced his resignation.

Violence on the right erupted in New York City, when hundreds of students from NYU and Hunter College began gathering in the financial district early one morning for a day set aside by Mayor John Lindsay in memory of the four Kent State victims. All was peaceful until just before noon, when without warning the milling students were set upon by a phalanx of about two hundred well-organized construction workers from nearby buildings. Swinging their helmets as bludgeons, the burly workers ignored the thin line of police and began beating every long-haired head in sight. The police ignored them right back....

At hundreds of colleges, in circumstances not noticeably different from those in which violence broke out, no blood flowed at all. And in many cases, paradoxically, it was the very intensity of the reaction to Cambodia and Kent State that forced a peaceful course, because it brought out great numbers of moderates who had never been involved in any of the earlier demonstrations. "The Cambodian invasion has stirred up this campus more than anything else that has taken place in a decade," said a pretty, pigtailed Berkeley sorority girl named Maggie Cheatham.

In several places, demonstrations that started out in the hands of militants were taken over by the weight of moderate numbers. At Harvard, SDS leaders headed a march of five hundred students on the ROTC building. Within minutes a large number of moderates turned up and stopped the rock-throwers after a few windows had been broken. "For the first time on campus," said a Harvard junior, "moderates asserted themselves during a march, and SDS saw it was outnumbered."

There were also those striking instances of eloquence and poignance that any crisis seems to summon forth. At MIT, Klaus Liepmann, chairman of the music department, arose to address his cautious colleagues.

> This is the only time I have spoken in a faculty meeting during my twenty-three years at MIT. . . . However, there are times when "business as usual" becomes a crime. All this reminds me sadly of the Hitler years in Germany . . . when citizens were turned against each other, one side calling the other "Communists, traitors, bums," when atrocities were committed in the name of law and order. . . . In Germany great masses of people, notably the intellectuals, remained passive—they called it nonpolitical. . . . I feel it is our duty as intellectuals and artists to speak up now and to act now.

The faculty rose in a standing ovation, and subsequently passed resolutions supporting a university strike and—for the first time—condemning Mr. Nixon's war policies.

The commitment of others was not so clear. At Yale, Northwestern, Stanford, many students simply went home when classes were suspended, and took no part in any organized movement. At Columbia, Wayne State University, NYU, there was a heavy counterpressure to keep classes and exams going—especially by seniors heading for graduate school and all those others to whom traditional academic achievement is still important. As different universities played out the different permutations of strikes, suspensions, lockouts and reopenings, it was often difficult to tell who favored what, or why. In several schools, students who had forced a strike then turned around and demanded that the campuses stay open so that the strikers would have a base to work from. . . .

Demonstrations, indeed, were only part of the tactical arsenal. At the same time that scores of thousands of young people headed for the Ellipse, several thousand others were organizing into seemingly instantaneous new political action groups. Out from Princeton radiated an idea called the Movement for a New Congress, which calls upon students to organize themselves 1968-style to try to elect as many individual antiwar congressmen as possible this fall; within a week there were dozens of chapters.

NEW TURMOIL AT UNIVERSITIES [3]

Two things seem clear after the killing of four Kent State University students by National Guardsmen. The splintered left on the campuses has been suddenly reunited. And the nation has become more polarized.

What this will mean in coming days and coming months is unclear, however. At the moment, the nation's collegians are angry and confused. Some talk of violence—and some practiced it at scattered campuses . . . and others talk of political action. . . .

The issues of war in the jungles of Southeast Asia and death on the grassy commons in Kent, Ohio, are inextricably bound, collegians say. The four dead youths—already known as "the Kent State Four" on many campuses—were shot Monday [May 4] by Guardsmen called out to quell rioting by Kent State students who were protesting President Nixon's decision to send United States troops into Cambodia. Thus, to many college students, President Nixon is responsible for the deaths.

"The President has baited people into violence. When the President refers to students as 'bums,' as he did Friday at the Pentagon, it becomes much easier for a National Guardsman to look down the barrel of his rifle at one of them and pull the trigger," says Sam Brown, leader of the disbanded National Moratorium Committee and of the 1968 McCarthy youth campaign.

[3] From "Campus Crisis—Widening War, Deaths at Kent State Produce Turmoil at Universities." *Wall Street Journal.* p 1+. My. 6, '70. Reprinted with permission of *The Wall Street Journal.*

Mr. Brown thinks the only chance for "constructive, rational action" will come if the Senate cuts off appropriations for the war. A bipartisan group of Senators introduced legislation . . . seeking to do just that, but political observers give the bill little chance of survival. If the Senate doesn't act, Mr. Brown warns, "we'll all be back in the streets—and there is very little hope for continued existence of moderate peace sentiment.". . .

Everywhere, there is a new solidarity. Groups that have been bickering with each other for months have suddenly found a common cause. "Nixon has done what all the assorted radical movements have been unable to do since 1968. He has brought the students together in a militant radical mood. It's like he was a secret SDS agent," says Immanuel Wallerstein, professor of sociology at Columbia University in New York and a member of a hastily formed Faculty Peace Action Committee. . . .

The decision to send troops to Cambodia and the killing of the four students seem to have ended any hope for a rapprochement between the student majority and the "silent majority." "This will polarize the students even further against the Establishment and the military. It just can't help things at all," says Ted Allpich, a student at the Stanford Business School.

If America is becoming more polarized—which at the moment seems certain—all sorts of political problems and possibilities arise. Princeton's faculty voted overwhelmingly . . . to juggle vacation days next fall to give students two weeks off in late October to work in political campaigns. Other campuses surely will follow. But will politicians embrace the youths? If collegians work hard for a candidate, they can do much good for him. Eugene McCarthy wouldn't have got far in 1968 without his youth corps, for instance.

Yet, the youths are a liability, too. The opponent of their candidate can run against them instead of against their man. That can mean almost certain defeat. So far, at least, politicians have discovered they can make more votes running against youths than with them. At the moment, it seems as if the Administration will pass the word that Republican candidates this fall can run against these youths. Statements by the President and the Vice President following the Kent State killings already indicate this, in the view of political analysts in Washington. Certainly students feel the statements offered them little solace.

LETTER FROM SECRETARY HICKEL TO THE PRESIDENT [4]

I believe this Administration finds itself, today, embracing a philosophy which appears to lack appropriate concern for the attitude of a great mass of Americans—our young people.

Addressed either politically or philosophically, I believe we are in error if we set out consciously to alienate those who could be our friends.

Today, our young people, or at least a vast segment of them, believe they have no opportunity to communicate with Government, regardless of Administration, other than through violent confrontation. But I am convinced we—and they—have the capacity, if we will but have the willingness, to learn from history.

During the Great Depression, our youth lost their ability to communicate with the Republican party. And we saw the young people of the 1930s become the predominant leaders of the forties and fifties—associated not with our party, but rather with those with whom they felt they could communicate. What is happening today is not unrelated to what happened in the thirties. Now being unable to communicate with either party, they are apparently heading down the road to anarchy. And regardless of how I, or any American, might feel individually, we have an obligation as leaders to communicate with our youth and listen to their ideas and problems.

[4] Letter from Secretary of the Interior Walter J. Hickel to President Nixon dated May 6, 1970. Text from New York *Times*. p 18. My. 7, '70.

About two hundred years ago there was emerging a great nation in the British Empire, and it found itself with a colony in violent protest by its youth—men such as Patrick Henry, Thomas Jefferson, Madison and Monroe, to name a few. Their protests fell on deaf ears, and finally led to war. The outcome is history. My point is, if we read history, it clearly shows that youth in its protest must be heard.

Let us give America an optimistic outlook and optimistic leadership. Let us show them we can solve our problems in an enlightened and positive manner.

As an example, . . . December 16 [1969], I wrote to you suggesting that April 22, Earth Day, be declared a national holiday. Believing this would have been a good decision, we were active on university campuses over the Christmas holidays with a program called SCOPE (Student Councils on Pollution and the Environment). It was moderately successful, and it showed that it was possible to communicate with youth. I am gratified that on April 22, I, and approximately one thousand Interior employees, participated in Earth Day commemorative activities all over the United States.

I felt, after these meetings, that we had crossed a bridge; that communication was possible and acceptable. Likewise, I suggest in this same vein that you meet with college presidents, to talk about the very situation that is erupting, because before we can face and conquer our enemies, we must identify them, whether those enemies take physical or philosophical form. And we must win over our philosophical enemies by convincing them of the wisdom of the path we have chosen, rather than ignoring the path they propose.

In this regard, I believe the Vice President initially has answered a deep-seated mood of America in his public statements. However, a continued attack on the young—not on their attitudes so much as their motives—can serve little purpose other than to further cement those attitudes to a solidity impossible to penetrate with reason.

Finally, Mr. President, permit me to suggest that you consider meeting, on an individual and conversational basis, with members of your Cabinet. Perhaps through such conversations, we can gain greater insight into the problems confronting us all, and most important, into the solutions of these problems.

VIOLENCE IN THE SOUTH [5]

Summers are longer and hotter in the Deep South than in any other part of the country, and with much of the region's urban black population strangled by poverty and discrimination, seed beds of explosive racial disorder are present in the sultry slums of every major city.

Yet the South has remained largely free of convulsive rioting. There was Tampa and Atlanta in 1967, and Memphis and Miami in 1968; but these were shortlived outbursts with low loss of life and minor property damage compared to the great racial sieges that ravaged Northern cities in those years.

But last week, after twenty months of calm, violence broke out again in the South, this time in the small (under 100,000) Georgia city of Augusta, a usually placid community on the Savannah River famous for a golf course (the Augusta National—scene of the Masters Tournament) and a pair of ex-shoeshine boys, boxer Beau Jack and multimillionaire soul singer James Brown.

It started as many of the other riots have started, with the death of a Negro.

When Augusta police announced last Sunday that a sixteen-year-old mentally retarded boy accused of murder had died after being beaten and tortured in his jail cell, the black community was angered and outraged. Although the police later charged two of the teenager's cellmates with his murder most of the Negroes in Augusta either held the police directly responsible for the death or blamed the police for placing minors in overcrowded and unsupervised cells.

[5] From "After Long Calm Violence Again in the South," by Jon Nordheimer, staff reporter. New York *Times*. p E 3. My. 17, '70. Copyright © 1970 by The New York Times Company. Reprinted by permission.

On Monday five hundred blacks marched on the Augusta municipal building and tore down and burned the state flag. When the police arrived, the crowd dispersed in a wild, window-breaking rampage back to the ghetto where looting, arson and sniping shattered the night.

What exactly precipitated the violence was difficult to assess. The march had been peaceful until the crowd zeroed in on the Georgia flag, which contains the Confederate Stars and Bars. Then the young people lunged forward to rip it down, and kicked it on the ground, and set fire to it, as if it represented a repugnant, intolerable creed. And then, in a moment rare in the history of southern blacks, they reached out for an American flag, too, and burned it into a curling black fabric, as though the Stars and Stripes now symbolized the same emotions as the rebel battle flag.

By morning, after Governor Lester Maddox had called in state police reinforcements and a National Guard unit of two thousand heavily armed soldiers with orders to shoot to kill, the trouble had subsided. But in its wake, dozens of buildings in a one-hundred-square-block area had been burned or looted and six men were dead in the blood-stained streets. It was the worst racial disorder in the South after a decade of civil rights progress. . . .

Before the week was over, the unrestrained attitude of white police in the South when confronted with a hostile black crowd was tragically demonstrated when [on May 15, 1970, following two nights of campus disorder] the police in Jackson, Mississippi, opened fire on a collection of students at Jackson State College, an all-black institution, killing two students and wounding five, after the police said a sniper fired a gunshot from a dormitory window.

But there may be another factor which led to the breakdown of reason in Augusta. On the day after the riot the black community bypassed its own elected officials at city hall (three blacks sit on a sixteen-man council) to ask for a ten-man *ad hoc* committee to negotiate with white officials and air grievances, many of which for some strange reason seemed to catch the whites by surprise. "We discovered that perhaps the old leaders had just been telling us what they thought we wanted to hear," a white politician explained simply.

If the episode served to demonstrate how the gap between the black community and its own formal political leadership had widened, it also held the discouraging promise that the cities of the South may yet have to undergo the summer agonies of the North to purge the established leadership of apathy and neglect. For as the fires flickered in the rubble of the ghetto last week a shudder ran through the South with a realization that if civil strife could break out without warning in this sleepy city on the banks of the Savannah River it could happen anywhere, from Charleston to Mobile to Shreveport.

WHAT IS A UNIVERSITY? [6]

Suddenly, in just about a week's time, national trauma has catapulted colleges and universities into an active, over-riding political role that raises with new urgency the question, "What is a university?"

In the words of Professor Kenneth Keniston of Yale University, a member of the Carnegie Commission on Higher Education, there has been a "quantum jump" in the level of political activity emanating from the campuses since the United States moved into Cambodia and National Guardsmen killed four students at Kent State University.

School after school has shut down as thousands of students converged on Washington for . . . antiwar demonstrations.

At Yale, students are canvassing New Haven neighborhoods on behalf of the antiwar movement and a fair trial for Black Panthers. Political scientists there are using the resources of their departments to determine which political

[6] From news analysis by William K. Stevens, staff reporter. New York *Times*. p 9. My. 9, '70. Copyright © 1970 by The New York Times Company. Reprinted by permission.

campaigns are critical to the antiwar movement, and are helping to place students in those campaigns.

At Princeton and at the Harvard Graduate School of Education, the faculties are rearranging next fall's calendar so that students and teachers can work for candidates.

For the first time, many universities begin to look in some ways as much like the highly political Japanese model as the more sedate American model.

This is leagues away from the classical view of Cardinal Newman, who in the mid-1800s expressed a liberal ideal education that greatly influenced American colleges at the outset. In this view, a university is an assembly of scholars, testing and sharing ideas, creating a general intellectual atmosphere in which undergraduates—whatever their specific fields—can develop sound and creative habits of mind.

Over the years, other functions were added in American universities, two of the main ones being the fulfillment of society's need for professionals and technicians and the provision of expertise to government.

Judging by conversations with some leading educators, the question of whether the university's newly magnified role as a political staging ground can coexist with the older roles promises to become one of the central issues in higher education during the months ahead.

Many neoclassicists still hold to Cardinal Newman's ideal. At the opposite end of the scale are the New Left radicals who see the university as a base from which to launch their revolution.

A more moderate school of thought, represented by Yale's president, Kingman Brewster Jr. holds that the university cannot remain neutral in the face of compelling social issues. Thus, Mr. Brewster is expected to ask the Yale Corporation . . . to ratify his decision to allow use of Yale's faculty and resources in helping to assure a fair trial for the Black Panthers in New Haven.

"This really marks a possible change in the definition of a university's relationship to a society, and a change in what the institution itself does," says Mr. Keniston.

Another view is represented by Christopher Jencks and David Reisman, co-authors of *The Academic Revolution,* a widely hailed 1968 examination of higher education.

Mr. Jencks believes that a university is well suited to political action over the short term, because it can provide a vast number of recruits with the necessary time and independence. But over the long term, Mr. Jencks believes, the university is "simply not a well-fortified political base from which to launch an attack on the status quo," because in time it becomes vulnerable to reprisal by those who supply it money.

Students and faculty should be encouraged to take political action as individuals, Mr. Riesman says, but the university itself should not sponsor such action or give students time off for it.

"Even more than before, they are turning the universities into political forums in which the serious and the skeptical have very little chance," he says. "There's a temptation to burn the seed corn when the famine is going to last a long time. And the universities are very significant seed corn."

In the end, some feel, the character of the universities is likely to be shaped by events. "I just think the universities are up for grabs right now," says the Rev. Theodore M. Hesburgh, president of the University of Notre Dame. "There is no great, overwhelming wisdom coming out of anywhere right now as to where we're going.

"I think we're at some kind of a watershed in American history," Father Hesburgh said. "Until we can somehow get this generation convinced that the system can work, we cannot get back to education as we have known it. The university's proper role in this? I don't know. Everybody's living on adrenalin these days."

BIBLIOGRAPHY

An asterisk (*) preceding a reference indicates that the article or a part of it has been reprinted in this book.

Books, Pamphlets, and Documents

Aldridge, J. W. In the country of the young. Harper's Magazine Press. '70.

Ali, Tariq, ed. The new revolutionaries; a handbook of the international radical left. Morrow. '69.

American Bar Association. Commission on Campus Government and Student Dissent. Report. The Association. 1155 E. 60th St. Chicago 60637. '70.

*American Bar Association. Law Student Division. Model code for student rights, responsibilities & conduct. The Association. 1155 E. 60th St. Chicago 60637. '69.

American Civil Liberties Union. Academic freedom and civil liberties of students in colleges and universities. The Union. 156 Fifth Ave. New York 10010. '70.

*American Civil Liberties Union. Statement on campus demonstrations. The Union. 156 Fifth Ave. New York 10010. '68. mimeo.

American Council on Education. Special Committee on Campus Tensions. Campus tensions: analysis and recommendations. The Council. 1785 Massachusetts Ave. N.W. Washington, D.C. 20036. '70.

Aron, Raymond. The elusive revolution; anatomy of a student revolt; tr. from the French by Gordon Clough. Praeger. '69.

Avorn, J. L. and others. Up against the Ivy Wall; a history of the Columbia crisis. Atheneum. '68.
    Review articles: New York Times Book Review. p 6+. D. 15, '68. Columbia students look at their school and some visitors do, too. S. V. Roberts; New York Review of Books. p 15-17. Ja. 30, '69. Who cares for Columbia? Allan Silver.

Bell, Daniel. The reforming of general education: the Columbia College experience in its national setting. Columbia University Press. '66.

Bell, Daniel and Kristol, Irving, eds. Confrontation; the student rebellion and the universities. Basic Books. '69.

261

Birmingham, John, ed. Our time is now: notes from the high school underground. Praeger. '70.

Black studies in the university: a symposium; ed. by Armstead L. Robinson [and others]. Yale University Press. '69.
  Sponsored by the Black Student Alliance at Yale.

Bourges, Hervé, ed. The French student revolt; the leaders speak [by] Daniel Cohn-Bendit [and others]; tr. from the French by B. R. Brewster. Hill & Wang. '68.

*Brewster, Kingman, Jr. The politics of academia; remarks at Yale Political Union, September 24, 1969. The Author. Yale University. New Haven, Conn. 06520. '69. mimeo.

*Brock, Bill and others. Report of campus unrest submitted June 17, 1969, to the President following a tour of campuses by 22 congressmen. W. E. Brock. 115 Cannon House Office Bldg. Washington, D.C. 20515. mimeo.
  Same. Congressional Record (daily ed.) 116:S3520-5. Mr. 11, '70.

Brownfeld, A. C. The New Left; memorandum prepared for the Subcommittee to investigate the administration of the internal security act and other internal security laws of the Committee on the Judiciary, United States Senate. 90th Congress, 2d session. Supt. of Docs. Washington, D.C. 20402. '68.

Califano, J. A. Jr. The student revolution: a global confrontation. Norton. '69.

Cantor, Norman. The Columbia revolution and the crisis in American higher education. Cornell University Press. '69.

Cockburn, Alexander and Blackburn, Robin, eds. Student power: problems, diagnosis, action. Penguin. '69.

Cohen, Mitchell and Hale, Dennis, eds. The new student left; an anthology. Beacon. '66.

Cohn-Bendit, Daniel and Cohn-Bendit, Gabriel. Obsolete communism: the left-wing alternative; tr. by Arnold Pomerans. McGraw. '69.

Corson, W. R. Promise or peril; the black college student in America. Norton. '70.

Cruse, Harold. The crisis of the Negro intellectual. Morrow. '67.

Divoky, Diane. How old will you be in 1984? Expressions of student outrage from the high school free press. Avon. '69.

Douglas, W. O. Points of rebellion. Random House. '70.

*Editorial Projects for Education. Who's in charge? report on the national picture of college governance. The Organization. 3301 N. Charles St. Baltimore, Md. 21218.
  Text in Simmons Review. Spring-Summer '69.

Fact-Finding Commission on Columbia Disturbances. Crisis at Columbia. Vintage. '68.

Feuer, L. S. The conflict of generations; the character and significance of student movements. Basic Books. '69.
Review: New York Times Book Review. p 3+. Mr. 30. '69. R. P. Wolff.

Foley, J. A. and Foley, R. K. The college scene; students tell it like it is. Cowles. '69.

Fortas, Abe. Concerning dissent and civil disobedience. World Pub. '68.
Excerpt. New York Times Magazine. p 28-9+. My. 12, '68. Justice Fortas defines the limits of civil disobedience.

Fortune, Editors of. Youth in turmoil. Time-Life Books. '69.

Foster, Julian and Long, Durward, eds. Protest! student activism in America. Morrow. '70.

Frankel, Charles. Education and the barricades. Norton. '68.
Excerpts. Saturday Review. 51:23-5+. N. 2, '68. Student power: the rhetoric and the possibilities.

Graham, H. D. and Gurr, T. R. eds. History of violence in America: historical and comparative perspectives; a report submitted to the National Commission on the Causes and Prevention of Violence. Praeger. '69.

Grant, Joanne. Confrontation on campus: the Columbia pattern. New Am. Lib. '69.

*Hesburgh, T. M. Letter to Notre Dame faculty and students, February 17, 1969. The Author. University of Notre Dame. Notre Dame, Ind. 46556. '69.

Hook, Sidney. Academic freedom and academic anarchy. Cowles. '70.
Review. New York Review of Books. p 5-9. F. 12, '70. Yes men. H. D. Aiken.

Jencks, Christopher and Riesman, David. The academic revolution. Doubleday. '68.
Review. New York Review of Books. p 30-2. Jl. 11, '68. The revolting academy. H. D. Aiken.

Kahn, Roger. The battle for Morningside Heights; why students rebel. Morrow. '70.

Kelman, Steven. Push comes to shove: the escalation of the student protest. Houghton. '70.

Keniston, Kenneth. Young radicals: notes on committed youth. Harcourt. '68.

Kennan, G. F. Democracy and the student left. Little. '68.

Lipset, S. M. ed. Student politics. Basic Books. '67.

Lipset, S. M. and Altbach, P. G. eds. Students in revolt. Houghton. '69.

McGuigan, G. F. and others. Student protest. Methuen. '68.

Mannes, Marya. They. Doubleday. '68.
   Review. Saturday Review. 51:36-7+. N. 2, '68. Their own thing. Glendy Culligan.

Marcuse, Herbert. An essay on liberation. Beacon. '69.

Margolis, J. D. comp. The campus in the modern world: twenty-five essays. Macmillan. '69.

Mead, Margaret. Culture and commitment; a study of the generation gap. Doubleday; Natural History Press. '70.

Methvin, Eugene. The riot makers. Arlington House. '70.

Metzger, W. P. and others. Dimensions of academic freedom. University of Illinois Press. '69.

Neustadt, R. M. and others. The Harvard strike. Houghton. '70.

New York University. School of Law. Student conduct and discipline proceedings in a university setting; proposed codes, with commentary. The School. Washington Sq. New York 10003. '68.

Orrick, W. H. Jr. Shut it down! A college in crisis: San Francisco State College, October 1968—April 1969; a report to the National Commission on the Causes and Prevention of Violence. Supt. of Docs. Washington, D.C. 20402. '69.

*Plimpton, C. H. Letter to President Nixon, April 29, 1969. The Author. Amherst College. Amherst, Mass. 01002. '69.
   Same. New York Times. p 23. My. 3, '69.

Rader, Paul. Professor Wilmess must die. Dial. '69.

Roszak, Theodore. The making of a counter culture; reflections on the technocratic society and its youthful opposition. Doubleday. '69.
   Review: New York Times Book Review. p 3+. S. 7, '69. R. P. Wolff.

Rothblatt, Sheldon. The revolution of the dons: Cambridge and society in Victorian England. Basic Books. '68.

Rubenstein, R. E. Rebels in Eden: mass political violence in the United States. Little. '70.

Schlesinger, A. M. Crisis of confidence: ideas, power and violence in America. Houghton. '68.

Schwab, J. J. College curriculum and student protest. University of Chicago Press. '69.

Seale, Patrick and McConville, Maureen. Red flag/black flag: French revolution, 1968. Putnam. '68.

Seidenbaum, Art. Confrontation on campus: student challenge in California. Ward Ritchie Press. '69.

Spender, Stephen. The year of the young rebels. Random House. '69.
  Review: New York Times Book Review. p 5+. My. 11, '69. Jack Newfield.

Taylor, Harold. Students without teachers; the crisis in the university. McGraw. '69.

United States. National Commission on the Causes and Prevention of Violence. Task Force on Violent Aspects of Protest and Confrontation. The politics of protest; a report submitted by Jerome H. Skolnick, director. Simon & Schuster. '69.

University of California. Study Commission on University Governance. The culture of the university; governance and education. Jossey-Bass. '68.
  Majority report by Caleb Foote and others; the dissenting report by Albert Fishlow and David Freedman.

Von Hoffman, Nicholas. We are the people our parents warned us against. Quadrangle Books. '68.

Wallerstein, I. M. University in turmoil; the politics of change. Atheneum. '69.

Waskow, A. I. Running riot; official disaster and creative disorder in American society. Herder & Herder. '70.

Weaver, G. R. and Weaver, J. H. eds. The university and revolution. Prentice-Hall. '69.

Wolff, R. P. The ideal of the university. Beacon. '69.

Zinn, Howard. Disobedience and democracy; nine fallacies on law and order. Random House. '68.
  Review: New York Times Book Review. p 18. F. 16, '69.

PERIODICALS

Academy of Political Science Proceedings. 29:1-190. Jl. '68. Urban riots: violence and social change. Robert Connery, ed.

American Association of University Professors Bulletin. 56:33-5. Mr. '70. Draft statement on student participation in college and university government.

American Scholar. 38:548-61. Autumn '69. Black studies: an intellectual crisis; address. J. W. Blassingame.

*American Scholar. 38:588-605. Autumn '69. Living with crisis: a view from Berkeley. H. F. May.

Amherst Alumni News. Jl. '69. Special issue: The moratorium.

*Atlantic. 224:43-53. Jl. '69. The campus crucible: student politics and the university. Nathan Glazer.

Atlantic. 224:53-6. Jl. '69. Moralists against managers. F. G. Hutchins.

Barron's. 48:1+. My. 20, '68. Campus or battleground? Columbia is a warning to all American universities. R. Hessen.

*Boston Sunday Herald Traveler. p 33. O. 12; p 28. O. 19, '69. Dr. Abram on education.

Christian Science Monitor. p 20. Je. 6, '68. The violent minorities.

Christian Science Monitor. p 3. Je. 19, '68. Student-run college coming? L. Garinger.

Christian Science Monitor. p 7. Je. 20, '68. Review of the academic revolution, higher learning in America and the commonwealth of learning.

Christian Science Monitor. p 15. Je. 20, '68. Student hagiocracy. G. Godsell.

Christian Science Monitor. p 7. Je. 29, '68. To further man's search for truth.

Christian Science Monitor. p 9. Jl. 19, '68. But are they allowed to do that? H. J. Morgenthau.

*Christian Science Monitor. p 9. Jl. 21, '69. Student power: can it help reform the system? K. G. Gehret.

Christian Science Monitor. p 9. Jl. 26-28, '69. The faculty must play its part. K. R. Bergethon.

Christian Science Monitor. p 9. Ag. 2-4, '69. Caught in a thicket of political pressures. J. W. Ryan.

Christian Science Monitor. p 5. Ag. 31, '68. How university lowers tensions. D. Holstrom.

Christian Science Monitor. p 10. Ja. 14, '70. I'm here because I have to be. Kingman Brewster, Jr.

*College Law Bulletin. p 43-6. F. '70. Joint statement on rights and freedoms of students.

Columbia College Today. p 29. Winter '67-'68. The power structure: sense and nonsense. J. W. Gardner.

Commentary. 46:29-55. N. '68. On the steps of Low library: liberalism & the revolution of the young. Diana Trilling.
    Discussion. Commentary. 47:4+. Mr.; 19-20+. Ap. '69.

Commentary. 47:33-41. Je. '69. Reflections on youth movements. Walter Laqueur.

Commentary. 47:42-9. Je. '69. Power in the academy. Dorothy Rabinowitz.

Daedalus. p 1-20. Winter '68. Students and politics in comparative perspective. S. M. Lipset.

Daedalus. p 116-36. Winter '68. British student politics. A. H. Halsey and Stephen Marks.

Daedalus. p 293-317. Winter '68. The student left in American higher education. R. E. Peterson.

Daedalus. p 318-41. Winter '68. An experiment in education. M. B. Duberman.

Denver Law Journal. 45 no 4:497-678. '68. Local aspects of student-institutional relationships [symposium].

Economist. 227:10-11. My. 25, '68. Hello, anarchists!

Economist. 227:23-4+. Je. 8, '68. Stanford sits in—and out.

Encounter. 31:22-30. Ag. '68. After the barricades: the meaning of the French university crisis. Raymond Aron.

Encounter. 33:25-32. Ag. '69. Tales of academe; down and out on the American campus. Ben Morreale.

Encounter. 33:29-42. S. '69. Obsolete youth. Bruno Bettelheim.

Encounter. 34:10-18. F. '70. Who killed the student revolution? Robert Nisbet.

Esquire. 72:1a-1d+. S. '69. Back to college issue.

Esquire. 72:140-4+. O. '69. The collapse of S.D.S. Roger Kahn.

Foreign Affairs. 48:414-26. Ap. '70. Youth and foreign policy. S. J. Kelman.

Fortune. 79:73-4. Je. '69. A special report to youth; dissidence among college students is still growing, and it is spreading beyond the campus. Jeremy Main.

George Washington Law Review. 37:835-47. My. '69. Black power and student unrest: reflections on Columbia University and Harlem. Eli Ginzberg.

Guardian Weekly (London). p 13. O. 25, '68. Open letter to a new student. Lord James of Rusholme.

Harper's Magazine. 239:69-72. Ag. '69. Harvard on my mind. Michael Holroyd.

*Harper's Magazine. 240:25-32+. Ja. '70. The failure of black separatism. Bayard Rustin.

Harvard Business Review. 46:49-60. S.-O. '68. What businessmen need to know about the student left. G. E. Bradley.

Harvard Law Review. 70:1406. Je. '57. Dismissal of students: "due process." W. A. Seavey.

Humanist. p 11+. My.-Je. '69. Student power: a symposium.

Journal of Legal Education. 21 no 2:222-3+. '68. Model code of procedure for academic freedom and tenure cases as approved by the A.A.L.S. Committee on Academic Freedom and Tenure, Dec. 29, 1967.

Journal of Legal Education. 21 no 5:547-59. '69. A suggested seminar in student rights. W. W. Van Alstyne.

Liberty. 64:8. My.-Je. '69. Anarchy on campus. W. L. Roper.

Life. 66:24-35. Ap. 25, '69. Academic calm of centuries broken by a rampage.

Look. 31:21-3. S. 5, '67. Dissent or destruction. Eric Sevareid.

Look. 31:27-31. O. 31, '67. The black revolt hits the white campus. Ernest Dunbar.

Look. 32:23-7. Ap. 2, '68. Campus mood, spring, '68; panel discussions ed. by Ernest Dunbar.

Look. 32:23-9. O. 1, '68. Vanguard of the campus revolt; Students for a Democratic Society. Ernest Dunbar.

*Look. 32:28. N. 12, '68. To an angry young man. Leo Rosten.

Look. 33:36+. F. 18, '69. Uproar hits the campus press. Jack Star.

*Look. 33:14. Ap. 29, '69. To an angry old man. Leo Rosten.

*Look. 33:13-14. My. 13, '69. Columbia: to be a revolutionary or not to be? J. L. Avorn.

*Look. 33:61-2+. My. 27, '69. Battle for a college—why San Francisco State blew up.
    Two views: We needed a revolution. Leo Litwak; An arrogant minority victimized the college. J. H. Bunzel.

Look. 33:73+. Je. 10. '69. Beyond campus chaos: a bold plan for peace. G. B. Leonard.

Look. 34:14. Ja. 13, '70. Why we need a generation gap. Roger Rapoport.

Look. 34:16+. My. 19, '70. Who speaks for the young? Some startling facts and fictions. Leo Rosten.

Michigan State Bar Journal. 47:29-33. Ap. '68. Faith, freedom and law. J. E. Hoover.

*National Review. 20:699. Jl. 16, '68. What's relevant? Russell Kirk.

National Review. 20:1224. D. 3, '68. Choose your own protest. Geoffrey Wagner.

National Review. 21:175-7+. F. 25, '69. Revolting students. John Sparrow.

National Review. 21:702. Jl. 15, '69. Students for education; California State College, Dominguez Hills. Russell Kirk.

National Review. 21:754. Jl. 29, '69. The student left: cause and consequence. Will Herberg.

National Review. 21:1212-13. D. 2, '69. The campus and the law. Ernest van den Haag.

New American Review. 5:81-101. Ja. '69. The unliberated university. E. Bentley.

New Republic. 159:19-22. N. 23, '68. Bringing about change. L. J. Halle.

New Republic. 160:17-19. Ap. 12, '69. Whose university? Michael Miles.

*New Republic. 160:16-18. Ap. 26; 13-14. My. 17; 31+. My. 24, '69. Whose university? the case for professionalism. Robert Brustein.
   Same. Current. 108:19-24. Je. '69.

New Republic. 160:23-6. My. 10, '69. Holden Caulfield meets the movement. Theodore Solotaroff.

*New Republic. 161:15-16. S. 20, '69. Student demands and academic freedom. A. M. Bickel.

New Republic. 162:15-17. Je. 13, '70. The tolerance of violence on campus. A. M. Bickel.

New Statesman. 75:865. Je. 28, '68. Home thoughts from home. J. B. Priestley.

New Statesman. 77:104. Ja. 24, '69. America's student class war. Andrew Kopkind.

New Statesman. 77:685-6. My. 16, '69. Upheaval at Harvard. Nora Sayre.

*New Statesman. 77:756-7. My. 30, '69. What kind of black studies? John Hatch.

New Statesman. 77:898+. Je. 27, '69. A new blueprint for revolution. Andrew Kopkind.

New York Magazine. p 34-5+. F. 9, '69. Do you remember La Pasionaria? Meet the women of the revolution 1969. Peter Babcox.

New York Post. p 46. My. 16, '68. Capers on the campus. Art Buchwald.

New York Post. p 38. My. 30, '68. The ultimate protest. Art Buchwald.

New York Post. p 42. Jl. 2, '68. The boy who came to dinner. Art Buchwald.

New York Post. p 54. D. 12, '68. A campus dialogue. Art Buchwald.

New York Post. p 45. F. 17, '69. The young rebels. Mary McGrory.

New York Post. p 46. F. 18, '69. The forgotten student. Drew Pearson.

New York Post. p 50. My. 5, '69. What we can do. Max Lerner.

New York Post. p 54. My. 8, '69. The class struggle. Art Buchwald.

New York Post. p 55. My. 8, '69. It worked at Chicago University. F. Mankiewicz and T. Braden.

New York Post. p 36. Ja. 26; p 50. Ja. 28; p 41. Ja. 30, '70. Student power—an analysis. Max Lerner.

New York Post Magazine. p 28. Je. 1, '68. Students in rebellion; a distinguished historian defines the challenge posed by the Columbia uprising. H. S. Commager.

New York Review of Books. p 21. Ag. 27, '68. Two cheers for the university. Lawrence Stone.

New York Review of Books. p 36. Ag. 27, '68. An exchange on Columbia II.   I. Morris and D. MacDonald.

New York Review of Books. p 20. S. 26, '68. The uprising at Columbia. F. W. Dupee.

New York Review of Books. p 29-31. Ap. 24, '69. The radical students. F. Crews.

New York Review of Books. p 25+. Jl. 31, '69. Technology: the opiate of the intellectuals. J. McDermott.

New York Review of Books. 14:7-11. Je. 18, '70. Princeton in the nation's service. Lawrence Stone.

New York Times. p 69. Ja. 9, '68. Courts playing a major role. M. Gansberg.

New York Times. p 41. My. 17, '68. Text of Declaration of Confidence by 35 at Columbia Law School.

New York Times. p 9. S. 1, '68. Students all over challenge the system. F. M. Hechinger.

New York Times. p 33. O. 7, '68. Cox reflecting on report of students disorder, regards Columbia as microcosm of U.S. B. L. Collier.

New York Times. p 35. N. 28, '68. The Columbia confrontation. E. Fremont-Smith.

New York Times. p 46. D. 5, '68. How far does free speech go? T. Wicker.

*New York Times. p E 3. D. 6, '68. Imprisoned in kidhood. Russell Baker.

New York Times. p 51. Ja. 9, '69. Rebellion reshaping the campus —at Columbia, a threefold aim.

New York Times. p 53. Ja. 9, '69. Reform at Berkeley brings its own problems.

New York Times. p 56. Ja. 9, '69. Toward a changed Columbia; two views: the provost, the students.

New York Times. p 79. Ja. 9, '69. Teenagers protesting too. M. Stern.

New York Times. p 1. F. 25, '69. High court upholds a student protest. F. P. Graham.

New York Times. p 30. Mr. 12, '69. Students occupy a Princeton hall.

New York Times. p 38. Mr. 13, '69. Stiff campus discipline backed in poll.

New York Times. p 54. Mr. 23, '69. Letter to administrators of universities and colleges. Robert Finch.

New York Times. p 54. Mr. 23, '69. Statement on campus violence. R. M. Nixon.

New York Times. p 64. Ap. 14, '69. Text of statement issued by the Harvard Corporation.

New York Times. p 4. Ap. 15, '69. Text of American Council on Education statement about disorders on campus.

New York Times. p 42. Ap. 17, '69. Campus protests and the courts. S. E. Zion.

New York Times. p 42. Ap. 18, '69. Campus activism [letter to editor]. Staughton Lynd.

New York Times. p 19. Ap. 19, '69. Statement by Harvard Corporation on strike issues.

New York Times. p 34. Ap. 22, '69. Excerpts from talk by president of Cornell University on student dissension.

New York Times. p 31. Ap. 23, '69. City College rebellion. F. M. Hechinger.

New York Times. p 46. Ap. 23, '69. Suppose the young revolutionaries really won. James Reston.

New York Times. p 29. Ap. 30, '69. Excerpts from the President's address on disruption by students.

New York Times. p E 14. My. 11, '69. Letter to a young female rebel from Smith.

New York Times. p 31. Je. 4, '69. Text of the President's address on the challenge of revolutionaries on campus.

New York Times. p 30. Je. 10, '69. Text of a statement on campus disorder by the National Commission on Violence.

New York Times. p 31. Je. 10, '69. Text of the resolution on rights and responsibilities adopted by Harvard faculty.

*New York Times. p 28. Je. 24, '69. Text of Board of Higher Education's rules on campus conduct.

New York Times. p 37. O. 30, '69. Text of [New York City] school board resolution on student rights.

*New York Times. p 18. My. 7, '70. Text of the Hickel letter.
  Letter from Secretary of the Interior Walter J. Hickel to President Nixon, dated May 6, 1970.

*New York Times. p 9. My. 9, '70. What is a university? W. K. Stevens.

*New York Times. p E 3. My. 17, '70. After long calm violence in the South. Jon Nordheimer.

New York Times Magazine. p 32-3+. My. 26, '68. What student power means. J. R. Kramer.

New York Times Magazine. p 56. Ag. 4, '68. Revolution, yes—anarchism, no [letter to editor]. Mark Rudd.

New York Times Magazine. p 25-7+. S. 15, '68. Confessions of a professor caught in a revolution. Amitai Etzioni.

New York Times Magazine. p 27-9+. O. 20; 72 N. 10, '68. The new confrontation politics is a dangerous game. Irving Howe.

New York Times Magazine. p 29-31+. O. 27, '68. Marcuse defines his new left line; interview, ed. by J. L. Ferrier and others; tr. by H. Weaver.
  Discussion. New York Times Magazine. p 12. N. 17, '68.

New York Times Magazine. p 50-1. D. 8, '68. A different way to restructure the university. Irving Kristol.

New York Times Magazine. p 28-9+. F. 16, '69. The eleven days at Brandeis, as seen from the president's chair. M. B. Abram.

New York Times Magazine. p 28-9+. F. 23, '69. The revolution (cont.) : at the University of Connecticut. Evan Hill.
  Discussion. New York Times Magazine. p 6+. Mr. 16; 110+. Ap. 13, '69.

New York Times Magazine. p 26-7+. Mr. 16, '69. Revolutionaries who have to be home by 7:30. Nicholas Pileggi.

New York Times Magazine. p 56-7+. Mr. 30, '69. What the rebellious students want. Stephen Spender.

New York Times Magazine. p 257+. Ap. 6, '69. The black studies thing. Ernest Dunbar.

New York Times Magazine. p 34-5+. My. 11, '69. The road to the top is through higher education, not black studies. Sir Arthur Lewis.
Reprinted from *University: A Princeton Quarterly*

New York Times Magazine. p 32-3+. My. 18, '69. The "ins" and "outs" at M.I.T. Richard Todd.

New York Times Magazine. p 28-9+. Je. 8, '69. A fairly old grad ('55) looks at Harvard (in '69). J. A. Lukas.
Reply. New York Times Magazine. p 2+. Je. 29, '69.

New York Times Magazine. p 9+. Ja. 18, '70. The two nations of Wesleyan university. R. J. Margolis.

New York Times Magazine. p 10-11+. Ja. 18, '70. What generation gap? Joseph Adelson.

*New York University Alumni News. 13:3. My. '68. Student revolts could destroy academic freedom. Sidney Hook.

Newsweek. 73:66-71. Mr. 10, '69. How to deal with student dissent.

*Newsweek. 73:68-73. Je. 23, '69. Class of '69: the violent years. Edwin Diamond.

*Newsweek. 75:28-30. My. 9, '70. The rebellion of the campus.

Observer (London). p 26. Mr. 31, '68. What can I tell my daughter? John Crosby.

Observer (London). p 10. My. 19, '68. What's it all about; the student revolt.

Observer (London). p 11. My. 19, '68. Soviets on the campus. Neal Ascherson.

Observer (London). p 21. Je. 2, '68. Free societies in ferment. Neal Ascherson.

Observer (London). p 21. Je. 16, '68. Crisis on campus.

*Observer (London). p 21. Je. 23, '68. Intolerable! Philip Toynbee.

Observer (London). p 21. Jl. 7, '68. John Osborne—interview.

Observer (London). p 29. Mr. 2, '69. The mind of the left. Julius Gould.

Observer (London). p 30. Ap. 20, '69. Ideologists of black power. J. Moynahan.

Observer (London). p 21. Je. 2, '69. The new heroes.

Playboy. p 89+. S. '69. Student revolt; a discussion.
Participants: Ewart Brown, Edgar Friedenberg, Buell Gallagher, S. I. Hayakawa, Tom Hayden, Christopher Jencks, P. A. Luce, Linda Morse.

*Prosecutor. 5:161-3. My.-Je. '69. Forward to chaos—or the New Left in action. J. E. Hoover.

Public Interest. 13:3-197. Fall '68. Special issue: The universities.

Public Interest. 15:10-39. Spring '69. Academic confrontations. G. P. Elliot; Sidney Hook.

Publishers' Weekly. 194:19-20. D. 16, '68. AEPI [American Educational Publishers Institute] discusses campus revolution.

*Saturday Review. 51:14-16+. Jl. 20, '68. A Federal judge digs the young: "It is quite right that the young should talk about us as hypocrites. We are." C. E. Wyzanski, Jr.

Saturday Review. 51:53-4. Jl. 20, '68. Voices in the classroom. Peter Schrag.

Saturday Review. 51:41-9+. Ag. 17, '68. Students against the world: student movement on three continents; symposium.

Saturday Review. 51:26+. N. 9, '68. The issues beyond the beards [editorial]. Norman Cousins.

*Saturday Review. 51:116-17. N. 16, '68. When the young lions roared. B. B. Stretch.
      Review of Crisis at Columbia, report of the Fact-Finding Commission on Columbia Disturbances.

Saturday Review. 51:61-2. D. 21, '68. Nothing has changed. Paul Woodring.

Saturday Review. 52:23-5+. Mr. 1, '69. The political thrust motivating campus turmoil. S. M. Lipset.

*Saturday Review. 52:68-71+. Je. 21, '69. Can the university survive the black challenge? James Cass.

Saturday Review. 52:56+. Jl. 19, '69. Feuer: Freud and the fathers. Otto Klineberg.

Saturday Review. 52:60. Jl. 19, '69. An optimistic view of campus unrest. Paul Woodring.

Saturday Review. 52:41-3+. Ag. 16. '69. Medical students: healers become activists. M. G. Michaelson.

Saturday Review. 52:50-1+. Ag. 16, '69. Gloom at the top. Peter Schrag.

Saturday Review. 52:54-6+. D. 20, '69. Will Everyman destroy the University [CUNY]? T. S. Healy.

Spectator (London). 220:809. Je. 14, '68. Student power: who failed whom? P. Cosgrave.

Spectator (London). 221:83. Jl. 19, '68. Goodbye to the Left. J. Braine.

Spectator (London). 221:88. Jl. 19, '68. The party's over now. Denis Brogan.

Spectator (London). 221:574. O. 15, '68. The treason of the vice-chancellors. Ian MacGregor.

Spectator (London). 221:540. O. 18, '68. Home truths on the campus. Ian MacGregor.

Spectator (London). 221:619. N. 1, '68. Save our universities. Ian MacGregor.

Spectator (London). 221:869. D. 20, '68. Students—ends and means. Ian MacGregor.

Spectator (London). 222:43. Ja. 10, '69. University follies of 1969. Denis Brogan.

Spectator (London). 222:107. Ja. 24, '69. Nominalism and realism in academe. Denis Brogan.

Spectator (London). 222:163. F. 7, '69. In defence of students. Auberon Waugh.

Spectator (London). 222:208. F. 14, '69. A generation of idiots. Denis Brogan.

*Spectator (London). 222:578. My. 2, '69. Misbehavioural sciences. Murray Kempton.

Student Lawyer. 14:12-14. Mr. '69. Mr. Dooley on student power. E. J. Bander.

This Week. p 2. F. 23, '69. The thinking Capp. Al Capp.

Time. 93:45-6. F. 28, '69. Signs of moderation?

Time. 95:50+. Ja. 26, '70. Black studies: a painful birth.

*Time. 95:12-14. My. 18, '70. Kent State: martyrdom that shook the country.

Times Literary Supplement. p 397. Ap. 18, '68. Student power [editorial].

Times Literary Supplement. p 597. Je. 6, '68. Campus prophet [editorial].

Times Literary Supplement. p 768. Jl. 25, '68. In France.

Times Literary Supplement. p 769. Jl. 25, '68. Students and revolution in Italy.

Trans-action. 6:29-36+. Je. '69. Confrontation at Cornell. W. H. Friedland and Harry Edwards.

*Trans-action. 6:3-4. S. '69. Universities on collision course. David Riesman.

Trial. 4:22-4. Je-Jl. '68. Masses of people. E. N. Griswold.

Tulane Law Review. 42:726-39. Je. '68. Dissent—1968. E. N. Griswold.

U.S. News & World Report. 66:47-8. Ap. 7, '69. States and schools
   fight back against riots.

U.S. News & World Report. 66:61-3. Ap. 7, '69. Too many misfits
   in college; excerpts from statement to the House Special Subcommittee on Education, March 20, 1969. Bruno Bettelheim.

U.S. News & World Report. 66:34-7. My. 26, '69. The quiet majority; the other side of campus revolt.

Vanderbilt Law Review. 22:1027-88. O. '69. The Constitution on
   the campus. C. A. Wright.

Vital Speeches of the Day. 35:410-13. Ap. 15, '69. A generation in
   search of a future. George Wald.
       Same. Representative American Speeches: 1968-1969; ed. by Lester
   Thonssen. (Reference Shelf. Vol. 41, no. 4) Wilson '69. p 33-44; *Excerpts.*
   New Yorker. 45:29-31. Mr. 22, '69.

Wall Street Journal. p 1+. Mr. 7, '69. Most university heads shun
   hard-line talk with student radicals.

*Wall Street Journal. p 1+. My. 6, '70. Campus crisis—widening
   war, deaths at Kent State produce turmoil at universities.

VERMONT COLLEGE
MONTPELIER, VERMONT